D1367469

Number Two: Environmental History Series
MARTIN V. MELOSI, *General Editor*

Environmental Politics and the Coal Coalition

ENVIRONMENTAL POLITICS
AND
THE COAL COALITION

By
Richard H. K. Vietor

Texas A&M University Press

COLLEGE STATION AND LONDON

Library of Congress Cataloging in Publication Data

Vietor, Richard H K 1945–
    Environmental politics and the coal coalition.

    (Environmental history series ; no. 2)
    Bibliography: p.
    Includes index.
    1. Coal mines and mining—Environmental aspects—
United States. 2. Industry and state—United States.
I. Title. II. Series.
HD945.V54   363.7'392   79–5277
ISBN 0–89096–094–1

Manufactured in the United States of America
FIRST EDITION

For
Cindy

Contents

List of Tables   xi

Acknowledgments   xiii

List of Abbreviations   xv

1. Introduction   3
2. The Coal Coalition: Synthesis of Corporate Power   13
3. Sportsmen and Strip Mining in Pennsylvania: The Fight
   for Controls   58
4. Strip Mining in Washington: A Tougher Fight   85
5. Air Pollution Becomes a National Problem:
   1958–1969   127
6. Administrative Politics and the Clean Air Act of 1970   155
7. Growth, Energy, and Air Pollution:
   America's Bicentennial Crisis   194
8. Coal and the Public Interest   227

Appendixes
A. Technical Aspects of Coal Surface Mining   237
B. Stationary Source Air Pollution: The Technical Issues   245
C. The Politics of Information: Two Issues   250
D. Who's Who in Coal   256

Bibliography   262

Index   275

List of Tables

1. Forty Largest Coal Producers by Industry Group, 1976   19
2. Forty Largest Coal Reserve Holders by Industry Group, 1976   20
3. Principal Rail Systems Involved in Coal, 1974   22
4. Banks Most Frequently among the Thirty Top Stockholders of Selected Coal-Related Corporations   31
5. Shared Membership in Coal-Related Industry Political Groups   37
6. Coal-Related Membership of the American Mining Congress, 1974   50
7. Pennsylvania Assembly Votes on 1961 Surface-Mining Control Bill   62
8. Summary Enforcement Data for Bureau of Surface Mine Reclamation, 1965–1972   73
9. Bureau of Surface Mine Reclamation Violation Record   74
10. Bureau of Surface Mine Reclamation Enforcement Record, 1965–1972   76
11. Strip-Mining Regulations Introduced during the 92nd Congress   89
12. Coal Consumption in the United States   129
13. National Ambient Air Quality Standards   162
D.1 Forty Largest Corporate Coal Producers, 1976   256
D.2 Forty Largest Coal Reserve Holders, 1976   258
D.3 Petroleum/Gas Interests in the Coal Industry   259
D.4 Memberships and Activities of Coal Interests Most Involved in Federal Environmental Policy Making   261

Acknowledgments

I WAS extremely fortunate to have studied history under the direction of Professor Samuel P. Hays. His analytical approach to history and his enthusiasm for multidisciplinary research indelibly marked my way of thinking. I am grateful as well for the critical advice Professors Peter Karsten, Charles Jones, and Van Beck Hall contributed to my work. Other teachers and colleagues, including Alice Harris, David Thelen, and Susan Flader, have helped me think about the relationships between business and government and the nature of reform. Philip Scarpino gave me invaluable criticism in a careful reading of the manuscript.

Much of my research was made possible through the cooperation of several private associations and public agencies. Executives of the American Mining Congress, the National Coal Association, and the National Coal Policy Conference granted me forthright interviews and limited use of their records. The directors of the Pennsylvania Coal Mining Association, the West Virginia Surface Mining and Reclamation Association, and the Environmental Policy Center provided similar help. The cooperation of the librarians of Bituminous Coal Research, Inc. was also valuable. H. R. Woolridge, president of the Moshannon Falls Mining Company, helped me to understand first hand the problems and techniques of surface mining. The employees of the Environmental Protection Agency, particularly Donald Walters, were invariably cooperative in providing records from their files. I am especially grateful to William Guckert, the director of the Pennsylvania Bureau of Surface Mine Reclamation, who opened up all his agency's records and files for my use and whose staff cooperated freely in my research. Funds from the Research Council of the Graduate School, University of Missouri-Columbia, and the division of Research, Harvard Graduate School of Business Administration, supported parts of my research.

Above all I have depended on the persistent patience and encouragement of my wife, Cindy. Her efforts provided a family environment that allowed me to do this work.

List of Abbreviations

AEC	Atomic Energy Commission
AISI	American Iron and Steel Institute
AMC	American Mining Congress
API	American Petroleum Institute
ASARCO	American Smelting and Refining Company
BACT	best available control technology
BSMR	Bureau of Surface Mine Reclamation (Pennsylvania)
CASM	Coalition Against Strip Mining
DER	Department of Environmental Resources (Pennsylvania)
EEI	Edison Electric Institute
EPA	Environmental Protection Agency
EQB	Environmental Quality Board (Pennsylvania)
FEA	Federal Energy Administration
FPC	Federal Power Commission
FGD	flue gas desulfurization
FWPCA	Federal Water Pollution Control Administration
GASP	Group Against Smog and Pollution
HEW	Department of Health, Education, and Welfare
NAM	National Association of Manufacturers
NAPCA	National Air Pollution Control Administration
NAS	National Audubon Society
NCA	National Coal Association
NCPC	National Coal Policy Conference
NERA	National Economic Research Associates
NIPCC	National Industrial Pollution Control Council
NPC	National Petroleum Council
NRDC	Natural Resources Defense Council
NSD	no significant deterioration
NSPS	new source performance standards
OCR	Office of Coal Research
OMB	Office of Management and Budget
PCMA	Pennsylvania Coal Mining Association
PEA	Pennsylvania Electric Association
TVA	Tennessee Valley Authority
UMW	United Mine Workers
USCC	United States Chamber of Commerce
WSCC	Western Systems Coordinating Council
WVSMRA	West Virginia Surface Mining and Reclamation Association

Environmental Politics and the Coal Coalition

1

Introduction

WASHINGTON weather was at its worst on a late July day in 1973. Near one hundred degrees, the heat was unbearable, the humidity stifling, and an air stagnation alert was in effect. Motorists waited miserably in long lines at Washington gas stations. But in its coolly air-conditioned hearing room, the Senate Committee on Public Works was holding a special hearing entitled "Nondegradation Policy of the Clean Air Act." The committee members listened as Carl Bagge, president of the National Coal Association, and Lawrence Moss, president of the Sierra Club, voiced antithetical views on the future of the nation's public policy concerning coal energy. Bagge, who spoke for industrialists interested in mining and burning coal, argued that if coal were to rescue America from its impending energy crisis, then rigorous environmental controls would be disastrous. Existing air quality standards and the pending federal strip-mining regulations were bad enough, Bagge said. But a policy of nondegradation, requiring clean air to be kept clean, threatened to halt industrial growth. Moss, on the other hand, appeared undaunted by the energy crisis. He urged that the Congress give first priority to guaranteeing Americans a clean and healthy environment. He seemed unconcerned with any implications that such priorities might have for the costs and technological feasibility of maintaining clean air or with their possible impact on industrial growth.[1] A reflective senator must have wondered how the Congress

---

[1] U.S. Congress, Senate, Committee on Public Works, *Hearings on Nondegradation Policy of the Clean Air Act*, 93rd Cong., 1st sess., July 24, 1973.

could reconcile such a conflict of values as it determined national policy.

However, political decisions made during the past fifteen years had already largely defined the contents of that policy, and by 1977 Congress finished setting forth its principal elements. The evolution of federal environmental policies relevant to coal energy and the political processes that guided that evolution are the subjects of this book. When it amended the Clean Air Act and mandated federal strip-mining controls, the Ninety-fifth Congress adopted policies unimaginable in the Eisenhower years. Those new national policies reflect considerable change in social values, in the financial and political organization of the energy business, and in the performance of the American political process.

Coal is a primary industry that, since the late nineteenth century, has been essential to America's industrial economy. By 1970, 45 percent of the electric power generated in the United States was being produced by the combustion of coal.[2] Since World War I, the steel industry has been dependent on coal for electricity, process heat, and coke; it consumed 87 million tons of coal in 1973.[3] Railroads, which once relied on coal for locomotion, have come to rely on coal haulage for more than 10 percent of their revenues. As advanced mining technologies developed after World War II, the coal industry also came to support a huge equipment manufacturing industry. And, finally, as corporate ownership patterns became increasingly interlinked during the 1960's, many large companies and commercial banks developed substantial vested interests in coal.

Coal's greatest natural shortcoming is that it is a dirty fuel when burned and an environmentally destructive resource when strip mined. Industrial air pollution damages human health, property, and natural resources. Strip mining destroys natural topography, ruins plant and animal habitats, and causes acid mine drainage that pollutes the nation's streams and rivers. Although coal has been mined in as many as twenty-five states and consumed in all fifty, its environmental ill effects have been traditionally regulated at the

---

[2] U.S. Congress, House, Congressional Research Service (prepared for the Committee on Science and Technology), *Energy Facts II*, p. 61.

[3] National Coal Association, *Coal Facts, 1972*, p. 60.

state and local levels. By 1880, America's urban dwellers had begun seriously to resent the health and aesthetic problems coal created, and some tried to use nuisance laws to control them. At the turn of the century and again in the late 1940's, local urban reform movements repeatedly tried to curb industrial smoke from coal. Not until the 1950's, however, did health officials and environmental activists begin to perceive air pollution as a national problem that, unsolved by local initiatives, required a national solution. But, since the problems of strip mining resulted from relatively new technologies of scale that developed during and after World War II, they did not impinge on the environment of most Americans until the late 1950's.

During the last two decades, two changes seem most responsible for the evolution of national policies for regulating coal's environmental problems: increasing criticism of capitalism's growth ethic and the modernization of pluralist political institutions. A historic shortcoming of industrial capitalism has been the failure of the market mechanism to assure the internalization of all costs of production. Adam Smith's assertion that the market price should account fully for all production costs was seldom realized during the course of America's industrialization.[4] Those costs not fully internalized in the price equation and so passed on to the consumer became "social costs"—costs that must be borne by the society at large. Deforestation and erosion from timber cutting, workmen's disabilities, abuses of child labor, salmon depletion, and oil spills exemplify industrialism's social costs. In the past, such deleterious side effects have periodically stimulated reform movements aimed at forcing the production process to account for them.

During the 1960's, a spreading public unwillingness to suffer such problems was increasingly channeled through organized groups of conservationists and public health officials who were most sensitive to coal's social costs. Such groups began a political campaign, marked by the first national conference on air pollution in 1958, to encourage and eventually force the coal industries to mitigate the costs of air pollution by controlling it. At the same time, groups of sportsmen, conservationists, and journalists began promoting politi-

---

[4] Adam Smith, *The Wealth of Nations*, chap. 5.

cal action in several states to reduce the social costs of strip mining. They were soon joined by groups of citizens angered by the disappointing results of local regulation. As the new regulatory legislation escalated the costs of controlling air pollution and strip mining, affected businessmen hardened against the growing drain on their retained earnings, their principal source of growth capital.

By 1970, some environmental activists, especially in larger groups like the Sierra Club, Friends of the Earth, and the Natural Resources Defense Council, had begun to move beyond policies that merely forced internalization of costs. More and more supported policies like nondegradation that appeared likely to constrain needed energy developments and to threaten industrial growth in an absolute sense. Especially after Earth Day in April, 1970, public opinion provided broad constituent support for the political goals of organized environmental interest groups.[5] Nevertheless, corporate values continued to evolve in the opposite direction, becoming more preoccupied with growth capital and devoted to intensely centralized, ever-larger systems for producing energy. Utilities, oil companies, and banks started laying plans for huge, 3,000-megawatt coal-fired power plants, 12-million-ton-per-year strip mines, and 500-acre energy centers for gasifying and liquifying coal. The clash between these two sets of values was inherent in much of the heated political conflict over federal environmental policies.

This book is as much a case study of the political economy as it is a history of environmental politics and coal. As used here, the term *political economy* describes that interaction between business and government aimed at bringing order to the market economy. Rapid industrial and economic growth like that which followed World War II has invariably heightened competition and induced uncertainty in the business environment. Planning future investments is difficult, market shares fluctuate, and corporate fortunes become tenuous. The established interests of large corporations and federal administrative bureaus are frequently threatened by this market instability. Historians and political scientists have con-

---

5 *New York Times*, August 3, 1970. A Gallup poll, conducted May 2–3, 1970, showed air and water pollution to be the second most important social problem after crime. In 1965, pollution had ranked only ninth.

structed numerous models that explain public policy in terms of business control over government decision making.[6] Obviously, the reality of corporate political power is scarcely news. But none of the available models seems accurate or complete enough to describe the immensely complex political organization of coal-related interests and the ways in which they have affected government decision making since 1945. Opposition to environmental controls brought together a large number of previously diverse corporate interests in loosely cooperative political action. This study is especially devoted to describing that cooperation as a newly "modernized" stage in the evolution of the political economy.

With the assent of the federal government, the coal interests have developed a network of institutions for coordinating their combined political influence. The rudiments date from the 1870's, when large-scale businesses of all kinds began trying a succession of organizational devices—pools, trusts, and trade associations—in hopes of attaining economic stability and market control. In the long run, the trade association proved to be the most successful mechanism, both for providing business cooperation among companies in the same industry and for focusing corporate influence on governmental decision making. Trade associations grew and proliferated, especially when the government sought to mobilize industry in support of World War I. Then, as commerce secretary during the 1920's, Herbert Hoover encouraged business organization and peacetime cooperation with government to fulfill his vision of an "associative state."[7] Franklin Roosevelt's New Deal contributed as well. Many of the recovery agencies funneled their economic remedies through business organizations: the American Farm Bureau Federation delivered agricultural adjustments, the American Bankers' Association medi-

[6] See for example, Grant McConnell, *Private Power and American Democracy* and *The Decline of Agrarian Democracy*; Ronald Radosh and Murray Rothbard, eds., *A New History of Leviathan*; Robert Wiebe, *Businessmen and Reform*; Samuel P. Hays, *The Response to Industrialism*; Robert Engler, *The Politics of Oil*; Phillip Foss, *Politics and Grass*; and Marver Bernstein, *Regulating Business by Independent Commission.*

[7] Ellis Hawley, "Herbert Hoover, the Commerce Secretariat, and the Vision of the Associative State, 1921–28," *Journal of American History* 61 (June, 1974), 116–140; see also Robert Cuff, "Herbert Hoover, the Ideology of Voluntarism and War Organization during the Great War," *Journal of American History* 64 (September, 1967), 358–372.

ated banking reform, and hundreds of trade associations helped write and enforce the National Recovery Administration's codes. By the outbreak of World War II, cooperative decision making by business and government agencies was an everyday occurrence. War mobilization extended business organization into every sector of the economy. Patriotism gave legitimacy to the new business-government interface.

The post-1945 plethora of business organizations constitutes the foundation of "pluralism"—the process of formulating public policy through the countervailing self-interests of political pressure groups. Students of pluralism, both critics and apologists, have described the activities of trade associations without finding evidence of significant cohesion between industry groups. Adolph Berle, for one, claimed that "there is no high factor of unity when several hundred corporations in different lines of endeavor are involved. . . . dominance by them over the political state in major matters is not a present possibility."[8] Marxists, however, do sense interindustry cohesion, but only as an ill-defined aura of class self-interest. But, beginning in the late 1950's, coal-related industries did indeed develop new organizational structures that provided political cohesion among several industrial sectors. In the coal-energy community, trade association membership diversified, specifically interindustry associations developed, and corporate executives willingly served on government-appointed councils to advise the president and his cabinet. This systematization of interest-group politics replaced countervailing balance with internal coherence, thereby undercutting the traditional justification for pluralism.

Information and those who control it have become the second crucial element of decision making in the political economy. Since the 1880's, as corporate systems have grown in scale and complexity, government administrators, regulators, and even presidents have found it increasingly difficult to master, or even gain access to, the economic and technical information necessary for sound policy decisions. In 1903, President Theodore Roosevelt established the Bureau of Corporations to gather the information necessary to deal

---

[8] Quoted in McConnell, *Private Power*, p. 252. See also Adolph Berle, *The American Economic Republic*.

with the trusts. But bureau administrators quickly learned that worthwhile information was available only from the trusts themselves, and the price for getting it was selectivity and confidentiality. The bureau's dependency hamstrung the president in his desire to regulate or prosecute the "bad" corporations.

By the 1960's, in a greatly advanced industrial state, technical and economic data had become the essence of environmental politics. Industry's control and use of data repeatedly overwhelmed environmentalists, impressed congressmen, and convinced state and federal regulators. Such data have been the stock-in-trade of industry's network of trade associations and advisory councils. Partly for this reason, most industrialists, and especially the coal interests, have preferred state rather than federal regulatory authority. As laws to control both strip mining and air pollution have been worked out, industry mastery of data has been thoroughly intimidating at the state level, where resource and expertise have been pitifully limited. This was particularly evident when Pennsylvania officials tried to set up rules for controlling air pollution in 1972. Even at the federal level, hard technological and economic data have been the meat of political debate over environmental controls since 1967. "Best available technology," health criteria, coal reserves, "new source performance standards," and energy-crisis particulars have been at the heart of political conflict over national environmental policy.

Even more than legislation, administrative policy making occurs beyond the purview of the public, often appearing to be the disembodied output of a faceless bureaucracy. In most accounts of the political economy, one is left with the impression that after the legislative battle ends, unnamed bureaucrats implement the fully articulated policy impartially and without influence from pluralist pressures. But as the modernizing process has shifted more and more responsibility for complex policy from legislators to administrators, the political process has been subtly altered in several fundamental ways. More crucial decisions are made in secret, without the knowledge of the electorate or the approval of their representatives. The personal values and ambitions of individual, unelected civil servants have a greater influence on important public policies. And, finally, technocratic resources—data, expertise, and financial strength—afford corporations a unique role in lengthy implementation procedures.

The problem of secrecy in government is hardly new, but the increasing emphasis on administrative policy making has been changing its character. The National Industrial Pollution Control Council, advising Richard Nixon on matters of environmental policy, exhibited the most blatant aspects of this tendency toward closed policy discussions between government administrators and corporate managers. A related sort of secrecy, that of interagency bargaining, accounted for the extraordinary revision of the Environmental Protection Agency's guidelines for implementing the Clean Air Act. In both instances, the smoke-filled rooms were occupied by technocrats, not bosses, deciding what was best for the national interest. Even when nongovernment interests were not involved, the bureaucracy's expanded authority to make policy in a closed environment is worth noting. Middle-level staff in the National Air Pollution Control Administration developed the policy concept of "no significant deterioration." It seems that while successive reforms, such as the Freedom of Information Act and the Advisory Council Act, hack away at government secrecy, the modernizing process, stimulating a drift toward more technical, administrative decision making, reinforces it.

In many other nations, such as France, Egypt, or Mexico, the power and autonomy of bureaucrats, both individually and collectively, is widely and commonly recognized. Careful studies of public policy in those countries rarely ignore the role of civil servants. For some reason, however, analytical literature on American public policy most often disregards the bureaucrats' influence on interpreting and implementing the law. Nevertheless, quite real people do make and carry out policy. They staff congressional committees, regulatory agencies like the Environmental Protection Agency, and administrative departments like Interior. Only to a limited extent does the written law of congressional mandate constrain their decisions. This study makes an effort, although inadequate, to get some sense of how individual bureaucrats, governed by their own values and ambitions, contributed to environmental policy. We shall examine, for example, the autonomy of a state strip-mining administrator and the extent to which his personal values and authority affected the outcome of policy and the important role that one or two EPA bureaucrats played in changing the course of air pollution control policy from a reductive, health-oriented minimum, to an expansive, growth-limiting ideal.

As environmental issues became more complex and controversial, the Congress wrote laws necessarily general and without adequate precision. The government agencies that must apply and enforce the law have been given great leeway to construct the technical details of policy. Corporate expertise and technical data have been of critical importance to these administrative executors of the law. For example, the Clean Air Act of 1970 simply mandated that the nation's air quality be improved to a condition not detrimental to human health.[9] By itself, that mandate was scarcely more than a stated goal, at best, an undefined criterion for regulation. However, more than fifteen years of administrative regulation will be necessary to implement that goal. Thus far the Environmental Protection Agency has promulgated specific health criteria for various pollutants, developed air-quality baseline measurements and control districts, established standards for ambient air quality and new source performance standards for each important industrial process, and federal guidelines to the states for enforcing federal rules. It is still developing a centralized federal enforcement program and modifying state regulatory requirements. Likewise, now that the Department of the Interior has begun implementing the federal strip-mining control act, the politics appear to be just as complicated.

At every stage of this regulatory process, the focused expertise of coal's political organization has persistently exerted its influence on policy decisions. For beyond their more traditional lobbying activities, coal-related trade associations, advisory councils, and consulting firms can bring their financial resources, permanent structure, data, and personal and institutional ties most effectively to bear over the long haul of administrative implementation. At least during the 1960's, the amateurs who represented the interests of environmentalism lacked the time, money, data, and organization to monitor, let alone influence, the seemingly dull and endless pro-

[9] P.L. 91-604, 84 Stat. 1676, 42 U.S.C. Sec. 1857-18571.

cess of implementing environmental policy. Not until 1971 did any of the environmental groups grow large enough in membership, political experience, or staff expertise to provide consistently effective, countervailing power in administrative politics.

Scholars who have focused exclusively on policy formation have usually misunderstood how business and government actually interact. A good example is the heated academic debate over the federal "reforms" enacted during the Progressive era. The disagreement among historians over the nature of the Progressive era seems to derive from their preoccupation with the sources, purposes, and conflicts behind those national policies. While certainly important, that emphasis has distorted the significance of such legislation, the concerns of its opponents, and, most of all, the subsequent effects of its administrative application. To understand the evolution of national environmental policies over a period of two decades, this study attempts reasonably to integrate the politics of policy formation with those of administrative implementation.[10]

[10] If the reader is interested in the technical aspects of coal-related, environmental issues, he should refer to appendixes A, B, and C. Appendix A describes strip-mining processes, reclamation techniques, and the enviromental problems that strip mining causes. Appendix B, a primer on stationary-source air pollution, describes the various air pollutants, their effects on health and the natural environment, and the available pollution control techniques. Appendix C explains two of the most volatile information issues of the political debate over strip mining and air pollution—the distribution of coal reserves and the effectiveness of flue gas scrubber devices.

2

The Coal Coalition:
Synthesis of Corporate Power

BY 1954, long before environmental regulations began to affect production, coal had become a sick industry. Annual coal production in the United States had slumped to a low of 391 million tons, down from its postwar level of 630 million tons. The coal industry earned a total of $32 million in 1952. "Unbelievable as it may seem," complained Harry LaViers, president of South-East Coal, "the amounts spent for research by some of the industrial groups is almost ten times larger than the total amount of net profit made by our entire industry."[1] New technologies, competition from other fuels, labor problems, the coal industry's own weak financial structure, and government policies all seemed to conspire its ruin. During World War II, railroad locomotives converted from coal power to diesel fuel. The government built huge oil pipelines and spent $2 billion on nuclear research. Oil companies, invigorated by war profits, expanded exploration and development of both domestic and foreign petroleum reserves. The United Mine Workers, led by John L. Lewis, thwarted the industry's efforts further to mechanize underground mining. And the coal business, diversified by four thousand vigorously competitive mine operators, lacked the scale, management skills, and cash flow needed to keep up with the rapidly expanding economy.

[1] U.S. Congress, House, Special Committee on Coal Research, *Coal*, 84th Cong., 2nd sess., June, 1956, p. 38.

Most of all, coal men needed the power to influence public policy. Government energy policies were killing the coal industry and draining its profits. Federal research and development policy was especially harmful. Before Eisenhower became president, there had been real hope for subsidized coal research. In 1944, the Congress had passed the Synthetic Liquid Fuels Act, a coal promotion that Interior Secretary Harold Ickes and several coal-state senators had jointly sponsored.[2] Between 1944 and 1953, the act authorized more than $75 million for research and commercial demonstration of coal liquefaction and synthesis of gasoline from oil shale. In 1950, the Bureau of Mines reported that its two demonstration installations at Louisiana, Missouri, had produced gasoline from coal at costs competitive with the wholesale price of petroleum gasoline.[3] But as supporters of liquefaction in Interior and Congress clamored for a half-billion dollar development of ten commercial plants, the petroleum industry became concerned with the prospect of federally sponsored competition. Coal liquefaction threatened to create an independent supply of gasoline that would undercut that industry's control of world supplies. The prestigious National Petroleum Council (NPC) undertook a study of synthetic fuels and concluded that the Bureau of Mines had grossly understated costs. The NPC forcefully recommended that Interior and the White House withdraw support from the program.[4] When they did, the Congress terminated the funding for liquefaction and mothballed the plants in 1954.

Meanwhile, the Congress since 1946 had been pumping more

2 Correspondence between Michael Straus and Harold Ickes, 1943–1944, Record Group 48, Department of the Interior, Office of the Secretary, Central Classified Files, 1937–1953, section 11-34 "Synthetic Fuels" (pt. 3), in National Archives, Washington, D.C. See also U.S. Congress, Senate, Select Subcommittee of the Committee on Public Lands and Surveys, Synthetic Liquid Fuels, 78th Cong., 1st sess., August, 1943.

3 U.S. Bureau of Mines, Annual Report to the Secretary of the Interior, 1949, Part II, p. 145. At this point, the Bureau of Mines director estimated the price of coal-derived synthetic gasoline at 10.2 cents per gallon.

4 National Petroleum Council, Subcommittee on Synthetic Fuels Production Costs, "Report of the NPC's Committee on Synthetic Liquid Fuels Production Costs" (unpublished), October 31, 1951, p. 12, National Petroleum Council, Administrative Records, Department of the Interior, Washington, D.C. See also Bruce K. Brown, Deputy Administrator, Petroleum Administration for Defense, to Secretary of Interior, July 30, 1951, in RG 48, section 11-34 "Synthetic Fuels" (pt. 8).

than $100 million annually into developing nuclear power. In 1958, commercial reactors were becoming practical; Congress passed the Price-Anderson Act to spare would-be reactor investors from accident liability. With no significant research and development of their own, coal people faced a grim future of nuclear competition as expanding utilities turned to reactors instead of coal.

Besides stimulating new competition, federal tax and regulatory policies were further stacking the deck against coal. Since 1938, the Federal Power Commission (FPC) had regulated the price of interstate natural gas. Not only did the FPC hold residential gas rates below coal-generated electricity rates, but it also, through special discounts, encouraged bulk consumption of natural gas by utilities and manufacturers. At the same time, oil tax policies dating from World War I provided the petroleum industry huge profits and cash flows for growth from the oil depletion allowance, intangible drilling expenses, and, after 1955, large foreign tax credits.[5] This last perquisite, along with State Department cooperation, tremendously stimulated development of Middle Eastern petroleum, providing low-cost heating oil for New England and residual oil for industrial and utility boilers. Even after four years of "voluntary" imports restrictions, the flood of cheap foreign oil was penetrating coal markets as far west as Pittsburgh by 1958.

Coal's biggest problem was not economic, however. It was a problem of power, and that realization began to dawn on coal men. Former congressman Carter Manasco, chief lobbyist of the National Coal Association (the coal industry trade group), clearly understood the situation. Through its research and development, tax, regulatory, and import policies, said Manasco, "The Federal Government has

[5]The deduction for intangible drilling expenses was established by an Internal Revenue Service ruling in 1916. This provision amounted to as much as $650 million in tax loss in 1972 (see John Blair, *The Control of Oil*, p. 413, n. 19). The oil depletion allowance was established in the Revenue Act of 1918. This provision allowed a tax loss of as much as $1.7 billion in 1972. The foreign tax credit, also established in 1918, became significant to oil companies after an IRS ruling in 1950. During the 1950's and 1960's, foreign tax credits for oil importers amounted to tax losses in the hundreds of millions annually (IRS Statistics of Income, 1967, Supplementary Report, "Foreign Tax Credit Claimed on Corporation Income Tax Returns" [Washington, D.C.: Government Printing Office, 1967], cited in Blair, *Control of Oil*, p. 195).

done as much to hurt the coal industry . . . as any competing fuel."[6] The coal industry needed to restructure its basis of economic and political power if it was to survive, let alone compete, in the rapacious environment of energy's political economy.

First, the larger coal companies commenced a wave of mergers to reduce competition, develop management efficiencies, and generate larger cash flows. These changes were necessary for capital expansion, research and development, and sustained political activity. In the decade after 1955, Peabody Coal Company acquired ten other coal producers, Consolidation Coal Company bought eight, Island Creek Coal seven, and Pittston Company six.[7] These four companies and a few others emerged in the mid-1960's as sound energy-fuel corporations and consequently as likely targets for takeovers by noncoal corporations.

Also beginning in 1955, coal operators began sustained, albeit modest, pressure on Congress in support of federally funded coal research, equalization of depletion allowances, and mandatory quotas on oil imports. By the end of the decade, coal's political reinvigoration began to bear fruit. In March 1959, President Eisenhower, pressured not only by coal interests but also by domestic oil producers and independent refiners, ordered mandatory oil import quotas. For the next fourteen years, Washington restricted oil imports, at least in principle, to 12 percent of domestic oil consumption. In the fall of 1959, Senator Robert Byrd (D-W.Va.) and Congressmen Wayne Aspinall (D-Colo.) and John Saylor (D-Pa.) successfully guided the Coal Research Act through both houses. The act would have established an office of coal research as an independent agency to sponsor coal research. Oil interests were quick to see the analogy between an office of coal research and the Atomic Energy Commission. An independent office of coal research, with adequate funding and joint congressional backing, might create an entirely new fuel industry. They opposed the bill, preferring legislation that would establish the coal research agency as a modest and dependably controlled bureau within the Department of Interior.

[6] U.S. Congress, House, Special Committee on Coal Research, *Coal*, 85th Cong., 1st sess., February, 1957, pp. 566–567.
[7] Federal Trade Commission, *Concentration Levels and Trends in the Energy Sector of the U.S. Economy*, pp. 80–81.

President Eisenhower agreed and vetoed the bill. However, a year later he did sign a bill authorizing an office of coal research within Interior.

A range of coal interests joined in 1959 to incorporate a new trade association, the National Coal Policy Conference (NCPC). The NCPC was an innovation for organizing business power. Conceived as an interindustry association, the NCPC included representatives from the coal producers, electric utilities, railroads, mining equipment manufacturers, and United Mine Workers. The NCPC blended the political clout of broad membership with the effectiveness of sharply focused purpose. Its objectives were straightforward: ". . . [to] articulate the problems and the requirements of coal to the legislative and exectuive branches and other institutions of the government, thereby establishing a positive and constructive public policy toward coal. . . . [and to] assist in the formation and establishment of policy when the mutual interests of coal and related industries are affected, and to aid in and direct the execution of such policies."[8]

Seemingly, then, 1959 was a landmark year for the coal industry. Coal production was on the upswing, labor was cooperating, mergers were providing a firmer financial footing, and the largess of federal policy had at least begun to benefit coal. But these very developments made the coal industry ripe for plucking, marked the beginning of the end of an autonomous coal industry, and assured the emergence of the coal coalition. The larger industrial community had enjoyed a decade of rapid growth and healthy corporate profits, but at the expense of depleting energy resources. Coal became a prime target for diversification. Manufacturers, utilities, metals producers, and especially oil producers had excess capital for investment, and the coal industry was certainly capital-starved. Moreover, predictions by the Geological Survey, the interruption of Middle East supplies by the Suez crisis, and a downturn in new exploratory drilling for oil and gas reminded corporate planners that energy resources were neither limitless nor completely dependable. With General Dynamics Corporation's purchase of Freeman Coal

---

[8] Joseph Moody, president, National Coal Policy Conference, in National Coal Policy Conference, *NCPC, Purposes, Platforms, Objectives,* p. 4.

Company in 1959, an unprecedented merger movement began, and by 1978 the coal industry had virtually lost its corporate identity. Following General Dynamics' lead were Gulf Oil (Pittsburg & Midway Coal), Continental Oil (Consolidation Coal), Kennecott Copper (Peabody Coal), Occidental Petroleum, Standard Oil of Ohio, Exxon, General Electric, and dozens of others.[9] In less than two decades, coal ownership passed to a larger corporate control by oil and gas, utilities, steel, manufacturing, and railroads. And this new ownership was just the first of many systematic links that would bind together a new and powerful community of business interests whose alliance would strongly influence federal environmental policy.

Who Owns America's Coal?

At the heart of what has become the coal coalition are those corporations that own coal-producing facilities and control future coal reserves. Except for a couple of the largest integrated steel companies, the leading coal producers in the 1950's were all independent companies, and not very large at that. By 1976, all but three of the biggest producers were subsidiaries of larger, noncoal corporations, and the forty largest such firms produced nearly two-thirds of the nation's coal. Those forty largest coal producers (see appendix table D.1 for ranking of companies) mostly rank among the five hundred largest corporations in America and are dominated by oil and gas firms, primary metals interests, and diversified corporations (see table 1).

Future capacity to produce coal depends on ownership of untapped coal reserves. Just a decade ago, the federal government, Indian tribes, and land-grant railroads owned most of the coal reserves in the West. Patterns of reserve control in the East were less concentrated though exceedingly complex. Railroads and coal operators had, in the later nineteenth century, acquired thousands of acres of coal rights, at rockbottom prices, in broad-form deeds signed over by desperate Appalachian farmers. The remaining eastern re-

---

[9] Federal Trade Commission, *Concentration Levels*, p. 202. McGraw-Hill Co., *1976 Keystone Coal Industry Manual*, pp. 738–739.

TABLE 1

Forty Largest Coal Producers by Industry Group, 1976

Type of Industry	Number in Group	Annual Tonnage	Percentage of Top 40 Annual Tonnage
Petroleum/gas	12	150,550,000	37
Utilities	6	45,443,000	11
Steel/smelting	10	52,472,000	13
Diversified corporations	9	121,868,000	30
Independent coal producers	3	32,090,000	9
TOTAL	40	402,443,000*	100

SOURCE: Compiled from McGraw-Hill Co., *1976 Keystone Coal Industry Manual.*
* Sixty-three percent of total U.S. production.

serves were retained by landed families and realty speculators. As the 1960's wore on, as an oil and gas supply problems mounted, interest in coal reserves picked up. The new corporate coal interests seemed to be anticipating the crisis in energy that was soon to emerge. They commanded the necessary venture capital, as well as the capacity for long-range planning investments, and commenced acquiring both public and private coal rights. Moreover, since the oil-gas-uranium price spiral had not yet begun, coal leases could still be had at bargain rates. And the Department of Interior was willing, since coal leases generated needed revenue for the Bureau of Land Management and provided a source of quick cash that might alleviate pressures from hard-pressed Indian tribes to do something about their poverty and unemployment. Most important, since the oil companies themselves were leading the buying, they raised no significant political opposition that otherwise might have stayed the enthusiasm of Interior officials.

So, between 1966 and 1974, the new energy interests went on a coal-reserve-buying spree. By January, 1974, the Bureau of Land Management had leased more than 700,000 acres of coal from the public domain. The Bureau of Indian Affairs had approved leases amounting to 200,000 acres of Crow, Navajo, Cheyenne, and Ute lands. And a variety of coal interests, especially electric utilities, snapped up thousands of coal acres in the East. By 1976, the forty

Table 2

Forty Largest Coal Reserve Holders by Industry Group, 1976

Type of Industry	Number in Group	Reserves (billion tons)	Percentage of Total U.S. Reserves*
Petroleum/gas	19	43.313	38
Railroads	3	22.800	20
Utilities	6	6.413	6
Steel/smelting	3	4.900	4
Diversified corporations	4	12.559	11
Independent coal producers	5	9.235	8

Source: Compiled from McGraw-Hill Co., 1976 Keystone Coal Industry Manual.
* Based on 112 billion tons of reserves known to be under private control.

largest coal reserve holders (see appendix table D.2 for ranking of companies) controlled more than 99 billion tons, about 87 percent of proven reserves in private hands (see table 2). A handful of oil companies and two railroads, the Burlington Northern and Union Pacific, have intensively concentrated control of the coal reserve base for America's energy future.

During the 1960's, several financial interdependencies evolved among coal-related corporations, wedding them even more to mutual concern for coal prosperity. The complexity of new energy technologies forced cooperation. For example, a decision to utilize a unit train required intense joint planning and contractual arrangements between the railroad, the coal-mining operator, equipment suppliers, engineering firms responsible for building preparation and loading facilities, and the consuming utility.[10] The huge size of modern energy enterprises often involved several parties. Long-term contracts and consortium arrangements became necessary to secure their joint interests. Growing concern for assuring long-range energy

[10] A unit train is one devoted exclusively to delivery of trainloads of coal directly from the mine to the consuming power plant. Rolling stock is often owned by the utility, and portions of track may be specially designed and committed to the unit operation. Special loading facilities are designed to meet the particular needs of the mine, the utility, and the railroad. See John T. Starr, Jr., The Evolution of the Unit Train, 1960–1969, University of Chicago, Department of Geography, Research Paper No. 158 (1976).

supplies led to contractual and ownership ties between coal consumers (steel and electric utilities) and producers. Most important was the immense need for capital over long lead times (five to seven years), which drew commercial banks into a lasting involvement with coal. Just building a modern coal mine may cost more than $100 million. The largest coal-fired power plants can exceed $2 billion in price. Even equipment like strip-mining shovels and draglines can cost upwards of $40 million. And as coal interests began seriously planning gasification and liquefaction complexes, capital requirements skyrocketed. By the mid-1970's, an identifiable coalition of coal interests had emerged, its foundation resting on seven industrial sectors: coal production, oil and gas, metals, electric utilities, railroads, mining equipment manufacturers, and commercial banks.

The railroad business has had the oldest proprietary interest in coal. Railroads own, mine, and transport coal. In particular, five of the largest rail systems carry 55.2 percent of all coal shipped by rail and own reserves in excess of 24 billion tons—enough coal, at the current rate of consumption, to fulfill the total national demand for forty-five years (see table 3). For some of these rail lines, their tremendous reserves are their most valuable asset. Executives at Burlington Northern face a coal-energy future with vibrant enthusiasm: "Ours is both a transportation and a natural resources firm. . . . In the face of new demands for coal, Burlington Northern is a prime example of a firm that has good reason to marshal its coal facts and figures—it has rights to a good share of America's large western coal resources and as the nation's longest railroad it has the trains to move it."[11]

While these railroads are wedded to the coal coalition, they have not always shared identical views on environmental policy. The western roads have been most concerned with restrictive aquifer and revegetative aspects of federal strip-mining regulations, provisions that would injure their western freight. In 1974, while Congress debated strip-mining controls, Burlington Northern appealed

[11] George R. Rowe, assistant vice-president, commodity marketing, Burlington Northern, Inc., "Economics of Using Western Coal in Appalachian Markets," a paper delivered at 1974 Coal Convention of the American Mining Congress, Pittsburgh, Pennsylvania, May, 1974.

TABLE 3

Principal Rail Systems Involved in Coal, 1974

Rail Systems	Percentage of Total Rail Coal Tonnage	Coal Affiliate	Reserves (billion tons)
Burlington Northern	4.2		11.4
Union Pacific	1.1	Rocky Mountain Energy	10.8
		Union Pacific Mining	
		Medicine Bowl Coal	
C&O/B&O system*	22.2	Galley Coal Land Co.	250,000 acres
		New River Coal	amount unknown
Penn Central	14.5	Clearfield Bituminous Coal	amount unknown
		Chicago and Harris Coal	amount unknown
Norfolk & Western	13.2	Pocahontas Land Co.	1.4

SOURCES: Federal Trade Commission, *Concentration Levels and Trends in the Energy Sector of the U.S. Economy* (1974); Cleveland *Plain Dealer*, January 6, 1974; Davitt McAteer, *Coal Mining Health and Safety in West Virginia* (1970); *1976 Keystone Coal Industry Manual*.

* Includes Western Maryland and Reading railroads.

for public support of existing state legislation in full-page magazine advertisements: "Burlington Northern holds substantial reserves of clean-burning, low-sulfur coal to help supply the energy needs of our nation. But we also recognize our responsibility to the future. . . . As BN coal deposits are removed, extensive reclamation—contouring, fertilizing, and seeding—restore surface mined lands to further usefulness."[12] And because their coal is relatively low in sulfur content, these western railroads have not opposed restrictive air pollution standards except for the no-significant-deterioration policy, which might hurt western mining and industrial development. On the other hand, Penn Central and its eastern competitors have been more concerned by the steep-slope provisions of surface-mining regulations and with the ambient and emission standards for sulfur oxide in eastern industrial cities. When assemblymen in Pennsylvania were writing state regulations for air pollution in 1972, Penn Central executives effectively warned of the "drastic and unbelievably expensive consequences" rigorous rules would have on freights, revenues, and employment.[13] Advocates of pluralism might seize on such differences to justify a model of countervailing powers, but that model does not fit. While the different environmental policy interests of eastern and western coal railroads did conflict, their political opposition to strip-mining controls did not. As coalition members, they focused political pressure on the particulars of the national legislation that most concerned them, neither opposing nor supporting the concerns of their counterparts. The net effect was to weaken the overall policy package in the absence of intracoalition haggling.

Like the railroads, the primary metals industry have been involved with coal since the nineteenth century. Some steel producers own what have ironically been called "captive" coal mines. More realistically, metals smelters and especially steel producers have become captives of their coal sources, since coal, either for coking or electric generation, is essential for making steel. Prior to the mid-1950's, only U.S. Steel and Bethlehem Steel owned coal subsidiaries.

---

[12] *Business Week*, July 13, 1974, p. 3.
[13] Public Hearings on Air Pollution Regulations, December, 1971, III, 68, Pennsylvania Environmental Quality Board, Harrisburg, Pa.

But by 1976 at least nineteen metals producers had acquired substantial interests in coal-mining affiliates, reserve properties, or both. Ten metals producers mined about a tenth of domestic coal production and owned a significant share of reserves.

Market conditions account for this development and for steel's active participation, as part of the coal coalition, in environmental politics. In the 1960's, metallurgical-grade coal became more scarce and rose in price. At the same time, competition from foreign steel intensified. Domestic producers found themselves in a cost-price squeeze that made low-cost coal supplies essential. More than ever, steel companies needed controlled sources of coal. To make matters worse, rigorous strip-mining regulations threatened to escalate coal costs, and air pollution controls began adding staggering cost burdens to mill operations. Because these environmental costs were, according to steel men, uniquely American and not imposed in foreign nations, they aggravated the problem of competing with imports. Firms like Bethlehem Steel, with older and more polluting facilities, faced stunning declines in profitability and market share after 1975. Management placed a large part of the blame for their problems on environmental policy.

Even though nuclear electric generation became commercial in the 1960's, the electric utilities industry remained dependent on coal for 54 percent of their fuel consumption in 1971.[14] As cost problems and environmental opponents began plaguing nuclear-electric development, public and investor-owned utilities across the nation scrambled to secure coal resources. Western utilities could not wait to build coal-fired plants in order to meet the surging demands for electricity that rapid population growth and air-conditioning stimulated. Utilities in eastern and central states were coping with nuclear delay and cancellation and dwindling natural gas supplies. Then, in 1973, when the price of foreign residual (boiler) fuel oil skyrocketed, the entire demand pattern changed drastically. More than ever, eastern utilities needed to secure coal supplies to avoid reliance on independent producers charging spot market prices of more than forty dollars per ton. By 1976, six utilities had entered

---

[14] National Coal Association, *Coal Facts, 1972*, pp. 66–67.

the ranks of the top forty coal producers, and nine controlled 11 percent of privately held reserves.[15]

Long-term fuel supply contracts bound many of the other electric utilities to the coal coalition. Many contracts contain cost escalation provisions which pass on to the utility added costs for environmental reclamation. Other utilities that began planning efficient, mine-mouth generating projects frequently entered into joint ventures with coal producers. Duke Power, for instance, financed a new captive mine to be operated by Belco Petroleum's Hawley Fuels, and Carolina Light & Power financed 80 percent of a new Pickands-Mather mine.[16] Through these and other ties, including stock ownership and directorate interlocks, electric utilities became even more integrated with coal prosperity than they traditionally had been, and at the same time became active politically on coal-environmental issues.

Of all the electric utilities, the Tennessee Valley Authority (TVA) was unique among members of the coal coalition. In its own words, the "TVA, as a Federal Agency, as the nation's largest electric power producer and as the nation's largest coal purchaser, recognizes that it has a significant role in the national environmental effort."[17] Ironically, that role has been one of leading corporate opposition to effective federal controls of strip mining and air pollution. Senator George Norris conceived of the TVA as an experiment in public power and environmental engineering. President Franklin Roosevelt, who turned Norris' vision into a reality, valued it also as a source of employment and a way to revitalize the pitiful economy of Appalachia. Between 1934 and 1945, TVA built dozens of hydroelectric dams on the Tennessee River and its tributaries. That cheap power, together with the war, was too successful at attracting industry. By 1950, demand for TVA power was rising dramatically, and since practical dam sites were depleted, TVA turned to abundant local coal to provide new electricity. Following its congressional mandate to supply power at the lowest rates possible, TVA bought

[15] McGraw-Hill Co., *1976 Keystone Coal Industry Manual.*

[16] *Bluefield Daily Telegraph*, April 21, 1974, and *Mining Congress Journal* 60 (April, 1974), 15.

[17] Tennessee Valley Authority, *Environmental Statement: Policies Relating to Sources of Coal Used by the TVA for Electric Power Generation*, p. 1.

coal on competitive bids that encouraged rapid development of strip mining. When no laws controlled its environmental costs, strip mining was more efficient than deep mining. Likewise, TVA power plants, operating as cheaply as possible, burned high-sulfur coal and disregarded air pollution. Somewhere in the rush of postwar industrial growth, TVA directors had lost sight of the TVA's other guiding principle, environmental engineering.

By 1971, TVA burned 32.5 million tons of coal to generate 74.3 billion kilowatts of electricity for ten million people.[18] Nine energy corporations and one independent coal operator supplied three-fourths of TVA's coal.[19] And, like the other coal interests, the TVA had meanwhile been acquiring coal reserves of its own, 412 million tons by 1976.

Although the TVA did encourage strip mining by competitive coal bidding, it has not been unaware of environmental damage. The authority has consistently advocated state regulation of strip mining, and after 1965 it required some reclamation standards of the mine operators who sold it coal. But when it came to federal controls, TVA functionaries, especially Chairman Aubrey Wagner, balked. During the years of state and federal legislative hearings, TVA spokesmen always endorsed "realistic" environmental control policies. Euphemistically, "realistic" meant mild state standards for reclaiming strip mines (rather than rigorous federal requirements), ambient rather than source-emission standards for controlling air pollution, and use of tall stacks or "intermittent control techniques" to disperse rather than eliminate air pollutants. TVA executives did not hesitate to participate in coal coalition political activities, wielding special influence as government insiders and as directors of immense economic power in most of seven states.

Caterpillar Tractor, Dart Truck, and Bucyrus Erie are among the hundreds of companies that sell mining equipment and are a part of coal's coalition. Although few of these companies directly own coal resources, all to some degree depend on coal prosperity. Some of the companies—for instance, Marion Power Shovel and Joy

18 Ibid.
19 U.S. Congress, House, Committee on Small Business, *Hearings on Concentration by Competing Raw Fuel Industries in the Energy Market*, 92nd Cong., 2nd sess., October, 1971, pp. 10–17.

Manufacturing—primarily produce mining equipment. Such firms are the most devoted to a healthy coal industry and most actively participate in environmental politics. Other manufacturers, such as Caterpillar Tractor and Westinghouse, enjoy profits on coal-related sales but do not depend entirely on them. These corporations, many of which are quite large, add prestige to the coalition, contribute to the coffers of its trade associations, and occasionally reinforce coal's views in legislative hearings. And they help shape the policy goals of the organizations that conduct coal's political activity and public relations.

Each year thousands of executives from the companies that manufacture mining equipment attend the conventions of the American Mining Congress and the National Coal Association. Besides negotiating sales, these businessmen attend and participate in seminars and panel discussions on surface-mining regulations, air pollution control policy, and a dozen other subjects relating to national energy policy. Out of these meetings, equipment people learn the issues of environmental regulation and take home advice for political action. And there is scarcely a congressional district in the United States where the mining equipment manufacturers do not have a plant and with it the political clout of jobs and payroll. In a nationally circulated advertisement on behalf of strip mining, Caterpillar Tractor succinctly explained the equipment manufacturer's role in the coal coalition: "Surface mining may not be the total answer [to the energy crisis]. But done carefully, responsibly, it is a good way to get the coal we need. Caterpillar is concerned because we make machines used in the mines."[20]

When international oil companies began investing in coal, it was the surest sign that energy conditions in America were changing. Unlike the other industries entering the coal business, the petroleum industry had no prior involvement. In fact, oil and gas were coal's chief competitors. But domestic oil and gas reserves had reached their peak by the late 1950's, and new exploration and drillings began to level off. During the 1960's, they dropped off sharply, so that by 1973 domestic proven reserves had declined to critical

[20] *Time Magazine*, July 15, 1974, p. 17; *Business Week*, July 13, 1974, p. 32k.

levels. Prudent oil managers knew that declining reserves would eventually force rising fuel prices, and coal looked like a sure investment for the future. Moreover, as prices rose, processes to liquify and gasify coal were bound to become competitive, and synthetic gasoline and gas could eventually supplement the oil industry's supply of fossil fuel.

Drawing on their huge cash flows and solid investment credit, petroleum and gas companies raced to buy up coal producers and coal reserves. By 1976, at least fifty-eight oil-gas-energy corporations had bought into some form of coal ownership. Thirty-three oil and gas companies own coal-producing subsidiaries, and at least nineteen of the largest integrated oil companies acquired coal reserves (19 percent of all federal coal leases went to oil companies). Now at the top of the coal industry, twelve petroleum and gas companies control one-fourth of all coal output (see appendix table D.3). Those which could not buy mining subsidiaries developed their own mining divisions or entered into joint ventures with coal producers seeking to expand their output. Several of the larger oil companies accelerated their planning and development of projects to gasify and liquify coal. So, after years of struggling against the power of the oil industry, coal men quite suddenly found themselves working for it. And they relished the change as doors began opening in Wall Street and Washington. Credit grew easier, previously intransigent congressmen from Texas and Louisiana became allies, and federal policy, through the Federal Energy Agency and then the Department of Energy, began to favor coal.

Not everyone was pleased by oil's swift involvement in the coal industry. Several groups whose interests clashed with those of coal operators now faced and feared the power of "Big Oil." The United Mine Workers of America (UMW) vehemently attacked oil's new role in the coal business. UMW leaders quickly realized that oil company ownership drastically improved the bargaining position of coal operators, whose losses in a strike could now be absorbed by the parent company's profits. In 1973, an editorial in the *UMW Journal* warned that "the coal barons have changed, but the need to organize against their power remains much the same. . . . The fight against oil domination of coal is not one the UMW can wage alone.

. . . A coalition with other unions, environmental organizations, and consumer groups would be necessary to lobby for . . . anti-trust actions which President Miller has demanded."[21] By 1975, just such a coalition did convince Senators Edward Kennedy and Phillip Hart to sponsor a bill to force major oil companies to divest themselves of their coal and uranium properties. The Marine Engineers' Beneficial Association was another union that actively disapproved of oil's investment in coal. This group sought increased oil imports to stimulate jobs on oil tankers and feared that oil money would help develop sources of domestic fuel. The union engaged consultant Stanley Ruttenberg to appraise the economic impact of oil's entry into other fuel areas. The result was a book that criticized the oil industry for eliminating interfuel competition and highlighted the antitrust aspects of oil involvement in the coal business.[22]

As early as 1971, the House Committee on Small Business had held a hearing to air complaints about oil's growing dominance of the coal industry.[23] Distributors of electric power, represented by the Tennessee Valley Public Power Association, the American Public Power Association, and the National Rural Electric Cooperative Association, spoke adamantly against the merging of coal and oil interests. They believed that oil companies were raising the price of coal, and they asked the Justice Department to investigate the possibility of coal price-fixing by the oil companies.[24]

As one might expect, oil and gas people viewed their coal ventures quite differently. In 1966, when Continental Oil swallowed up the nation's largest coal company, L. F. McCollum, Continental's chairman, explained his company's goal: "We are convinced that the coal industry has attractive long-term prospects, particularly in supplying increasing requirements for generation of electric power. The acquisition of the Consolidation Coal reserves will strengthen the basic energy raw material position of the economy."[25] By 1972, oil

[21] "The New Energy Barons: How Big Oil Controls the Coal Industry," *United Mine Workers Journal*, July 15, 1973.

[22] Stanley H. Ruttenberg and Associates, *The American Oil Industry: A Failure of Anti-Trust Policy.*

[23] House, *Concentration Hearings*, 92nd Cong., 2nd sess., October, 1971, p. 18.

[24] Ibid., p. A437.

[25] *Time Magazine*, October 22, 1965, p. 106.

men were using the imminent energy crisis to justify interfuel mergers in the face of pending investigations by Congress and the Federal Trade Commission. John McLean, president of Continental Oil and a member of the National Petroleum Council, cautioned that "if coal is to play its proper role in bridging our pending energy gap . . . oil companies, gas companies, coal companies, and uranium companies should be free to shift their capital, manpower, and technological capabilities from one energy field to another as future circumstances may require."[26] And that same year, at the National Coal Association's annual convention, a West Coast utility executive won applause when he praised the "emerging partnership of coal and the gas industry." For certain, the petroleum-gas industry had moved to preeminence in the new coal coalition.

The picture of coal's new financial structure would be incomplete without considering the substantial involvement of America's largest and most influential banking houses. A dozen banks, seven based in New York, have substantial investments, trust accounts, and directorate interlocks with coal interests. And they are convinced that coal must play the crucial role in the orderly economic growth to which commercial banks are committed. The banking establishment, both locally and nationally, has lent coal not only its money, but also its huge prestige and institutional power.

Confidentiality makes it difficult to evaluate the role of banks in the merger movement that has reinvigorated the coal business. Most data on bank investments are proprietary, and open political intercession by banks has been rare. A recent congressional investigation of corporate ownership has at least shed some light on control of stock and shared directorships. Table 4 gives a sense of stock ownership by large commercial banks in a sample of twenty coal-related corporations. They include five coal-hauling railroads, six petroleum-gas corporations with coal reserves and production subsidiaries, and seven electric utilities, all of which have lobbied on federal environmental issues. On the average, the fifteen banks listed were among the top thirty stockholders of 80 percent of the twenty sample corporations. While it is true that banks rarely exercise the

[26] John G. McLean, "A Special Role for Coal," in National Coal Association, "Proceedings: 55th Annual Convention," June, 1972.

TABLE 4

Banks Most Frequently among the Thirty Top Stockholders
of Selected Coal-Related Corporations*

Rank	Bank	Number of Coal Interests
1	Morgan Guaranty Trust (NY)	18
2	Chase Manhattan Bank (NY)	18
3	Manufacturers Hanover Trust (NY)	18
4	First National City Bank (NY)	16
5	Bankers Trust (NY)	15
6	Bank of New York (NY)	13
7	U.S. Trust Co. (NY)	12
8	Chemical Bank (NY)	9
9	Girard Trust (Philadelphia)	9
10	Fidelity Bank (Philadelphia)	8
11	Bank of Delaware (Wilmington)	7
12	Provident National (Philadelphia)	7
13	Mellon Bank (Pittsburgh)	6
14	Northwestern National (Minneapolis)	4
15	First Pennsylvania (Philadelphia)	4

SOURCE: Compiled from U.S. Congress, Senate, Committee on Government Operations, *Disclosure of Corporate Ownership*, 93rd Cong., 2nd sess., 1974, S. Doc. 93-62.

* The twenty sample corporations are listed in order of the percentage of their stock (indicated in parentheses) held jointly by the seven biggest New York banks: Burlington Northern R.R. (21.7), Southern Railway (18.1), Mobil Oil (17.0), Pennzoil Corp. (16.2), Virginia Electric & Power (14.5), Caterpillar Tractor (13.2), Union Carbide (12.9), Continental Oil (11.8), American Electric Power (11.0), Atlantic Richfield (10.8), Allegheny Power (9.3), Norfolk & Western R.R. (8.2), Baltimore Gas & Electric (4.5), C&O/B&O R.R. (4.1), Cleveland Electric (3.2), Ashland Oil (2.7), Transcontinental Gas (2.5), Pennsylvania Power & Light (2.1), Penn Central R.R. (0.9), and Pacific Power & Light (0.4).

voting rights of their portfolios, they nonetheless have rights and the influence that accompanies them. Obviously, these banks have an overriding interest in securing the financial well-being of their coal interests. It has been in the mutual interest of commercial banks to oppose environmental policies that might threaten their coal commitments.

As larger corporate interests absorbed coal management, directorship interlocks on corporate boards proliferated. And as bankers became coal directors and vice versa, their business goals and political needs coalesced. This new relationship between coal and banking enhanced the prestige and effectiveness of coal men, who had rarely enjoyed much cosmopolitan influence. In local coal capitals like Charleston, West Virginia, and Cleveland, Ohio, banking and coal executives came jointly to dominate the business establishment of the entire region. In 1972, for example, the Oglebay-Norton Coal Company's board of directors was thoroughly interlocked with the Cleveland financial community. Ten coal directors held twelve directorships in seven regional banks. They also held a variety of other corporate directorships, several related to coal. One of Oglebay-Norton's directors, Herbert Richey, was also a director of the Union Financial Corporation, president of Valley Camp Coal (shortly to be acquired by Quaker State Oil), a director of the National Coal Association, chairman of the Natural Resources Committee of the U.S. Chamber of Commerce, and a member of the coal subcouncil of Nixon's National Industrial Pollution Control Council. Representing all these interests, Mr. Richey lobbied hard in Washington and also in state capitals against rigorous air pollution and strip-mining controls.

At the national level, banking interlocks with coal interests became pervasive. In 1972, directors of Morgan Guaranty Trust sat on the boards of ten coal-related corporations, and Morgan was a major stockholder in at least six of these companies.[27] The Burlington Northern Railroad, an important political activist in the coal coalition by 1972, was governed by a board of directors that held sixteen directorships at thirteen major banks, including the First National City Bank (New York), Morgan Guaranty Trust, and the federal reserve bank of Minneapolis.[28] Moreover, such links between coal and banking served as the basis for political as well as economic

---

[27] Data compiled from Dun & Bradstreet, *1973 Million Dollar Directory*. See also U.S. Congress, Senate, Committee on Government Operations, *Disclosure of Corporate Ownership*, 93rd Cong., 2nd sess., 1974, S. Doc. 93-62. The directors of Morgan Guaranty Trust ($27.4 billion in trust assets, 1973) served as directors of Atlantic Richfield, Burlington Northern, Continental Oil, Exxon, Southern Railway, Union Carbide, U.S. Steel, Duke Power, Cities Service, and Niagara Mohawk.

[28] Senate, *Disclosure of Corporate Ownership*, 93rd Cong., 2nd sess., 1974, S. Doc. 93-62, p. 387.

power. For example, Continental Oil's directors sat on the boards of Bankers Trust, Morgan Guaranty Trust, Mellon Bank, and Continental Illinois Bank. Collectively those banks owned 10 percent of Continental Oil. The directors of Continental's subsidiary, Consolidation Coal, held two other banking directorships as well as directorships of six other coal-related corporations.[29] And the men who filled those chairs had some strong convictions about the environment. The president of Continental Oil, John McLean, was also a director of the Boston Company and Consolidation Coal and chairman of the National Petroleum Council's Committee on Energy Outlook. He believed that the biggest problems facing the coal industry were "availability of manpower, anti-pollution requirements, environmental restraints, and the mine health and safety laws." The way to solve these problems, according to McLean, was to "seek a reasonable balance between our economic requirements and our social aspirations. . . . with respect to pollution controls, we need pragmatic compromises, compatible with our society's economic necessities." In 1972, McLean's National Petroleum Council committee produced *U.S. Energy Outlook*, the most comprehensive recommendation for energy policy ever prepared for the federal government.[30] The chairman of the policy committee for that report was Andrew Tarkington, another director of Continental Oil, Consolidation Coal, and Bankers Trust.

During the 1970's, bankers themselves played increasingly active roles in the affairs of the coal coalition. They warned against environmental policies that might upset stability in the coal business, shake the confidence of potential investors, and cause growth capital to dry up. George Kruger, a vice-president of Chase Manhattan Bank, explained this theme carefully to an audience of congressmen holding hearings on strip-mining controls in 1973. "Among the basic elements of risk evaluation are predictability of costs and consistency of government regulatory controls," said Kruger. To avoid upsetting bankers, "reclamation requirements should be prudently developed . . . based on careful cost/benefit analysis." The

[29] Compiled from Dun & Bradstreet, *1973 Million Dollar Directory* and Ruttenberg, *The American Oil Industry*, app. 3.
[30] McLean, "A Special Role for Coal," p. 11, 12; National Petroleum Council, *U.S. Energy Outlook: A Summary Report* (1972).

Chase Manhattan Bank was a member of both the National Coal Association and the American Mining Congress, and its concern for sound policy was, in Kruger's words, self-evident: "Chase Manhattan Bank is one of the nation's leading lenders to the mining industry."[31] In November, 1973, the National Coal Association sponsored a special conference in Chicago to establish a "timely dialogue among coal industry principals, financial specialists, [and] financial community lenders." Top executives from Chase Manhattan, Continental Illinois National, and the Fidelity Bank of Philadelphia discussed the problems that new environmental policies created for generating enough growth capital.[32] And when the American Mining Congress convened a year later, Norman Robertson, a senior vice-president of Mellon Bank and director of Pennsylvania Power and Light, spoke on how shifting federal policies created an atmosphere of instability that was the worst problem for independent coal operators and a major reason for the coal coalition: "Unlike the oil and gas industries that can support a substantial portion of new investment from internal cash flows, the independent coal firms at present have to rely heavily on external financing." Notwithstanding the present policy problems, the banker from Mellon earnestly hoped that "with responsible government policies and sound management, the coal industry will . . . be able to attract the financing it needs."[33]

The giant commercial banks have contributed far more than their self-interest to the coal coalition. Their considerable prestige now stands behind the coal lobby on most policy issues. The banks have lent coal their management skills and have negotiated the mergers that built the coalition. Their financial ties weave together the interests of all the coal-related corporations. The Senate Committee on Government Operations summarized the banking community's pervasive influence in even broader terms: "The multiple levels of corporate management available to institutional investors present fundamental questions regarding public policy . . . they present

[31] U.S. Congress, Senate, Committee on Interior and Insular Affairs, *Hearings—Regulation of Surface Mining Operations*, 93rd Cong., 1st sess., March, 1973, pp. 834–835, 833.
[32] National Coal Association, Announcement Bulletin, "Financial Conference," 1973.
[33] Reprinted in *Mining Congress Journal* 60 (June, 1974), pp. 70–71.

questions about the nature of our industrial society—how it will be directed and controlled."[34]

Coal's New Political Machine

As the economic interests of seven coal-related industries overlapped more and more, so did their political commitments. It was only logical that the corporate leaders with a stake in coal would converge in a political coalition to protect their mutual interest. By coordinating their political efforts, they could best "assure the development of a healthy coal industry."[35] After 1959, as each new environmental issue arose, more corporate members joined the coal coalition, pooled their political resources, and tried to stop the costly and impractical drift of federal environmentalism.

By 1970, the political organization of coal had assumed a four-tiered structure. State and regional trade groups constituted the industrial equivalent of grassroots political organization. There are several dozen of these associations that lobby legislatures and regulatory agencies in state capitals. There are also a number of smaller trade groups representing coal operators or equipment manufacturers from a few counties or a single coal field. While these organizations are devoted to serving the financial and labor-relations needs of their members, they have invariably taken an active interest when their state officials have had to develop strip-mining and air-pollution controls. Because their interests are not always consistent, there has been little interaction between coal-related trade associations of different states or between state and national groups. At one time in the 1960's, the National Coal Association did try to broaden its constituency by affiliating state coal associations into the Mined Lands Conservation Conference, but nothing lasting came of it.

National trade associations make up a second level of coal's political structure. During the 1960's, quite a number of such organizations had lobbied autonomously on coal-related environmental

---

[34] Senate, *Disclosure of Corporate Ownership*, 93rd Cong., 2nd sess., 1974, S. Doc. 93-62, p. 2.
[35] Moody, in *NCPC, Purposes*, p. 3.

issues. By 1970, however, four national associations emerged as the principal defenders of coal interests at this level. For three of these, the Edison Electric Institute (EEI), American Petroleum Institute (API), and the American Iron and Steel Institute (AISI), air pollution controls were the principal concern. But for the National Coal Association, strip mining was also a major policy problem. These groups have been most responsible for the hardcore lobbying, cost and technology studies, and publicity the coalition has aimed at federal policy.

Interindustry associations can be distinguished as a third level of political organization. Four of these have actively participated in air pollution and strip-mining policy formation. Two are general business groups—the National Association of Manufacturers (NAM) and the United States Chamber of Commerce (USCC). Both have consistently opposed every serious new development in stationary-source air-pollution regulation by the federal government. Far more influential, however, have been the National Coal Policy Conference (NCPC) and the American Mining Congress (AMC). The former was established explicitly to cross industry lines, and the latter's membership diversified during the 1960's much like the coal coalition itself.

It has been through industry advisory councils, such as the National Industrial Pollution Control Council (NIPCC) and the National Petroleum Council (NPC), that coal interests have had their most legitimate, semiofficial channel for affecting environmental regulation. Ostensibly, President Richard M. Nixon's rationale for creating the NIPCC in 1970 was that "the same energy and skills which have produced quantitative gains in our economy must be used to improve the environment and to enhance the quality of life."[36] Dozens of the most active and influential coal-related industrialists worked through the NIPCC and the Department of Commerce on the technical details of implementing federal environmental policies. By 1975, more than twenty other coal-related advisory councils were helping six government agencies with their policy decisions.[37]

[36] U.S. Congress, Senate, Committee on Government Operations, *Hearings on Advisory Committees*, 92nd Cong., 1st sess., July, 1971, p. 501.
[37] U.S. Congress, Senate, Committee on Government Operations, Subcommittee on Reports, Accounting, and Management, *Energy Advisory Committees*, 94th Cong., 1st sess., August, 1975, p. 501.

Since the late sixties, these councils and trade groups have cooperated formally and informally in the unified promotion of the environmental policy goals of all the coal-related industries. That these goals have been reasonably consistent over time is due, in large part, to the shared membership of the various political organizations. Table 5 offers a partial indication of the interlocking of trade association and advisory council memberships that has accounted for this consistency. Moreover, these five groups have extensive membership interlocks and joint political undertakings with such allied organizations as the Edison Electric Institute, the American Iron and Steel Institute, the American Petroleum Institute, and the Coal Advisory Committee to the Federal Energy Administration. Since all the elements of this coalition share a common interest in greater coal development and consumption, its diversity implies no significant internecine friction over public environmental policies. It is especially interesting that over the years, fifteen corporations in particular have distinguished themselves by the intensity and persistence of their political activism and organizational membership (see appendix table D.4). Of these fifteen firms, seven were oil companies (by 1976), five basic metals, two independent coal producers, and one electric utility. The extent and, as we shall see,

TABLE 5
Shared Membership in Coal-Related Industry Political Groups

| Coal-Related Industries | Number of Corporation Memberships | | | | |
	NCA	AMC	NCPC	NIPCC	USCC
Steel/smelting	8	15	—	17	4
Utilities	4	4	4	4	4
Petroleum/gas	29	15	—	6	5
Railroads	12	4	14	4	1
Mining equipment manufacturers	19	43	8	6	—
Independent coal producers	24	12	18	4	3
Commercial banks	2	22	—	—	—

Source: Membership data compiled from membership lists (cited in bibliography) of the National Coal Association (1972), American Mining Congress (1973), National Coal Policy Conference (1965), National Industrial Pollution Control Council (1972), and the U.S. Chamber of Commerce Natural Resources Committee (1967).

effectiveness of this political activism is a far cry from the sorry efforts of the autonomous coal industry of the mid-1950's.

COAL POLITICS AT THE GRASS ROOTS

Only a morning's drive from Washington, D.C., Harrisburg, the capital of Pennsylvania, is another world in the politics of coal. The same can be said of Charleston, West Virginia. These cities host no Coal Building, no DuPont Circle ringed with the offices of national trade groups, no lobbyists receiving six-figure salaries. In cities like Harrisburg and Charleston, strip mining and air pollution are not abstract issues of national policy. Instead, they are specific, painful problems that have called forth harsh regulations reaching out into the countryside, affecting the behavior and income of mine operators, coal truckers, sportsmen, consumers of electricity, bankers, and foundry workers. Until the 1970's, however, the most meaningful environmental policy decisions were made by the assemblymen and bureaucrats who worked in these and other state capitals. Indeed, even after coal's environmental problems became national issues demanding federal solutions, the daily implementation of these solutions still sifted down through the politics of state institutions.

Out in the individual states, the coal business has been politically organized at two distinct levels. At least in Pennsylvania and West Virginia, three-fourths of the coal has generally been mined by a handful of large corporations. By 1973, nine of the ten largest producers in both states were diversified corporations, primarily steel, petroleum, and electric companies.[38] These large firms have been the dominant members of the Keystone Bituminous Coal Association and the West Virginia Coal Association. The large producers, together with allied interests in railroads, banking, and equipment manufacturing, constituted at the state level a sort of local chapter of the national coal coalition. In West Virginia, for example, twenty-one of the twenty-three largest coal producers have had a national political perspective through their memberships in the National Coal Association, the American Mining Congress, or both.

[38] Compiled from McGraw-Hill Co., *1973 Keystone Coal Industry Manual.*

This upper tier of state coal interests, while part of the larger coalition, has nonetheless maintained local financial and political cohesion. Three railroads, the Penn Central, Chesapeake & Ohio/ Baltimore & Ohio, and the Norfolk & Western, dominate rail freight in Pennsylvania and West Virginia and depend heavily on coal revenues.[39] Their officers have vigorously backed the coal producers whenever strip-mining or air pollution controls have seemed to threaten the general regional prosperity. Likewise, local and regional bankers have been intimately tied to coal prosperity through financing, investments, and directorships. For example, in 1972, two directors of the Rochester and Pittsburgh Coal Company (Indiana, Pa.) also served on the board of the largest local bank.[40] Westmoreland Coal, another big Pennsylvania company, has been a major economic force in that state for more than a decade. It is a subsidiary of the Penn-Virginia Corporation and through its board of directors has been tied to the Fidelity Bank of Philadelphia, St. Joseph Minerals' Massey Coal Company, the Philadelphia National Bank, and the Louisville and Nashville Railroad. One director in particular, W. Graham Clayton, was the third largest shareholder of the Southern Railway and a director of the Morgan Guaranty Trust Company. In Charleston, West Virginia, nine of the seventeen directors of the Kanawha Valley Bank were also directors or chief officers of major coal producers.[41] Thus, in a regional as well as a national sense, coal-related industries became interknit first financially, and then politically.

The structure of the coal industries in Pennsylvania and West Virginia, in many ways similar, have one outstanding historical difference. In Pennsylvania, the coal business has been only a fraction of the state's economy, while in West Virginia, coal and related industries constituted the entire social and economic fabric of the state. It is probably this difference more than any other which accounted for Pennsylvania's early enactment of an effective strip-

---

[39] Davitt McAteer, *Coal Mining Health and Safety in West Virginia,* chap. 6.

[40] Compiled from Dun & Bradstreet, *1973 Million Dollar Directory.*

[41] Ibid.; Senate, *Disclosure of Corporate Ownership,* 93rd Cong., 2nd sess., 1974, S. Doc. 93-62; *Moody's Industrial Manual, 1972* (New York: Moody's Investors Services, Inc., 1972).

mining reclamation law. Besides the strip mine operators and their utility customers, there was little vigorous opposition to reforming strip mining from the corporate community. In sharp contrast, however, virtually the whole industrial establishment of West Virginia opposed effective strip-mining controls, delayed passage of a meaningful law for years after Pennsylvania's (1963), and had by 1976 convinced the governor to oppose air pollution control statutes mandated by the federal government. Moreover, the upper echelon of West Virginia's coal industry has been dominated by out-of-state corporations, which, according to local environmentalists, meant that those industrialists had scarcely any personal sympathy for the social and environmental well-being of West Virginia.[42]

In both Pennsylvania and West Virginia, there has been a second level of coal organization made up of the several hundred small surface-mine operators, the related equipment and trucking firms, small banks, and electric utilities. With activist trade groups of its own, this level of the coal business consistently took the lead in statewide political conflicts over strip mining. And again, the different status of coal in each state's economy considerably affected the breadth and vigor of coal politics. By 1971, nearly 400 strip mine operators produced 39 percent of Pennsylvania's coal. Excepting a few large operators (500,000 tons or more), most of these mines yielded an average of 85,000 tons yearly. Unlike the state's larger coal interests, Pennsylvania surface mine operators, like most other small businessmen, had few ties to the larger business community. That is to say, no "coalition," economic or political, had crystallized around small-scale coal in Pennsylvania. The Pennsylvania Coal Mining Association (PCMA) was the single political agency of Pennsylvania's small surface operators. It originated from a 1964 fusion of two regional groups that decided, after the 1963 enactment of a state surface-mining law, that there was strength in numbers. With 120 members, the PCMA claimed to represent operators of all sizes.

[42] Of all coal producers in Pennsylvania and West Virginia that produced more than 700,000 tons annually, 70 percent in West Virginia were controlled from out-of-state. Only 44 percent in Pennsylvania were out-of-state corporations. Also, 94 percent of West Virginia's sixteen largest producers were diversified corporations, while only 50 percent of Pennsylvania's seven large producers were.

However, available evidence suggests that few very small operators have been members. PCMA director Frank Mohney confirmed this, pointing out that small operators (under 20,000 tons per year) did not appreciate the PCMA's goals. Without the nearly 200 such small operators as potential PCMA members, only Pennsylvania's largest independent operators were left to fill the estimated membership rolls of 120.[43] For the firms headed by PCMA's eighteen previous directors for which data were available, the average annual tonnage was 302,000. The significant point is that it has served the PCMA's political interests to exaggerate the inclusiveness of its membership. Claims of serving the little man helped obviate charges of elitism that could only have undermined the PCMA's special relationship with Pennsylvania's Bureau of Surface Mining Reclamation. The PCMA conducted a simple operation compared with its West Virginia counterpart. Frank Mohney, a lobbyist registered in Pennsylvania, headed a staff of three whose principal responsibility was to serve as intermediary between operators and the Reclamation Bureau. In that capacity, PCMA established an excellent working relationship with state regulators, a process to be described at length in chapter 3.

Political organization of surface mine operators and related coal interests in West Virginia has been entirely different from Pennsylvania's experience. In 1963, some of West Virginia's independent surface mine operators formed the West Virginia Surface Mining and Reclamation Association (WVSMRA) by merging, as in Pennsylvania, two nearly defunct regional groups. It was increasingly evident to the few politically conscious operators "that many problems of the industry could best be handled by an active association."[44] By 1972, the WVSMRA represented 44 percent of the surface operators and 60 percent of the surface-mined coal in West Virginia. Its 80 operating members averaged 146,000 tons per year, nearly twice the average annual production of nonmembers. And

---

[43] Estimated from figures compiled from Commonwealth of Pennsylvania, Department of Environmental Resources, *Annual Report, 1970*, and from interview with Frank Mohney, director of PCMA, Harrisburg, Pa., August, 1973.

[44] West Virginia Surface Mining and Reclamation Association, "Semiannual report of the executive director," 1967, p. 1, West Virginia Surface Mining and Reclamation Association, Administrative Records, Charleston, W. Va. (hereafter cited as WVSMRA Administrative Records).

the membership was geographically varied, assuring a wide base of political influence in state politics. In contrast, the PCMA constituency was quite narrow, coming from only four or five rural counties.[45] However, WVSMRA was more than just a trade group of strip miners. Several of its operating members were among the nation's largest corporate coal producers, and 26 of them were also members of either the National Coal Association or the American Mining Congress. According to Ben Lusk, WVSMRA's director, his organization was informally affiliated with both the NCA and the AMC, as well as being a prominent member of the West Virginia Chamber of Commerce.[46] But perhaps the most interesting aspect of the WVSMRA membership were the 121 "associate" members. These included steel, utility, railroad, equipment manufacturing, and petroleum interests operating in West Virginia, and together with the surface mine operators constituted an active and powerful miniature version of the coal coalition.

As might be expected, the political activities of the WVSMRA were considerably more sophisticated and wide ranging than those of the PCMA in Pennsylvania. Public relations and informational lobbying have been the special strength of the WVSMRA. According to its 1972 annual report, "The West Virginia Surface Mining and Reclamation Association contacted each of the federal and state lawmakers personally, offering them informational assistance that would aid them in their consideration of the surface mining issue. Each state legislator, U.S. congressman, and senator regularly received copies of *Green Lands Quarterly* and our news releases, along with several other pieces of information."[47] Although Mr. Lusk claimed that the organization had no budget for public relations, it nonetheless managed to distribute 278,500 copies of ten magazines and pamphlets as well as 35,000 bumper stickers between 1971 and 1973. Moreover, the WVSMRA "contacted every civic group, school, and college in West Virginia, offering a speaker (and the response

45 Compiled from McGraw-Hill Co., *1973 Keystone Coal Industry Manual* and West Virginia Surface Mining and Reclamation Association, "Annual Report, 1972–73," WVSMRA Administrative Records.

46 "Annual Report, 1972–1973," WVSMRA Administrative Records; Ben Lusk, director, WVSMRA, interview, Charleston, W. Va., November, 1973.

47 WVSMRA, "Annual Report, 1972–1973," p. 24, WVSMRA Administrative Records.

exceeded all expectations)." It arranged nearly fifty mine tours in 1972, including several for state and federal legislators.[48] Besides issuing propaganda, both the staff and members of WVSMRA lobbied actively in state and federal legislatures. In 1972 and 1973, WVSMRA representatives testified at both House and Senate hearings on pending strip-mining bills. In a single year, WVSMRA lobbyists were busy with sixty bills in Charleston and a dozen in Washington, all of which potentially threatened their members' prosperity. Scripps-Howard newspapers credited the WVSMRA with blocking enactment of the federal surface-mining control bill of 1972. Although a WVSMRA spokesman denied that accomplishment, he did acknowledge that WVSMRA had worked "diligently in an attempt to get a fair and responsible bill from Congress."[49]

COAL'S NATIONAL POLITICAL MACHINERY:
NCPC, NCA, AND AMC

In 1959, the idea of a permanent trade association for the explicit purpose of combining the political resources of several different industries was quite original. The industrialists who organized the National Coal Policy Conference (NCPC) seem to have recognized not only the growing interdependence of corporate interest groups, but also the paramount significance of federal policy for business prosperity. The NCPC's forty-five members represented four industries: coal, mining equipment, electric utilities, and coal transport (railroads and barge lines). The capstone of the organization was cooperation by the United Mine Workers, represented by W. A. "Tony" Boyle. The eight-man executive board included Boyle, Joseph Moody (the founder of the NCPC), and the presidents of the two largest coal companies, American Electric Power, Joy Manufacturing (mining equipment), and the Pennsylvania Railroad. (There was also a staff secretary.)[50] In its own words, the NCPC sought to serve "the national interest by promoting the use, and

[48] Ibid., p. 25.
[49] Ibid.
[50] National Coal Policy Conference, directors and membership lists, National Coal Policy Conference Papers, Office of W. W. McClanahan Co., National Press Club Building, Washington, D.C.

the economic welfare, of bituminous coal."[51] Realistically translated, this meant the pursuit of a national fuels policy that would favor coal over petroleum, gas, and nuclear power. During the first half of its twelve-year life, the NCPC sought to present a united political front against the flood of cheap fuel-oil imports and the noncompetitive price ceiling on natural gas for industrial use.

But as the clamor over environmental issues increased during the 1960's, NCPC officials began devoting more and more of their efforts to dampening the impact that federal air pollution controls threatened to have on coal's competitive position. By 1967, when Senator Edmund Muskie's subcommittee on air and water pollution held hearings on stationary-source air pollution, the National Coal Policy Conference assumed a position of leadership in coal's opposition to federal regulation and enforcement. The NCPC coordinated testimony and lobbying by railroads, utilities, coal producers, the National Coal Association, and the United Mine Workers. An NCPC spokesman summarized the position of the emerging coal coalition: adamant opposition to federal air-quality standards tempered by a willingness to tolerate regulation and enforcement at the state level.[52]

As environmental regulatory procedures grew more complex, the NCPC provided its members essential advice on the meaning of various technicalities and reminded them of their potential for participating in the process of administrative decision-making. Early in 1968, NCPC legal counsel prepared a *Guide to the 1967 Air Quality Act* for its members. This sophisticated handbook for political action described for coal industry leaders the crucial areas of administrative implementation in which businessmen ought to participate. The NCPC booklet wisely suggested that "industry members should be prepared to do all they can to help develop sound criteria and accurate control information. Those invited by HEW to be a consultant or to work with an advisory committee . . . will not be acting as industry representatives as much as experts in their fields." The NCPC advised that no one should shirk: "Other members of indus-

[51] Moody, in *NCPC, Purposes*, p. 1.
[52] U.S. Congress, Senate, Committee on Public Works, Subcommittee on Air and Water Pollution, *Air Quality Act of 1967—Hearings on S. 780*, 90th Cong., 1st sess., 1967, III, 2129.

try not serving such committees must also seek an opportunity to present their points of view. This may be done by contacting members of an advisory committee . . . or in consultation with state and local officials. . . ."[53] The NCPC guide astutely recognized that the formulation of criteria was a crucial point in developing policy to control air pollution. And after the criteria were set, coal men were to continue their vigilance through the development of state implementation standards: "State and local authorities should establish their own mechanisms for hearings and consultation. . . . Businessmen should prepare to participate in any such organization and should be alert to the need to present their view at all appropriate State, local and interstate levels—particularly at the public hearings."[54] And finally, an especially prescient strategy set down by the NCPC staff anticipated the problem of future plant siting. Coal men should take special care in helping to determine air quality control regions:

> If a sound job is done in establishing the regions, much additional flexibility will be gained in improving air quality while avoiding the setting of rules which are unnecessarily restrictive and oppressive. For example, including in a region only those areas absolutely necessary, may permit a wider choice in location of new power plants outside of the area . . . *this would permit plant location to be a meaningful alternative to substitution of fuels or other controls* [emphasis added].[55]

In other words, the NCPC guide advised maximum industry pressure to gerrymander air control regions to suit future needs. It was precisely this approach to compliance that in 1973 engendered the no-significant-deterioration conflict, finally resolved in the 1977 Clean Air Act Amendments (discussed in chapter 7). Advice and direction rather than overt lobbying characterized the NCPC program and the emerging coal coalition's political style in the technically intricate politics of the environment during the 1970's.

In 1971, the National Coal Policy Conference dissolved itself.

[53] National Coal Policy Conference, *A Guide to the Air Quality Act of 1967*, p. 5.
[54] Ibid.
[55] Ibid., p. 12.

There seem to be several reasons for its demise. Former NCPC officials claimed that cooperation between coal producers and the UMW, always tenuous, simply collapsed.[56] While this may well have threatened corporate-labor cooperation in the NCPC, it does not explain why the principle of interindustry cooperation could not have continued effectively. In hindsight, two other explanations seem more likely. The most significant unifying factor in the origins of the NCPC had been the common opposition of coal interests to the expansion of petroleum and gas markets. In the late 1950's, coal men unanimously believed that government subsidies to oil and gas companies were killing coal's markets. But by 1971, oil and gas company acquisition of coal interests was well along toward ending interfuel competition. In fact, six of the NCPC's largest coal-producing members had become subsidiaries of oil companies, and federal environmental policies had become a common concern of all corporate energy-fuel interests. Moreover, the National Coal Association had, by 1971, thoroughly reorganized and revitalized its political activities under the new leadership of Carl Bagge, former member of the Federal Power Commission. Thus, NCA and the rapidly growing American Mining Congress seemed capable of handling coal's political problems, and, when the NCPC folded, many of its members joined the National Coal Association.

Coal men had founded the National Coal Association 1917 as a basis of industrial cooperation to meet the fuel crisis of World War I. Until the late 1960's, the NCA had remained a stodgy, politically ineffective trade group that had periodically offended federal legislators with its heavy-handed and outmoded political tactics. But by 1971, stimulated by new leadership, by the developing environmental policy crisis, and by the abundant resources and political sophistication of its expanded membership, the NCA had changed. In 1972, NCA membership numbered 56 major coal producers, 23 "resource developers," and a variety of associate members that included coal merchants, railroads and barge lines, equipment manufacturers, banks, and engineering consultants.[57] Although the NCA's

[56] William McClanahan, past director, National Coal Policy Conference, interview, Washington, D.C., February 7, 1974.
[57] National Coal Association, *Coal Facts, 1972*, pp. 46–47.

membership included only 1.4 percent of the estimated 4,000 coal producers in the United States, it did include half the 40 largest producers. Small eastern coal producers have occasionally accused the NCA, and particularly Carl Bagge, of favoring the big Western surface-mining/energy corporations, but NCA management denies any such internal frictions.[58]

One reason for the NCA's improved political profile was its development of better personal ties with federal policy makers. By 1972, the NCA employed a full-time staff for both congressional and administrative government relations. Moreover, the NCA's two chief spokesmen, Carl Bagge and Carter Manasco, had superb credentials. Manasco was a former congressman who spent so much time on the Hill that many of his old congressional colleagues still called him "Congressman." After 1970, Manasco increasingly devoted most of his energies to air pollution problems and, after 1972, to surface-mining controls. Carl Bagge, president of the NCA since 1971, is a doctor of law who served until 1965 as an executive with the Atchison, Topeka, and Santa Fe Railroad. President Lyndon Johnson appointed Bagge to the Federal Power Commission in 1965, where he served twice as vice-chairman. By the time he took over leadership of the NCA, Bagge was a Washington insider and an expert on federal energy policies.

The National Coal Association is typical of its genre, organized for activity in six service areas: government and congressional, environmental, economics and transportation, informational, research and technical, and legal.[59] In the past decade, information services has absorbed approximately one-third of the NCA budget.[60] *Coal News*, a weekly newsletter, is its most important publication, and its distribution is "restricted to NCA members and others with a well-defined interest in coal."[61] *Bituminous Coal Facts*, published biennially, is a statistical report on the coal industry and the National Coal Association and is widely distributed among members, libraries, and others. Two sporadic newsletters, *Letter of the Law*,

---

[58] Rex Chaney, vice-president for information services, National Coal Association, interview, Washington, D.C., February 5, 1974.
[59] National Coal Association, *Coal Facts, 1974–1975*, p. 49.
[60] Rex Chaney, interview.
[61] National Coal Association, *Directory of Organization and Services*.

and *Congressional Highlights*, supplement the principal publications. One particularly interesting NCA publication was an environmentally oriented magazine entitled *Mined Lands Quarterly*, published for seven years until 1972. It was a product of the Mined Lands Conservation Conference, an unsuccessful attempt by the NCA to affiliate with state and local associations of surface mine operators. The magazine, through the skills of its photographers and writers, praised the industry's efforts at surface-mine reclamation. Every two months, the magazine displayed shopping centers, corn fields, camping, recreation, and wildlife areas flowing from the cornucopia of private reclamation. There was never a hint of problems or a need for firmer statute.[62]

Besides publications, press releases, editorial statements, and statistical studies, NCA public relations was perhaps most distinguished at the annual national convention. The NCA convention gives thousands of coal men the chance to get together to socialize, make new business contacts, and discuss common technical and policy problems. It also offers an opportunity to meet some of the people in government whose decisions are important. For example, at the 1972 convention, NCA members held an evening reception for government officials attended by forty-one congressmen, eleven senators, forty-six congressional staffers, thirteen committee staffers, and eighty officials from federal agencies, departments, and councils.[63] As would be expected, congressional guests from coal states were most abundant, and more than half represented the rapidly expanded coal interests in the West and Midwest. Members of the House Interior Committee and the Senate Interior and Public Works committees turned out in especially large numbers for the reception. The congressmen attending the NCA party had an average rating of 44 on the 100-point index of voting records published annually by the League of Conservation Voters (this compares, for example, with an average rating of 80 for the eighty-eight congressmen who cosponsored H.R. 1000, Representative Kenneth Hechler's (D-W.

---

62 Back issues of the *Mined Lands Conservation Conference*, National Coal Association, library, Coal Building, Washington, D.C.

63 Compiled from convention registration lists, National Coal Association Offices, Washington, D.C.

Va.) 1973 bill to abolish strip mining).[64] The eighty administrative officials who attended the reception represented twenty-one federal agencies and included a federal power commissioner, the director of the Bureau of Mines, two assistant secretaries from the Department of Interior, two atomic energy commissioners, and a host of lesser luminaries. The National Coal Association had certainly improved its political image since the 1950's.

As late as the mid-1960's, the American Mining Congress (AMC) was still the trade association of hard-rock mining. Its members were traditionally westerners whose businesses were uranium, silver, copper, and iron. The AMC was organized somewhat differently from the NCA, and members rather than staff were responsible for most of its political activities. Throughout the late 1960's, as diversified corporations bought into the coal business, AMC membership grew rapidly to 471 members by 1974. Of those, at least 135 shared an interest in the coal industry and the problems of environmental policy it faced.[65] Besides its 31 members whose principal business was coal mining, the AMC membership included 18 other industrials with significant coal-producing subsidiaries. Together, these 49 members included 23 of the 40 largest coal producers. But the most significant characteristic of the AMC's growing membership was its interindustry nature. As table 6 indicates, the whole range of the coal coalition seems to have converged in the American Mining Congress. Most of these AMC, coal-related companies were very large corporations primarily devoted to other industrial processes, such as metals smelting, petroleum refining, electric power generation, and commercial banking. For this reason, the AMC has had a more cosmopolitan orientation to federal environmental policy than has the NCA. Throughout the 1970's, the NCA's biggest concern was federal regulation of surface mining. But the American Mining Congress has devoted most of its political attention to the regulation of stationary-source air pollution, water problems relevant to coal-

[64] Compiled from League of Conservation Voters, Congressional Voting Records, in Ralph Nader Congress Project, *Citizens Look at Congress.* Cosponsorship list for H.R. 1000 from Office of Representative Ken Hechler, Rayburn Office Building, Washington, D.C.

[65] American Mining Congress, "American Mining Congress Membership, 1974."

TABLE 6

Coal-Related Membership of the American Mining Congress, 1974

Coal-Related Industries	Number of AMC Members
Primary coal producers	31
Transportation	4
Electric utilities	4
Petroleum/gas	15
Steel/metals	13
Mining equipment	43
Commercial banks	22

SOURCE: Compiled from American Mining Congress, *Membership List, 1974.*

energy development in the West, and constraints on minerals leasing on the public domain. In 1973, the AMC's board of directors had thirty-two members, twenty-two of whom were executives of corporations with coal-producing subsidiaries. And only two of those were *primarily* coal producers.

The AMC's annual coal convention (separate from its annual mining convention) has become the premier national celebration of the entire coal-industrial complex. In 1976, more than six thousand people, representing every conceivable element of the coal coalition as well as academic and governmental segments of the coal establishment, attended that meeting. Since 1973, the focus of AMC coal conventions has been disseminating information on problems of federal policy that affect AMC members. Principal among these have been environmental policies affecting coal mining and combustion. At the 1974 convention, for example, the key speakers were Rogers Morton, secretary of the interior; John Sawhill, administrator of the Federal Energy Agency; and Thomas Falkie, director of the Bureau of Mines. Several of the panel discussions dealt with government policies regarding minerals leasing, sulfur oxide pollutants, noise and dust control, and surface-mining reclamation.[66] At the AMC convention a decade earlier, more than three-fourths of the coal interests attending were independent producers, and there were

[66] American Mining Congress, "1974 Coal Convention Program, May, 1974."

only a dozen attendants from banking, petroleum, and electric utilities. But by the 1973 convention, only a third of the coal producers were independent of larger corporations, and the number of representatives from banking, petroleum, and utilities had tripled.[67] More than any other single institution, the American Mining Congress has come to represent the interindustry political coalition of coal.

COAL'S POLITICAL ELITE: NIPCC, NPC, AND OTHER
ADVISORY COUNCILS

After the Congress has spoken and environmental policies are turned over to the executive branch to be implemented, the coal coalition's final vehicle for affecting policy has been the industry advisory council. As previously mentioned, in 1975 more than twenty advisory committees were helping the federal government make its coal-related policy decisions. But at the beginning of the decade, only one, the National Industrial Pollution Control Council (NIPCC), provided the coal industry an effective voice against the profusion of new regulations precipitated by Earth Day and the public clamor for federal environmental solutions. The NIPCC was by no means limited to serving the interests of coal. Its thirty subcouncils represented virtually every major polluting industry, from steel to poultry rendering. However, of the sixty-one corporate executives on the main council, one-third represented corporations with substantial interests in coal. The NIPCC functioned primarily through its subcouncils, five of which were dominated by coal interests. Altogether, forty-five coal-related corporations held positions on NIPCC subcouncils: two-thirds of them owned coal-producing subsidiaries, and the others either owned coal reserves, consumed coal, or manufactured mining equipment.[68] The Coal Subcouncil focused its attention on the threat of federal strip-mining regulations, while the other

[67] Compiled from data in American Mining Congress, Coal Convention Registration Lists, 1964, 1973, American Mining Congress Records Office, Ring Building, Washington, D.C.
[68] National Industrial Pollution Control Council, Council Report, 1971, app. A, pp. 17–32. For example, of the eight corporate members of the NIPCC Metals and Mining Subcouncil, six owned coal-producing subsidiaries and a seventh owned a coal-minerals lease from the Bureau of Land Management. Of the nine members of the Steel Subcouncil, seven owned coal-producing subsidiaries and of course all nine burned coke in their mills.

coal-related subcouncils—electric utilities, mining and metals, steel, and railroads—were preoccupied with the ramifications of federal air pollution control.

In Executive Order 11523, which established the NIPCC, President Nixon explained that the NIPCC's purpose was to "advise on plans and actions of Federal, State, and local agencies involving environmental quality policies affecting industry which are referred to it by the Secretary [Department of Commerce], or by the Chairman of the Council on Environmental Quality through the Secretary." Environmental improvement was to be a "coordinated effort" by business and government.[69] For three crucial years, until environmentalist congressmen rescinded Department of Commerce budget authority for the NIPCC in 1973, coal leaders on the NIPCC enjoyed a privileged channel through the Department of Commerce for affecting environmental policy in the White House and the Environmental Protection Agency (some of those activities are described in chapter 6).

Besides advising, the NIPCC managed a public relations program of major proportions. The Department of Commerce published more than twenty-five subcouncil booklets, in thousands of copies, that described each industry's efforts at cleaning up pollution and warned of the economic risks of pushing environmentalism too quickly. Another project was a massive, three-volume compilation of commitments by industry to various aspects of pollution control.[70] These projects and dozens of other technical and cost-benefit studies promoted by the NIPCC were the objects of Senator Lee Metcalf's scorn when his Subcommittee on Intergovernmental Relations investigated the NIPCC in 1972. In those hearings, Bert Cross, chairman of the 3M Company and of NIPCC, defended his council's public relations activities. "I do not think that it is true," said Mr. Cross, "that this is a gimmick that takes the place of getting the job done.

69 Executive Order 11523, in U.S. Congress, Senate, Subcommittee on Intergovernmental Relations, *Hearings on Advisory Committees*, 91st Cong., 2nd sess., December, 1970, pp. 502, 501.
70 National Industrial Pollution Control Council, *Commitments: Industry Cleanup Actions in Progress*, vols. I–III, National Industrial Pollution Control Council, Administrative Records, Department of Commerce, Washington, D.C. (hereafter cited as NIPCC Administrative Records).

. . . On the other hand, I do not think there is a thing wrong in letting people know when you do a job, and that is what we're after."[71] Commerce Secretary Maurice Stans shared this same concern when he wrote to Bert Cross of his "sense of frustration . . . concerning the prevalent lack of understanding about what industry is really doing to clean up pollution."[72] Together, Cross and Stans used NIPCC publicity, frequently prepared by member-industry trade associations, to convince the public of industry's good offices.[73]

A third important NIPCC activity, especially with regard to stationary-source air pollution, was its preparation and dissemination of sophisticated studies of the costs and technical difficulties of environmental clean-up. During its brief tenure, the NIPCC, together with the American Mining Congress, the Edison Electric Institute, and various other trade associations, developed a series of environmental cost-impact studies. These studies, which hypothesized the costs of compliance with strict air pollution regulations, presented convincing arguments that neither environmental groups nor governmental agencies could easily refute.[74] The NIPCC-sponsored studies were widely circulated among government agencies—especially the Environmental Protection Agency. And Secretary Stans exerted considerable pressure to have these cost considerations accepted as partial criteria for air pollution standards and implementation guidelines.

These and other activities belied the president's contention that the NIPCC's purpose was to improve the environment. Moreover, the NIPCC steadfastly operated in secrecy until shortly before its demise. Throughout 1970 and 1971, environmentalists and newsmen

[71] Senate, *Hearings on Advisory Committees*, 91st Cong., 2nd sess., December, 1970, p. 423.

[72] M. Stans to B. Cross, July 29, 1970, Box No. 9, "Chairman Gen. Corr." file, NIPCC Administrative Records.

[73] See "Draft—Wood Products Sub-Council Report to the NIPCC, December 11, 1970," Box No. 1, "Wood Products Sub-Council" file; G. H. Lawrence to W. A. Hamilton, January 6, 1972, and T. W. Jackson to W. J. Young, April 6, 1971, Box No. 1, "Utilities Sub-Council Report" file; all in NIPCC Administrative Records.

[74] For examples of NIPCC-sponsored, environmental compliance-cost studies, see National Technical Information Service (Department of Commerce, Springfield, Va.) acc. nos. PB207147, PB207148, PB207168, PB207169, PB211917, PB211918.

leveled heavy pressure on Secretary Stans to open up the NIPCC meetings, but Stans refused. As the NIPCC *Council Report* explained, closed meetings had "facilitated expeditious conduct of the meetings and frank exchanges. . . ." NIPCC members "concluded that their work would not be forwarded more effectively by a change in this practice . . . [and] the Secretary of Commerce . . . has approved this conclusion."[75] In 1973, after the Federal Advisory Committee Act had prohibited closed meetings, NIPCC's director, John Sullivan, acknowledged its effect on NIPCC activities: "With the passage of the Federal Advisory Committee Act, which requires open meetings, many NIPCC members, including the Chairman, feel that this will lead to less than candid discussion and place members in potentially embarrassing situations. This being the case, these members are extremely reluctant to participate in open meetings."[76]

A final comment should be added about the NIPCC. Some of its members paid dearly for the council's political accomplishments. NIPCC members contributed approximately $707,000 to Richard Nixon's 1972 campaign.[77] In February, 1972, Maurice Stans resigned his Commerce secretariat to head the Finance Committee to Reelect the President—but not before putting the touch on a half-dozen corporate presidents after a February 16 NIPCC meeting in Washington.[78] Five NIPCC members were eventually investigated for their contributions by the Senate Select Committee to Investigate Presidential Campaign Activities, and four were convicted of breaking the Federal Campaign Financing Act of 1971. Orin Atkins, chairman of the board of Ashland Oil, a leading coal producer, explained to Ashland stockholders his reasons for making an illegal

---

[75] NIPCC, *Council Report, 1971*, p. 7.

[76] J. L. Sullivan to Under Sec. Commerce, June 9, 1973. Box No. 8, "Sec. Dent Corr." file, p. 4, NIPCC Administrative Records.

[77] Data on NIPCC and NIPCC-related campaign contributions were compiled from three sources: NIPCC membership was based on 234 members listed in NIPCC, *Council Report, 1971*; presidential campaign contribution figures from General Accounting Office, Office of Federal Elections, *Federal Election Campaign Act of 1971 (P.L. 92-235); Alphabetical Listing of 1972 Presidential Campaign Receipts*, vols. 1, 2; Citizens' Research Foundation, *Political Contributors and Lenders of 10,000 Dollars or More in 1972*.

[78] NIPCC, "Council Meeting, Feb. 14, 1972," p. 2, Freedom of Information Files, Department of Commerce Library, Washington, D.C.

contribution. In doing so, he also explained how the NIPCC worked: "There was a good business reason for making the contribution and, although illegal in nature, I am confident that it distinctly benefited the corporation. . . . its intention was to give us a means of access to present our point of view to the executive branch of the Government."[79]

Although entirely different from the NIPCC, the National Petroleum Council (NPC), the most prestigious and influential of industry advisory councils, emerged as an advocate for the coal coalition after 1970. By then, NPC members, although primarily devoted to oil and gas concerns, had absorbed a large portion of the coal industry and an even larger share of the nation's coal reserves. Furthermore, a dozen NPC corporations were leading the way in the research and development of coal liquefaction and gasification. The National Petroleum Council had been established in 1946 to advise the Department of Interior on policy matters pertaining to oil and gas. But by 1970, the NPC's leading members had become thoroughly involved in every aspect of the energy business, especially coal fuel and nuclear power. Accordingly, the Department of Interior had come to rely on the NPC for broad advice on energy and environmental policy. In 1971 and 1972, at the request of Interior Secretary Rogers Morton, the NPC organized a task force to prepare a massive report on the relationship of environmental conservation to national energy needs.[80] All the task force's twenty-seven corporate representatives were interested in air and water pollution from the standpoint of oil and gas refining, and fifteen of them also served corporations with substantial coal holdings. The multivolume report, published in 1972, was thorough and wide-ranging. The National Petroleum Council concluded that there were serious environmental problems which industry had to work toward solving. But it recommended that government not go overboard. In particular, the NPC made some crucial recommendations regarding the costs and technical feasibility of environmental regulation:

---

[79] U.S. Congress, Senate, Select Committee on Presidential Campaign Activities, *The Final Report*, 93rd Cong., 2nd sess., June, 1974, S. Rept. 93-981, p. 460.

[80] National Petroleum Council, *Environmental Conservation*, vol. 2; *The Oil and Gas Industries*, app. A, p. 377.

. . . The determination of environmental quality standards should, among other things, take into account the cost-benefit to society and the impact of that factor upon our economy.
. . . Where environmental quality does not meet prescribed standards, the constantly moving limits of technology and economics should be taken into account in setting realistic and stable timetables for achievement of the desired quality.
. . . Imposition of economic penalties is not an effective means of attaining optimum environmental conservation.[81]

As will be seen in chapters 6 and 7, these recommendations ran exactly counter to the premises of the 1970 Clean Air Act, the 1972 Water Pollution Control Act, and the 1972–1973 versions of the Federal Surface Mining and Reclamation bills.

In 1972, the National Petroleum Council undertook to prepare the largest single piece of advice ever requested by government from an industry advisory council. The end result, U.S. Energy Outlook, was a fourteen-volume study of energy needs, resources, and policy problems for the next fifteen years.[82] It was to serve as the definitive source of energy information and policy recommendations for federal decision-makers until at least 1975. More than five hundred experts from the energy industry contributed to the study. Six of the seven corporate officials who made up the policy committee for the project were oil men with substantial coal interests. Andrew Tarkington, the chairman, was a director of Consolidation Coal, and other committeemen represented Gulf Oil (parent of Pittsburg and Midway Coal), El Paso Natural Gas, Kerr-McGee, Continental Oil, and Exxon. Likewise, the task force on coal policy was entirely staffed by coal coalition people.[83] Thus, not surprisingly, the report concluded that coal was the most significant and accessible source of domestic energy, and that to avoid an energy crisis, "prompt action is needed to eliminate the serious delays that have been caused by environmental issues."[84] The coal availability report issued a stern warning to the secretary of interior and others responsible for public energy policy: "Use of coal for conventional markets is ex-

[81] Ibid., I, 16–18.
[82] National Petroleum Council, U.S. Energy Outlook: A Summary Report.
[83] Ibid., pp. 88–97.
[84] Ibid., p. 10.

pected to increase provided that pollution control regulations do not seriously restrict future use of coal in electric power generation. . . . Delays in the enforcement of severe air pollution regulations pending commercial availability of the respective technologies may be in the public interest."[85] In 1978, the level of nonattainment of air quality standards and the extensive revisions of the 1977 Surface Mining Control and Reclamation Act would suggest that this advice had not fallen on deaf ears.

There can be little doubt that by the mid-1960's a cohesive political coalition of coal-related industries was evolving from post–World War II financial and technological interdependencies. Interlocked trade associations and industry advisory councils provided the institutional order for the coalition's political activity. Environmentalism provided a common cause. The existence of this coalition and the scope of its political power has obviously not blocked significant progress in environmental reform, however. For indeed, environmentalists succeeded in constructing elaborate interest-group coalitions of their own. But for two decades, the coal coalition has considerably blunted the impact of the environmental movement and has rendered obsolete some of the rationale for democratic pluralism. The following chapters tell that story.

[85] National Petroleum Council, *U.S. Energy Outlook: Coal Availability*, p. 10.

3

Sportsmen and Strip Mining
in Pennsylvania:
The Fight for Controls

AFTER the coal industry reached its nadir in 1954, coal output gradually began two decades of recovery. But to survive as an energy fuel, coal had to compete with cheap imported oil and natural gas priced by federal regulators at bargain-basement rates. To do so, the coal industry turned more and more to surface-mining techniques that required less capitalization to start and would be more efficient than deep mining if the environmental costs to society could be ignored. During the 1940's, several Appalachian coal states had enacted cursory laws for controlling strip mining. They required little more than throwing some dirt back into the exhausted pits. By 1960, strip mining's toll was mounting more quickly than its output. Public environmental consciousness was stimulated by the increasing concern of scientists for the difficult problems of acid water, land reclamation, and revegetation. Pennsylvania was the first state in which strip mining became a serious political issue and so provides a suitable case for studying the rudimentary political organization and activities of both environmental and coal interest groups.

By 1961, hundreds of miles of streams and thousands of acres of land had been disturbed or ruined by surface mining in Pennsylvania. Although surface mining had been regulated perfunctorily for sixteen years, the wastage of Pennsylvania's woodlands and clean streams was accelerating exponentially with the expansion of strip mining. As public pressure for corrective legislation intensified, Pennsylvania's strip-mining regulations evolved in two phases between 1961 and 1963. These first meaningful controls of strip mining were achieved only in the wake of bitter political conflict and innovative political activities by citizens' groups.

The pressure for new surface-mining regulatory policies was solidly focused in Allegheny County, where Pittsburgh is the major urban hub of western Pennsylvania. The majority of surface-mining operations had developed in the nearby western counties. Spearheading this pressure was the state's principal sportsmen's organization, the Allegheny County Sportsmen's League, an activist branch of the Pennsylvania Federation of Sportsmen's Clubs. Besides the group's conservationist ideals, the Sportsmen had a vested interest in the woods and streams of western Pennsylvania, many of which were being devastated by the strip mining. Alert politicians on both sides of the partisan fence embraced this newly emerging political issue, especially in the Pittsburgh vicinity.

A second key factor in this surge of conservation enthusiasm in Allegheny County was a full-blown crusade by Pittsburgh's leading newspaper, the *Pittsburgh Press*. The *Press* saturated its readership with nearly daily editorials and a constant barrage of news articles covering every action of the legislature and the "strip-mine lobby." The Allegheny County Labor Alliance, backed by the United Steel Workers, the International Brotherhood of Electrical Workers, and the United Mine Workers, also supported regulatory legislation. Besides their conservationist concerns, these unions tried to use the issue to pressure independent surface mine operators, none of whom were unionized. Still another reason for Pittsburgh's preeminence in the surface-mining controversy was the fact that its economy was not tied in any way to the surface-mining industry. Since most surface mine operators marketed their coal to rural electric generating plants or outside the state, Pittsburgh area politicians were not pressured by local business constituents to bridle their regulatory enthusiasm. Finally, the urbanity of Allegheny County's population, influenced by several major educational institutions, stimulated a progressive political posture on behalf of surface-mining reforms.

Beyond Allegheny County, support for the 1961 regulatory legislation came from the Pennsylvania Federation of Sportsmen's Clubs, several newspapers, the United Mine Workers, the State Grange, and the Departments of Health and Mines and Minerals Industries.[1] This narrow base of support reflected the relatively embryonic development of public concern for such environmental issues as surface mining. Thus, even the limited legislative success achieved in 1961 is surprising in retrospect, especially considering the strong political opposition of the coal interests.

Besides the strip mine operators themselves, other economic interests actively opposed new surface-mining regulatory legislation. The two regional trade organizations of Pennsylvania's surface-mining industry lobbied against any form of legislation.[2] Railroads, particularly the New York Central and the Pennsylvania railroads, effectively backed the surface operators. These two giants testified at hearings and forecast grim economic problems for Pennsylvania if controls were enacted. Frank Saen, New York Central's vice-president for coal sales, testified that the proposed regulations would eliminate 80 percent of Pennsylvania's strip-mining production. His special concern seemed to be that "widespread layoffs would follow and extend even to white-collar workers." A representative of the Pennsylvania Railroad warned that "hundreds and perhaps thousands of employees" might have to be laid off. Executives of the smaller lines, including the Bessemer and Lake Erie and the Pittsburgh and Shawmut railroads, predicted "economic chaos" if the proposed bill passed.[3] Other interests affiliated with surface mining, such as equipment manufacturers and operators, and commercial interests in regions heavily dependent on surface mining, were also active.[4] In Clearfield County, where surface mining was the primary industry, both the Chamber of Commerce and the newspaper opposed controls.

Although both political parties claimed to support strong regu-

---

[1] *Pittsburgh Press*, July 16, 1961, p. 8. A survey of newspaper editorials cited showed most major papers favored legislation, including the *Philadelphia Inquirer*, *Harrisburg Evening Star*, *Scranton Times*, and the *Somerset Daily American*.

[2] The Independent Mineral Producers Association (Director Frank Mohney) and the Central Pennsylvania Open Pit Mining Association.

[3] *Pittsburgh Press*, July 11, 17, 1961.

[4] Ibid., June 29, 1961.

lation, neither party appears to have been united, and conflicting amendments and opaque political deals thoroughly obscured partisan lines. Although the principal bill was authored by House Democrats, the Democratic administration of Governor David Lawrence opposed its more vigorous provisions.[5] The sources of controversy dealt with limitations on acid water drainage, the size of the bond that would ensure reclamation, and the extent to which backfilling of the pit would reduce the highwall. In its original version, the bill provided for an increased bond of $500 per acre, backfilling to a slope no steeper than thirty degrees, and responsibility for acid mine drainage, even when it originated from abandoned deep mines underlying surface mine operations. Although numerous amendments were made, only three roll-call votes recorded the voting patterns. The first vote rejected an amendment to weaken the bill by 120 to 80. The second vote passed the Assembly bill by a 150 to 50 margin. The third vote, 147 to 53, gave final passage to the bill after the Senate had severely weakened it and the Sportsmen had come out against it. As evident from table 7, vote 1 was a Republican measure to weaken the bill. Of the twenty Republicans voting pro-regulation, however, four were from Allegheny County. Vote 2 was a Democratic measure supporting strong regulations, and the eight dissenting Democrats were all from surface-mining counties. Illustrative of this group was Harris Breth, himself a surface miner from Clearfield County and a leading opponent of controls. Of the thirty-three representatives who consistently voted to weaken the bill, all but three were Republicans and none were from either Allegheny County or Philadelphia. Every assemblyman from the top three surface-mining counties voted repeatedly against controls, reflecting not only the political control of surface mine operators in their own counties, but also their unanimous opposition to any government intervention.

Assemblymen from Allegheny County and Philadelphia overwhelmingly supported control legislation. One-third of the Pittsburgh assemblymen crossed partisan lines and voted consistently (three times) in favor of strong surface-mining controls. Thus in 1961, the bulk of support for a strong Pennsylvania control law came

[5] Ibid., July 9, 1961.

TABLE 7

Pennsylvania Assembly Votes on 1961 Surface-Mining Control Bill

| | Vote 1 | | Vote 2 | | Vote 3 | |
	Anti-regulation	Pro-regulation	Anti-regulation	Pro-regulation	Anti-regulation	Pro-regulation
Democrats	4	100	8	96	85	18
Republicans	76	20	42	54	62	35
TOTAL	80	120	50	150	147	53

SOURCE: Commonwealth of Pennsylvania, *Legislative Journal—House*, 1961, pp. 2430–32.

from the two major urban areas, where both Democrats and conservationists were prevalent and where economic interests were scarcely linked to the surface-mining industry. Reflecting United Mine Workers' (UMW) support for stringent controls, the assemblymen from Pennsylvania's three major deep-mining counties supported the conservationist measures. Deep-mining interests, which constituted 95 percent of UMW membership, could only benefit from costly economic strictures on surface mining that would slow the trend away from labor-intensive deep mining.

After its passage through the Assembly in a form satisfactory to most conservationists, the bill went to the Senate, where it met real opposition. Again, it appeared that Governor Lawrence's administration wanted credit for the bill, but got more than it bargained for from the Assembly. As the result of a closed meeting between the governor's secretary and several leading legislators, the bill was routed through the Committee on Local Government rather than the Committee on Mines.[6] The governor's office, responding to critical media speculation, denied agreement with that decision. Nevertheless, Senator John Haluska (D-Cambria Co.), as chairman of the Local Government Committee, became the central political figure in the 1961 legislative battle. According to his opponents, Haluska had openly boasted that the "strip mine bill was a dead goose now that it had gone to his committee."[7] Something of a scandal developed over Haluska's close financial relationship with C. E. Powell, one of Pennsylvania's ten largest surface coal operators. Haluska handled Powell's insurance policies, had permanent use of a Powell company car, and had previously interceded with the state fish warden, helping Powell avoid prosecution for a negligent acid discharge that killed 1,200 trout.[8]

During the summer, Haluska's committee bottled up the regulatory bill by exercising every conceivable tactic for delay and eventually reported the bill out. It was severely weakened by amendments that proposed to divide strip-mined lands into "productive" and "nonproductive" categories, to lower backfilling requirements on "nonproductive" (wooded, hilly) lands, to reduce the bond require-

6 Ibid., July 16, 1961.
7 William Guckert, quoted in *Pittsburgh Press*, July 7, 1961.
8 *Pittsburgh Press*, July 16, 1961.

ments from $500 to $360, and to provide for a 5-degree tolerance in backfilling requirements. Proregulation advocates in both parties countered with amendments to restore the bill to its original form. But no sooner had bipartisan support been organized than it collapsed; apparently a deal was worked out between senators from surface-mining counties and the eight-senator contingent of Democrats from Philadelphia.[9] Of those voting to kill the strong restoration amendments, eight were Philadelphia senators and eight were from twelve rural surface-mining counties. In contrast, all the Allegheny County area's nine senators voted in favor of the restoration amendments. Governor Lawrence, under tremendous media and conservationist pressure, promoted a compromise bill that the Senate approved by a 41 to 1 vote. Its provisions established a small bond increase, 45-degree backfilling in "productive" areas, and 70-degree backfilling in "nonproductive" areas.[10]

When the bill returned to the Assembly for final consideration, neither the Sportsmen nor anyone else could do much to reinstate the original provisions. In a series of high-pressure meetings in the governor's office, Joseph Yablonski of the UMW tried to restore some rigorous measures. But, fearing a negative Assembly vote and under the pressure of pending adjournment of the legislature, conservation interests capitulated to the compromise bill. Recognizing the emasculated nature of the bill, stalwart defenders of strip mining jumped at the opportunity to "support" the final bill. Assemblyman Paige Varner of Clarion, who had introduced the largest number of amendments to weaken the bill, now concluded, "This version of the House bill 1438 is one that I am going to support . . . legislation is the art of the possible."[11] Conversely, Assemblyman Austin Murphy, the bill's original author, spoke bitterly as he prepared to vote against his own disfigured creation: "This bill is as good as no bill at all . . . [it] will leave us in an even weaker position than the Act of 1945 [referring to the 5-degree tolerance provision]."[12] And so the mining

9 Both the *Pittsburgh Press* and minority leader Fleming speculated about this sudden tie-up between Philadelphia and surface-mining counties.
10 Commonwealth of Pennsylvania, *Legislative Journal—Senate*, August 21, 1961, p. 3542.
11 Ibid., August 28, 1961, p. 2743.
12 Ibid., p. 3745.

interests had successfully coopted much of the thrust of public policy.

The legislative battle over the 1961 Pennsylvania Surface Mine Reclamation Act shows that old-style politics was still alive. Close personal and financial ties between mine operators and politicians were blatant and effective, while the conservationist forces were very limited in scope and experience. But changes were in the offing that would stand the conservationists in good stead in 1963 when they reintroduced surface-mining legislation. The public, advised by the active media of the crude politics of the likes of Senator Haluska, was growing less tolerant. Moreover, the environmental issue of strip mining was looming even larger in the public awareness, and both parties realized the expediency of a strong platform stand on the issue.

Perhaps a more significant change was the political activation of well-organized interest groups in the area of environmental policy. Within weeks of the passage of the 1961 act, the Allegheny County Sportsmen undertook a political campaign against those legislators who had most actively supported the surface-mining interests. Beginning in September, the Sportsmen directed a vigorous campaign to unseat the twenty-seven senators and fifty-one assemblymen who had voted against strip mine reform in key instances.[13] Local chapters of the Sportsmen's Federation were responsible for ousting local strip-mine advocates during the pre-election campaigns early in 1962. The Sportsmen swung into action with an apparently new appreciation of their political strength and the kinds of local pressures that would facilitate successful conservation legislation in 1963. In Greensburg, Aliquippa, and elsewhere, Sportsmen spoke out against incumbent legislators who had stood by the surface-mining interests. In Johnstown, at a Sportsmen's banquet, John Laudadio, executive secretary of the Allegheny County Sportsmen and himself a candidate for the Assembly, called adamantly for Senator Haluska's defeat (although his term was not to expire until 1964).[14]

This politicizing of the strip-mining issue contributed to its

13 *Pittsburgh Press*, September 24, 1961.
14 Ibid., June 14, 23, 1962.

inclusion as a prominent plank in the platforms of both parties in 1962. In April, Republican candidate William Scranton convincingly announced, "We will put through a strong strip mine law in the 1963 legislature and that's an absolute pledge."[15] Likewise, the Democratic candidate, although standing on the Lawrence administration's record, recommended that the law could be strengthened.[16] According to the Sportsmen, the 1962 election results proved the effectiveness of their campaign and the political liability of being a strip-mining advocate. Four of the most active pro-strip-mining legislators were defeated in the November elections. These included Harris Breth of Clearfield, Varner of Clarion, Speaker of the House Hiram Andrews, and Senator Jo Hays (Clearfield Co.), the man who had been second only to Haluska in weakening the 1961 legislation. The aggregate figures indicate that attrition in the Senate was approximately the same for advocates and opponents of controls. But in the Assembly, where grassroots pressure was perhaps more significant, the Sportsmen's campaign evidently was more effective. The assemblymen who had consistently voted to weaken surface mining controls in 1961 suffered a 33 percent attrition rate. In contrast, those who never voted to weaken the legislation showed an attrition rate of only 14 percent, less than half that for the Sportsmen's enemies.[17] Democrat John Laudadio won an Assembly seat, having campaigned almost exclusively on the surface-mining issue as secretary of the Sportsmen's Federation. Republican William Scranton rode into the governor's office, partially on the back of the surface-mining issue. The surface-mining interests faced a difficult new legislative session.

Conservation interests were demanding legislation to control acid drainage and sedimentation, complete backfilling of the strip pit, and reduction of the highwall. Governor Scranton, true to his campaign promises, appointed a bipartisan legislative committee to prepare new control legislation.[18] The committee's seven members were from the Allegheny County vicinity, yet another reflection of

15 Ibid., April 1, 1962.
16 Ibid., September 6, 1962.
17 *Pennsylvania Manual*, 1961–62, 1963–64.
18 Ibid., January 10, 1963.

the urban impetus for serious regulation. This committee prepared S. 176, which required backfilling to approximate original contour, cleaning up acid drainage, increased bonds, centralized enforcement, and shared liability by property owners. In contrast to surface-mining regulations in other states, these measures were revolutionary.

Support for these proposals developed over a substantially wider range of organized interest groups that had backed the 1961 legislation. Numerous civic and conservation groups and others entered into the 1963 surface-mining debate.[19] These new sources of vocal and active support for control legislation broadened the base of support, which had been too narrow in 1961 to sustain radically new legislation. However, most of these groups were western Pennsylvania interests. This provincial orientation had been problematic in 1961 when eastern Pennsylvania voting blocs had not been secured, since no constituent pressure had been developed in the east.

The surface-mining interests responded to these pressures with a barrage of publicity and by renewing their traditional political influences. The two surface-mining trade associations jointly formed the Pennsylvania Conservation Association, allegedly to improve reclamation, seek better legislation, and guard against unscrupulous operators. In practice, the Pennsylvania Conservation Association, inspired by a Pittsburgh public relations firm, undertook a multimedia publicity campaign intended to improve the image of surface miners by advertising past reclamation successes.[20] Industry-sponsored tours for legislators and the governor displayed the best examples of controlled surface mining and good reclamation. After one such air tour, Governor Scranton spoke at the Pittsburgh airport, hedging on his platform pledges. One week later, Lieutenant Governor Raymond P. Schafer introduced a substantially weakened bill in the Assembly as a companion to the rigorous S.176.

The Sportsmen immediately denounced Governor Scranton's

---

[19] The following organizations actively supported Pennsylvania's surface mining control legislation in 1963; Pennsylvania Federation of Sportsmen's Clubs, Save Our State Conservation Association (Beaver County), Western Pennsylvania Conservancy, National Wildlife Federation, American Camping Association, House Builders Association of Greater Pittsburgh, International Brotherhood of Electrical Workers, and five local civic groups.

[20] Ibid., June 7, 1963.

bill as having "pulled the rug out from under" the tough reform bill.[21] Assemblyman William Buchanan from the surface-mining county of Indiana sponsored the governor's bill. Its provisions would have weakened every important control measure in the Senate bill. From throughout western Pennsylvania, accusations of "appeasement" were hurled at Governor Scranton. Although the differences between these two bills were substantial, both still represented ample improvement over the 1961 act and were opposed by surface-mining interests. But those interests clearly were far weaker politically than during the previous session. In May, after months of stalemate, a compromise was settled on by the conservation and administration forces. The conservationist forces agreed to drop the water quality measure from their bill, it to be dealt with in separate legislation. In return, provision for backfilling to "approximate original contour" was reinserted in the administration bill. But in the course of floor debate, a property owners' liability provision was removed along with an eminent domain clause (159 to 38). The 38 assemblymen voting against this amendment were the absolute core of support for tough control legislation.[22] They included 19 of the proregulation core group from 1961, but none of the 13 farmer-legislators who, as property owners, were adamantly opposed to joint liability.

The opponents of surface-mining controls were substantially reduced in number from 1961 and were singularly unsuccessful in further weakening the governor's bill with more amendments. Analysis of the voting on three major proposed amendments reveals the extent to which surface-mining support had eroded. These amendments, introduced by assemblymen from Clearfield and Clarion counties (surface-mining counties) were trounced 175 to 22, 174 to 23, and 179 to 84.[23] Voting repeatedly for all three amendments was a hard-core group of 14 Republicans, primarily from strip-mining counties. None of the 14 represented a major urban area. Thus, the core of pro-strip-mining legislators had shrunk by more than 50 percent, from 33 in 1961 to 14 in 1963. Only 5 legislators out of 249

[21] Ibid., February 22, 1963.
[22] Commonwealth of Pennsylvania, Legislative Journal—House, June 4, 1963, p. 858.
[23] Ibid., pp. 871–874.

voted against final passage of the bill. These few opposition votes were a mere shadow of the legislative power previously wielded by the surface-mining industry in Pennsylvania.

The surface-mining industry has frankly acknowledged its active opposition to those acts of 1961 and 1963, claiming that such opposition was mandated by unfair publicity and the conservationist refusal to listen to economic reason. The newly formed Pennsylvania Coal Mining Association (PCMA) lobbied against the bills and conducted advertising it felt was necessary to counteract the false impressions established by the news media.[24] A survey of western Pennsylvania mine operators revealed that about a third of the respondents had been politically active in the strip-mining contest.[25] Two of the larger PCMA member-directors explained their points of view. They had felt that no one in or out of the legislature would sit down and talk about the control provisions and the problems they raised for operators. The few who did were "heckled to death."[26]

Although the newspapers had complained bitterly about the heavy industry lobbying and secret deals, the surface mine operators themselves felt that they accomplished nothing and that costly reclamation regulations eventually resulted in putting 75 to 100 of their number out of business.[27] Nevertheles, those that continued to operate seem to have prospered and readily acknowledge having been able to pass on the cost of reclamation.[28] Furthermore, the resulting legislation and the failure of the surface-mining interests to insert many favorable amendments into the 1963 bill suggest in retrospect that the traditional political ties and pressures had, at least to some degree, dried up by 1963. The ground swell of public conservationist sentiment and the effectiveness of pressures exerted by civic and environmental groups had guaranteed at least the minimum regulatory policy for an improved state control program.

This formative period of Pennsylvania's surface-mining control

[24] Frank Mohney, executive director, Pennsylvania Coal Mining Association, interview, Harrisburg, Pa., August, 1973.

[25] Survey of Western Pennsylvania surface mine operators by author (a questionnaire of 27 questions mailed to 75 operators in October, 1973).

[26] Ray Walker and H. R. Woolridge, surface mine operators and directors of the PCMA, interview, Clearfield, Pa., August, 1973.

[27] Frank Mohney, interview.

[28] H. R. Woolridge, interview.

policies reflects several elements of change in post–World War II America. Most obvious is the genesis of the environmental movement. The environmentalism that has become such a significant part of the American scene since 1970 is something more than merely a continuation of the prewar conservation ethic. In Pennsylvania and elsewhere during the early 1960's, new interest-group coalitions were focusing on environmental quality rather than on efficient use. Moreover, these new interest groups, slowly at first, began developing mechanisms for effective political action. The Sportsmen's Federation's blacklisting was one such grassroots device. Cooperation by environmentalist interest groups through larger coalitions developed later in the 1960's, but the rudiments of such cooperation were apparent in Pennsylvania in 1963.

After 1964, the locus of environmental politics shifted from the legislative to the administrative arena. The Bureau of Surface Mine Reclamation (BSMR), which became a division of the Pennsylvania Department of Environmental Resources in 1972, was responsible for administering the Pennsylvania Surface Mining and Reclamation Act. The bureau's regulatory mandates under that act have since been supplemented by the acid drainage control provisions of the 1965 Clean Streams Act and by strip-mine revegetation requirements in a 1971 amendment. While the politics of implementing environmental policy is less spectacular than that of forming policy, it is equally crucial for eventually realizing public environmental goals. The central aspect of these administrative politics was the pragmatic relationship between the industry and the regulatory agency, which resulted in environmental controls defined by a bargaining process.

The Pennsylvania Bureau of Surface Mine Reclamation has been a relatively compact watchdog agency, run by a staff of about a dozen in Harrisburg and another two dozen or so field inspectors. The BSMR's primary responsibility has been to process mining permits and inspect and enforce the terms of those permits. Beyond in-house procedures for handling violations and revoking permits, enforcement and appeals have been handled outside the BSMR by an environmental strike force of attorneys and an environmental hearing board. Between 1964 and 1972, the bureau supervised about

350 surface mine operators annually. In order to surface mine coal in Pennsylvania, an operator had to obtain a license ($300 per year), a mine drainage permit, a mining permit, bonding (at $500 per acre), and permission from the land owner to mine.[29] The mine drainage permit has been the central guideline for the mine's operation. With bureau approval, this permit entailed an elaborate plan, describing with geologic and property maps the area to be mined, test borings and sample reports, run-off diversion channels, pumping equipment and storage capacity for accumulated water, sedimentation barriers, and descriptions of adjacent hydrologic sources. Accompanying this plan had to be a preliminary report by the mining inspector, a Bureau of Fish and Wildlife report, and evidence that the operation had been announced in local newspapers. The operator also had to acquire a mining permit approved by the BSMR, which described the reclamation plan in terms of backfill planning (e.g., original contour, terracing, or alternate use), backfill schedule, soil segregation provisions (topsoil to be separated from other overburden material), and revegetation. This mining permit, guaranteed by a per-acre surety bond, covered only the immediate acreage (usually from two to fifteen acres) in the next stage of mining.

The second phase of this regulatory process was the inspection of operating conditions and the issuance of violations and "cease orders."[30] In theory, depending on the nature of the violation, several different sanctions could result from the reporting of a violation. If the problems were minor and immediately remedied, no further action was taken. For a more serious violation, the BSMR issued a cease order, temporarily halting the mining operation. Where the problem was not immediately resolved, the BSMR called a formal or informal hearing, which might result in resolution of the problem or possibly in loss of the mining permit, loss of the mine drainage permit, failure to renew license, forfeiture of bond, or even legal action. In the event of a bureau hearing, mandated by only the most serious violations, the operator could defend or explain his

[29] These procedures were found in Pennsylvania Department of Environmental Resources forms ER-MI-BD-151, 152, 153.

[30] Explanation of the violation process is based on an interview with Charles Herwig, supervisor of the BSMR's violations section, Harrisburg, Pa., July, 1973.

problem, whereupon the bureau decided on the solution or penalty. If the operator chose not to abide by the bureau's decision, he could appeal the case to the Pennsylvania Environmental Hearing Board. If he ignored the hearing request, his bond was forfeited and his operating license revoked.

In practice, the Pennsylvania Surface Mining and Reclamation Act was implemented in a far more flexible and less formal manner. Data in tables 8, 9, and 10 analyze the BSMR's enforcement record between 1965 and 1972. For comparison, surface mine operations during those years were classified in seven size groupings. The data base includes 463 operators, 1,238 major violations by 285 operators, and the bureau records of 60 hearings and 48 cases of bond forfeiture. No one operator size group was disproportionately burdened by violations. The percentage of violators in each group increased steadily with increasing production, as did the number of violations per group. Bureau officials logically explained this in light of the increased opportunities for violations as the size of a surface mine operation increased. The number of violations per violator followed the same pattern because problem conditions often resulted in multiple violations. However, table 9 reveals that larger operators suffered a disproportionately smaller number of violations relative to their tonnage output. A class VI operator produced fifteen times as much coal-per-violation-received than did a class I operator. Supposedly, larger operators were more efficient and conscientious. At the same time, they were not heaped with multiple violations when a single one was sufficient to force a shutdown and correction of related problems not reported as separate violations.

Politically organized operators who were members of the Pennsylvania Coal Mining Association seem to have fared about the same as the nonmember mine operator. In class V, for example, the average was 3.4 violations per operator, while PCMA members averaged 3.6.[31] But when violations were related to production tonnage, a significant difference becomes evident. The PCMA class VI members averaged one violation per 39,000 tons, as compared to one violation

[31] Data based on twenty operators whose PCMA membership was determined. PCMA membership data remained confidential although every source was exhausted.

TABLE 8
Summary Enforcement Data for Bureau of Surface Mine Reclamation, 1965–1972

Operator Size Group	Number of Operators	Average Tonnage Forfeitures*	Number of Forfeitures	Percent of Total Forfeitures	Number of Forfeitures with Hearings	Percent of Hearings Resulting in Forfeitures	Number of Hearings**	Percent of Total Hearings	Number of Violators	Number of Violations
I (under 5,000)	86	2,439	10	21%	5	55%	9	15%	41	92
II (5,000–15,000)	106	9,019	13	27%	1	10%	10	17%	47	104
III (15,000–35,000)	69	24,165	9	18%	4	33%	12	20%	43	138
IV (35,000–65,000)	72	50,191	8	17%	3	60%	5	8%	49	165
V (65,000–150,000)	78	99,404	8	17%	4	25%	16	27%	60	272
VI (150,000–1 mil.)	51	265,490	—	—	—	—	7	11%	44	431
VII (1,000,000+)	1	2,300,000	—	—	—	—	1	2%	1	36
TOTAL	463		48	100%	17	28% (avg.)	60	100%	285	1,238

SOURCE: Compiled from Pennsylvania Department of Environmental Resources, Bureau of Surface Mine Reclamation permit files, violation records, and hearing records, Harrisburg, Pa.

* Average size of operator undergoing forfeiture: 30,726 t./yr.

** Average size of operator having hearing: 98,378 t./yr.

TABLE 9
Bureau of Surface Mine Reclamation Violation Record

Operator Size Group	Number in Group	Percentage of Violators Forfeiting	Number of Violations per Violator	Percentage of Group in Violation	Ratio of Violations to Hearings	Average Tons per Violation
I	86	25%	2.2	47%	1:10	2,280
II	106	27%	2.2	44%	1:10.4	8,801
III	69	21%	3.2	62%	1:11.5	12,257
IV	72	16%	3.3	68%	1:35	21,902
V	78	13%	4.5	77%	1:17	28,506
VI	51	—	9.8	86%	1:61.6	31,392
VII	1	—	36.0	100%	1:36	56,555

SOURCE: Compiled from Pennsylvania BSMR violations records, Harrisburg, Pa.

per 31,392 tons for all class VI operators. Thus for class VI operators, PCMA membership meant 24 percent fewer violations per ton; this probably means that PCMA members were better informed regarding the laws and perhaps even more conscientious.

The bargaining process, the pragmatic heart of environmental regulation, originated at the inspection-violation stage. Finding deficiencies at the mining site, inspectors usually went to the operator if a satisfactory personal relationship existed and tried to iron out the problem. This generally happened, according to bureau officials, in instances of minor and unintentional violations. The operator often tried to explain the problem, and the inspector could either accept or reject the explanation. Usually, a middle ground was agreed upon, a process that occurred repeatedly if the inspector wished to avoid citing the operator for a violation. Once a formal violation was reported to the bureau, the mine operator was notified, and in instances of unintentional violation, he needed only to inform the bureau of his intent to comply or of actual compliance, and the bureau dropped further action. In certain instances, where mines were operated without proper permits or beyond the parameters of the permit, the BSMR temporarily closed down the operation. This was usually the only sanction and could be alleviated merely by filing the proper applications. If the operator's relations with the bureau had been satisfactory, then he could have the application processed more quickly than under normal circumstances, especially if he indicated financial stress. Even after the thirty-day compliance period, a "regular" operator was usually extended a final chance to arrange a compliance schedule before a hearing was called.

The BSMR's enforcement procedure has been premised on several operating principles defined by the bureau's director, William Guckert: (1) offer fairness to all parties, (2) offer equal-handed dealings, (3) expedite and cut through red tape, (4) correct situations without punishment, (5) keep operators in business if at all possible, (6) clear up violations, don't prosecute or close down operations.[32] It is the philosophy expressed in the latter three of these goals that resulted in enforcement by a bargaining process. While

[32] William Guckert, director, BSMR, interview, Harrisburg, Pa., July, 1973.

TABLE 10

Bureau of Surface Mine Reclamation Enforcement Record, 1965–1972

Year	No. of Forfei- tures	No. of Hearings	Penalties from Hearings	No Penalties	Formal Hearings	Informal Hearings
1972	2	1	—	1	1	—
1971	3	1	—	1	—	1
1970	7	15	1	14	8	7
1969	3	21	2	19	12	9
1968	11	12	5	7	9	3
1967	11	10	9	1	10	—
1966	11	3	3	—	3	—
1965	9	1	1	—	1	—

SOURCE: Compiled from Pennsylvania BSMR violations records, Harrisburg, Pa.

bureau personnel seem to have recognized their responsibility to preserve Pennsylvania's natural environment, they felt nearly as strong a responsibility for sustaining the industry they regulated. In order to maintain the balance between these two goals, the BSMR, from inspector up to director Guckert, was willing to bargain. Static regulations were made fluid by daily modification to deal with the individual problems of each operation and, in fact, each violation. These informal allowances became the working essence of Pennsylvania's regulatory relationship with the strip-mining industry. There were sensible reasons, moreover, for avoiding the extreme sanction of bond forfeiture. In the event of bond forfeiture, the state assumed responsibility for completing reclamation, a job that cost the state two or three times the amount of the average bond ($500 per acre).

In terms of meeting the goal of correcting violations rather than punishing violators, the bargaining worked well. In only 66 instances did any of the 1,238 violations reach the serious stage of conducting a hearing.[33] That is to say, about 95 percent of the time violations of state law were corrected with no sanctions other than temporary shutdowns of operations (usually a matter of a few days or less). The annual incidence of BSMR hearings peaked in 1969 and de-

[33] Discrepancy due to six hearing transcripts missing from files.

creased precipitately after 1970. Bureau personnel explained that by then they had largely weeded out troublesome operators or brought them under control. Furthermore, the number of hearings that resulted in any sort of penalty decreased steadily (see table 10). These changes signify a trend toward less formal prosecutions of the regulations and a concomitant increase in the use of informal, pragmatic bargaining to resolve problems.

Smaller operators had disproportionately more hearings. This tendency, indicated in table 9, mirrors the more serious problems encountered with small operators whose limited resources were often inadequate to meet water control requirements in particular. The large operators (class VI) were especially immune to hearings, having had no more than one per every 61.6 violations. This probably reflects the large operator's willingness or ability to correct violations and perhaps also somewhat deferential treatment by the bureau. The threat of "ceasing" an operation was particularly effective for dealing with larger operators whose multiple mining operations were all jeopardized by a single violation. The expense of opposing a bureau request for compliance was rarely justified by principle or cost of compliance.

In the first eight years of regulation, seventeen hearings resulted in the ultimate penalty of bond forfeiture, eleven because the operators failed to attend the hearing. Thus, 87.5 percent of the fifty-six actual hearings were resolved in some way without putting the operator out of business. In nine cases besides those resulting in forfeiture, some form of penalty, usually license suspension, was imposed. In the other forty cases, the BSMR exercised no sanctions, and the problem was simply resolved. These figures reemphasize Guckert's operating rules 4 and 6. In five hearing cases, the operator was represented by PCMA's director, Frank Mohney. All five cases were resolved without penalty or forfeiture, four by informal agreement. The regulatory bargaining process was most evident in these hearings conducted by the BSMR, the Department of Environmental Resources, and a Pennsylvania district attorney. In one hearing, for example, a class VI operator had mined beyond his permit area and then ignored the inspector's "cease order." At the hearing, the operator, his attorney, and Frank Mohney (PCMA) all submitted to the bureau's charges. Director Guckert concluded that the operator had "willfully violated the inspector's order. . . ." Although this was "justification for suspending your license . . . ," said Guckert, "we do feel, however, that you have been penalized by ceasing your work. . . ."[34] Without further penalty, the operator agreed to rectify the problem. In another hearing, second in a series of three for the same large operator, the miner agreed to complete reclamation of his mining site, from which he had already withdrawn his equipment. Mr. Guckert fumed, "I should have suspended his license; I should have prosecuted him." But the operator was given fifteen days to return his equipment to the property and resume reclamation.[35] While such enforcement seems pretty weak, it nonetheless resulted in eventual reclamation and allowed the operator to continue mining coal. In only three instances did operators staunchly oppose the bureau's judgment at the hearing. In one such case, the operator's attorney left the hearing with the parting remark, "We will see you in court. . . ." But Guckert could not be bulldozed, and the operator finally submitted to correcting his acid drainage problem.[36]

As these representative examples suggest, resolution of most hearing cases was achieved through bargaining rather than rigid application of the regulations. In most cases, mutually agreed-upon compliance schedules were adopted without additional sanctions. Although the bureau extended itself to accommodate the operator's individual problems, compliance was still achieved in most cases.

This functional relationship did not develop immediately after the laws were passed in 1963. According to the surface mine operators, influence politics had allegedly played a role in implementation for several years before Guckert became director of the BSMR. Most responsible operators had refused to get involved in unsavory political dealings, and such conditions had resulted in inequitable en-

[34] Hearing on permit #73-16, January, 1971, Violation Hearings Transcripts, Pennsylvania Department of Environmental Resources, Bureau of Surface Mine Reclamation, Harrisburg, Pa. (hereafter cited as BSMR Hearing Transcripts.

[35] Hearing on permit #30-67, January, 1968, BSMR Hearing Transcripts.

[36] Hearing on permit #212-4, July, 1970, BSMR Hearing Transcripts.

forcement of the law.[37] When William Guckert took over in 1968, the operators had been pessimistic, since Guckert, as secretary of the Allegheny County Sportsmen's League, had led the campaign for regulatory legislation in 1963 and was considered a conservationist zealot. In fact, during his first year of administering the BSMR, he justified those fears by his "overly enthusiastic" application of every rigid detail of the law regardless of extenuating circumstances and economic realities.

However, after some exposure to the technical exigencies continually encountered in surface-mining operations, Guckert apparently settled into a more pragmatic regulatory relationship with the operators. Several crucial things made the relationship work. Guckert was, by all accounts, absolutely committed to eliminating external political influence from the regulatory process. Moreover, according to most operators, the BSMR under Guckert favored no operators over others. The data on violations, hearings, and forfeiture distribution would seem to substantiate this point. Most important, the bureau sought to expedite the regulatory process with a minimum of red tape. These various factors guaranteed the operators unprecedented stability, which they valued highly. Survey responses from Pennsylvania surface coal operators substantiated their satisfaction with the stability imposed by Guckert, although most operators still felt that the bureau enforced the laws too strictly.[38]

These conditions which served the surface-mining industry were obtained through the bureau's informal enforcement system, backed by Guckert's manipulation of cross-permit pressures. The PCMA's representative aptly dscribed this regulatory relationship as a "double-edged sword."[39] As the law was written, the mining permits, drainage permits, licenses, and violations were all interlocked. While in violation, the operator would not be issued any new permits on related operations. The bureau had to process permit alterations and cease orders resulting from violations. Not bound to expedite such changes, the BSMR could use its discretion to bring pressure on the

[37] H. R. Woolridge, interview.
[38] Frank Mohney, interview; author's questionnaire data.
[39] Ibid.

operator to comply. Furthermore, an inspector had the discretion to "cease" an operation, which, in effect, was an immediate punishment that resulted in short-term financial loss. When the threat of this power—to cease an operation for the smallest violation—was used coercively, as many operators felt had been the case with Guckert's administration, it resulted in efficient and informal regulation.[40] Through these practical methods, red tape was avoided and decisions were made quickly. While such expedition of bureaucratic procedure was generally favored by the operators, pressure tactics and circumvention of orthodox legal procedure were the price.

While the surface-mining regulatory system in Pennsylvania has generally been geared to sustaining responsible operations, the extreme sanction of bond forfeiture and concomitant revocation was exercised in 57 instances from 1965 to 1972. Slightly more than 10 percent of the operators active in the eight years studied were permanently shut down. Eighty-two percent of those foreclosures were conceded without opposition by "fly-by-night" operators or by operators whose businesses had collapsed. Seventy percent of these occurred during the first four years of regulation under the 1963 act. Two-thirds of the forfeitures involved small operators mining less than 35,000 tons per year. Many were of the strip-and-run variety, who took coal out of a single piece of property, never intending to perform satisfactory reclamation. In the forfeiture cases where there were hearings, most operators planned to comply or pleaded financial difficulties, and only one refused to accept the bureau's proposals. None appealed to either the courts or the Environmental Hearing Board.

One other noteworthy ingredient in the Bureau of Surface Mine Reclamation's regulatory formula was the bureaucratic impulse toward self-preservation and autonomy. As a minor regulatory bureau within the larger Pennsylvania Department of Environmental Resources, the bureau consistently acted to maintain its independence and to increase its autonomy. This characteristic was certainly a factor in Guckert's opposition to external political influences. Moreover, one function of the bureau's tight relationship with the

[40] Ibid.

surface mine operators and the informal, practical methods of enforcement that emerged as part of that relationship was precisely to close out other administrative and even legislative inputs from the regulatory process. Prior to the Sanitary Water Board's absorption into the new Department of Environmental Resources in January, 1971, Guckert's bureau was invariably at odds with that board. On more than one occasion Guckert used publicity, principally the *Pittsburgh Press*, to denigrate the Water Board's role in regulating surface mine operations where it impinged upon the BSMR's prerogatives. The bureau frequently clashed with the Fish Commission and occasionally with the Bureau of Forestry regarding interagency approval of mine drainage permits. Usually, this friction arose from criticism by either of these two bureaus of the BSMR's permit plan approval in instances where provision for adequate environmental protection appeared dubious. The BSMR, by dint of Guckert's bluster, the bureau's favorable record, its preeminence in this regulatory field, and the responsive support of the operators, usually prevailed. In 1973, the Pennsylvania Environmental Hearing Board, on a rare occasion, sustained an operator's appeal of a BSMR decision. Director Guckert, with the help of Fred Jones, the conservation editor of the *Pittsburgh Press*, and Assemblyman John Laudadio, responded by bringing some heavy publicity pressure on the hearing board. The *Press* published a Laudadio letter to the governor demanding the resignation of the hearing board's chairman.[41] This incident exemplifies not only the effectiveness of publicity as a political tool, but also the intense bureaucratic impulse for defending an agency's own prerogatives.

From 1965 to 1972 the Pennsylvania Bureau of Surface Mine Reclamation steadily reinforced its autonomy and, at the same time, established a condition of relative stability on which the mine operators came to depend. In return, the industry eventually approved of and came to support the bureau's authority in order to protect a generally desirable status quo. This close relationship has, of course, been mutually beneficial. In fact, it became a smoothly functioning "cliental" relationship, similar in some ways to those federal regula-

[41] *Pittsburgh Press*, August 5, 1973.

tory situations described by political scientist Samuel Huntington in his study, "Clientalism: A Study of Administrative Politics."[42]

The early regulation of surface mining in Pennsylvania may be seen as a precursor of environmental regulatory relationships at the federal level. Studies by Marver Bernstein, Grant McConnell, and others have suggested that federal agencies evolved similar regulatory relationships.[43] Bernstein's model of a regulatory life cycle fits the Pennsylvania case to a tee. Amid an outpouring of public concern for the environmental costs of surface mining, control policies established in 1961 and 1963 prescribed fairly rigid enforcement goals. The responsibility for implementation, however, was not precisely mandated by the Pennsylvania legislature. Even the 1963 act merely provided guidelines for BSMR regulation. After the early years of external political influences under the BSMR's first director and the reform zeal of Guckert's first months, public enthusiasm receded, and the bureau began dealing with, rather than dictating to, the strip-mining industry.[44]

At that point, perhaps in 1969, when the record reflects a sharp decrease in the incidence of bond forfeitures and formal hearings, a bargaining process began to characterize the environmental regulatory process. Bargaining was evident not only in the hearings and the inspectors' on-site discretionary activities, but also in the day-to-day operating procedures of the BSMR. The Pennsylvania Coal Mining Association's director, Frank Mohney, saw his role not only as a lobbyist, but also as an intermediary between operators and the bureau. This viewpoint was shared by the BSMR staff. According to one staff member whose relationship with Mohney was not particularly agreeable, the PCMA man was in the bureau offices practically every day. He expedited permit applications, smoothed out detailed problems, checked on violations, and sought to iron out any differences arising therefrom. Moreover, Mohney was usually present at informal meetings held in the bureau offices between regula-

---

[42] Samuel P. Huntington, "Clientalism: A Study in Administrative Politics" (Ph.D. dissertation, Harvard University, 1951), introduction, p. i.

[43] Marver Bernstein, *Regulating Business by Independent Commission;* Grant McConnell, *Private Power and American Democracy.*

[44] See, for example, Murray Edelman, *The Symbolic Uses of Politics.*

tors and mine operators with problems. At these sessions, which often preceded formal hearings, the details of a violation settlement were frequently worked out through consensus and compromise.[45]

The problem with this bargaining procedure, according to Mathew Holden, arises from "the accretion of many small exceptions in the policing process" that can amount to "a significant deviation from the policy norm from which the regulatory agency began." Furthermore, such a procedure leads to a siutation where "large amounts of regulatory action have little or nothing to do with the achievement of any overall systematic result, and much to do with achieving a tolerable day-to-day working arrangement."[46] This point is the crux of environmental regulatory politics, and one that was again evident during the federal implementation of air pollution statutes.

The apparent necessity of the bargaining process and the inevitability of the cliental relationship were, in the case of Pennsylvania, the two dimensions that defined environmental regulatory politics. In retrospect, one logically wonders to what extent clientalism and enforcement through pragmatic bargaining neutralized the effectiveness of the BSMR's mandate to protect the environment. A precise answer would depend on whether the yardstick was the ideal environmental condition or the minimum industrial practicability. There can be little argument that the bureau's enforcement record fell short of the reformers' initial goals. A trip through the rural areas of western Pennsylvania's coal region testifies to that fact. But, on the other hand, attainment of such goals in practice might well have meant closure of most strip-mining operations and severe damage to local economies, not to mention reduction of the energy supply. A second substantive question is whether the regulatory relationship became a conservative force that cast administrative government in a role of sustaining the status quo. Once again, the answer depends on the perspective. Environmentalist detractors of the Pennsylvania Bureau of Surface Mine Reclamation view the years of regulation since 1964 as merely the institutionalization of

[45] Frank Mohney, interview, and interview with BSMR staff member who asked to remain unidentified.

[46] Mathew Holden, *Pollution Control as a Bargaining Process*, pp. 28–30.

environmental degradation. The bureau's proponents, however, have seen the BSMR's legacy as a positive accomplishment of progressive environmental cleanup, precedential in contrast to the records of other Appalachian states. Both questions must be considered in light of pragmatic working relationships between government and business and the politics that guide the development of such relationships.

4

Strip Mining in Washington:
A Tougher Fight

In 1940, Everett M. Dirksen, senator from Illinois, introduced the first bill for federal control of coal surface mining. Nearly thirty years passed before federal responsibility for the social costs of strip mining became a serious public issue. Seven more years of political debate, expansion of strip mining, and inadequate state regulation finally yielded the Surface Mining Control and Reclamation Act of 1977.

Three stages, marked by significant changes in the context of larger public issues, determined the long evolution of a national policy for regulating strip mining. In all the years prior to 1971, concerns for strip mining's impact on the environment were offbeat and not consistent with the mainstream devotion to economic growth, resource exploitation, efficiency of scale, and the sanctity of contract. Even when acknowledged as a problem, strip mining was viewed as a local problem, best subject to local control. Those congressmen who introduced control bills or even sought studies of the environmental impact of strip mining were running against the tide, with no support from effective constituencies and no broad public concern. But the spring of 1970 clearly marked a turning point. Under the impact of the National Environmental Policy Act, the Clean Air Act, and, most especially, Earth Day, it became only a matter of time until federal authority would be leveled at coal strip mining. During the next four years, the coal coalition, federal policy makers, and an emerging coalition of environmental interest groups became immersed in the complexity of technical and economic issues implicit in the regulation of strip mining. By December, 1974, the Congress had compromised on the most difficult of these issues and delivered a bill to the desk of President Gerald Ford. But by then, the larger political context had again shifted and the energy crisis dominated public attention. The Ford administration and most of the business community contraposed environmental and energy problems. As President Ford vetoed the bill, a third stage of policy development commenced. For the next two years, political debate hinged on a "balance" between environmental quality and energy supply. By the summer of 1977, and many compromises later, the Congress enacted a federal law to regulate strip mining, thus signaling the start of a fourth stage, the politics of implementing the new national policy.

In the two and a half decades between V-J Day and Earth Day, the annual share of coal mined by surface removal methods had risen steadily, impelled by years of rapid economic growth, the superb technological efficiencies of giant machinery, and the productivity of a stable, nonunion labor force. Each year more acres of land were disrupted by the increasingly mammoth buckets of stripping shovels and drag lines. By 1971, strip-mining productivity cost 74,900 acres of land "utilized" per year, and many more thousands of adjacent acres "disturbed."[1]

To a growing number of people, strip mining was a blight spreading across the land, and the state reclamation law, even in Pennsylvania, seemed inadequate at best and utterly useless in many instances. Two phases of legislation generally defined control policies at the state level. A first series of laws, enacted in the mid-1960's, were halfway measures engendered by varying degrees of compromise between local environmentalists and industrial interests. Inadequate mandates for enforcement and the rapid emergence of cliental relationships neutralized the already limited goals of those statutes. Another round of regulatory reform evolved in the early 1970's, particularly in the western states. Those measures aimed at

---

[1] U.S. Department of the Interior, *Land Utilization and Reclamation in the Mining Industry, 1930–71*, Bureau of Mines Information Circular IC8642 (1974), p. 13.

improving revegetation requirements, increasing surety bonds, and improving on-site inspections. Nonetheless, to many environmentalists coal interests were simply too politically powerful at the state level for any significant reclamation progress to be made. The Tennessee Citizens for Wilderness Planning were among the many local groups in Appalachia that complained bitterly of inadequate state regulations. That group's chairman, Robert Peele, told the House Interior Committee that his organization had originally supported Tennessee's 1967 reclamation law. But four years had passed, and the Tennessee Citizens felt the law had been totally ineffective. New legislation was pending before the state assembly, but Peele's group was certain that it too would do little to restore the environment. So they vigorously supported federal regulation, which they hoped would be above manipulation by local coal interests.[2] Even in states with reasonably effective laws, citizen groups favored federal controls so that mine operators could not plead for relief in the face of competition from adjacent states with weaker strip-mining controls.

In the decades after Senator Dirksen's first effort, bills for coping with the social costs of strip mining were sporadically introduced in the Congress. In 1949 and again in 1951, an Arkansas representative proposed modest legislation to institute a survey of the damages from strip mining. Between 1959 and 1965, Pennsylvania delegates introduced a flurry of similar study proposals that would have examined coal property ownership, fish, wildlife, aesthetic damages, and even the effects of strip mining on public health. None of those bills moved beyond committee. Senator Gaylord Nelson (D-Wis.) began an annual drive in 1965 to promote a comprehensive control bill authorizing the secretary of interior to license strip mining and regulate reclamation. Although this proposal received token support from a handful of senators, it too withered from lack of broad-based public interest. Washington's Senator Henry Jackson (D) joined the bandwagon in 1969 with a bill to provide federal guidance for state regulatory programs.

2 U.S. Congress, House, Committee on Interior and Insular Affairs, *Hearings: Regulation of Surface Mining—H.R. 60*, 92nd Cong., 1st sess., October, 1971, pp. 711–723.

Although Interior Secretary Stewart Udall approved of Jackson's bill and it was the least noxious to the mining interests, it was not supported by conservationists, who preferred Senator Nelson's bill. And finally, there was an entry by Representative Kenneth Hechler (D-W. Va.) to abolish strip mining completely.

At the beginning of the Ninety-second Congress in January, 1971, legislators introduced more than two dozen bills relating to strip mining. These bills offered four basic approaches to a national regulatory policy (see table 11). Preeminence of the states was a major issue implicit in this range of options. The Type I proposals, supported by ranking members of the House and Senate Interior committees and the Nixon administration, basically offered state preeminence thinly masked by an overlay of federal guidance. This was the same issue that had dominated the air pollution control debate during the 1960's, and most coal industrialists, along with politicians who narrowly construed the interstate commerce clause, adamantly favored state, rather than federal, regulation of strip mining. In the fall, when House and Senate committees opened hearings on the question of strip mining, this issue of state versus federal preeminence quickly polarized interest-group positions. The coal people, represented by seven trade associations, a handful of coal producers, electric utilities, and the Tennessee Valley Authority, supported Senator Jackson's idea of federal guidelines. Speaking for the American Mining Congress, a Pickands Mather Company executive admitted to the Senate Interior Committee "that it is appropriate for the Federal Government to have and exercise the authority to establish guidelines for the regulation of surface mining."[3] Likewise, Carl Bagge, representing members of the National Coal Association, endorsed Senator Jackson's bill (S.630) because it "encourage[d] the states to develop their own programs based on broad federal criteria. . . ."[4] Such criteria would guarantee the necessary "flexibility," at the same time reducing inequities among the various state laws. Aubrey Wagner, chairman of the Tennessee Valley Authority, also endorsed this position, emphasizing the importance that "Federal

[3] U.S. Congress, Senate, Committee on Interior and Insular Affairs, *Hearings on Surface Mining*, 92nd Cong., 1st sess., November, 1971, I, 280.
[4] Ibid., p. 376.

TABLE 11

Strip-Mining Regulations Introduced during the 92nd Congress

Degree of Regulation	Principal Provisions	Industry Position	Environmentalist Position
Type I* Least rigorous	States to submit plans for approval by Secretary of Interior within two years	Support with reservations by NCA, AMC	Non-support or opposition by most groups
Type II Modest controls	Secretary of Interior to promulgate and enforce uniform national standards for reclamation	Opposition	Limited support by some groups, opposition by others
Type III Strict controls	EPA to promulgate and enforce strict uniform national standards	Strong opposition	Support by most environmental groups
Type IV Abolition	Strict regulating leading to gradual abolition	Adamant opposition	Support by most environmental groups, opposition by a few

* Sponsors of bills:

Type I—Henry Jackson (D-Wash.), Gordon Allott (R-Colo.), Robert Byrd (D-W.Va.), John Sherman Cooper (R-Ky.), John Saylor (D-Pa.), Craig Hosmer (R-Calif.), Nixon administration;

Type II—Mike Gravel (D-Alaska), Wayne Hays (D-Ohio);

Type III—Gaylord Nelson (D-Wisc.), George McGovern (D-S.Dak.), Edward Kennedy (D-Mass.);

Type IV—Kenneth Hechler (D-W.Va.) and eighty-eight co-sponsors.

legislation recognize state responsibilities."[5] And for this reason, all the coal people opposed every other bill that "would attempt to set out the specific reclamation requirements [which] would not be desirable."[6]

Most environmentalists were extremely suspicious of any provision for state regulation of strip mining, with or without federal guidance. Past experience had convinced local groups of strip-mining opponents that "Federal legislation is hopefully less subject to the type of industry manipulation we have witnessed on the state level."[7] And many of the national conservation groups, such as the Sierra Club, had already learned a hard lesson about state preeminence and federal guidance from their experience with the Clean Air Act of 1963 and the Air Quality Act of 1967. With the exception of the Conservation Foundation, which appeared not to understand the issues, the sixteen environmental interest groups that testified at the 1971 hearings unanimously opposed federal "guidelines"[8] Like the coal interests, environmental groups were fusing into a nationwide coalition. Six of the more established groups organized the Coalition against Strip Mining (CASM) in 1972 to pool their resources and centralize their political activities. Louise Dunlap, a young professional lobbyist for the Environmental Policy Center in Washington, took charge of CASM. During the next few years, she built CASM into a national information clearinghouse that mobilized hundreds of local citizens' groups across the nation to bring maximum grassroots pressure on their legislators on every key strip-mining issue.

A second important issue, evident in the differences between the Type II and Type III proposals, was the bureaucratic vehicle for federal control—the Department of Interior versus the Environmental Protection Agency (EPA). During both the Ninety-second and

[5] Ibid., III, 993.
[6] Ibid., I, 376.
[7] House, Surface Mining Hearings, 92nd Cong., 1st sess., October, 1971, p. 715.
[8] The most active groups included Friends of the Earth (Environmental Policy Center), Izaak Walton League, National Conservation Foundation, National Wildlife Federation, Natural Resources Defense Council, Sierra Club, Black Mesa Defense Fund, Appalachian Research and Defense Fund, Save Our Kentucky, and the Tennessee Citizens for Wilderness Planning.

Ninety-third congressional sessions, coal interests persistently sought to vest the Department of Interior with whatever administrative authority was to be mandated. Environmentalists, on the other hand, favored the EPA as the appropriate agent of control. For years, the mining industry had nurtured a favorable working relationship—in fact, a cliental relationship—with the Interior Department. Coal mining was the domain of the Bureau of Mines, the Bureau of Land Management, the Office of Coal Research, and the Geological Survey. More recently, as the petroleum-gas-energy interests had become involved in coal development, they had strong ties to the Department of Interior through their powerful National Petroleum Council. Secretary Rogers Morton's stalwart opposition to rigid federal reclamation standards reflected the empathy between the energy industries and Interior. And it seemed only natural to coal people that Interior Department staff, who were experienced in matters of coal mining and energy resource management, should rightfully administer any federal controls.

For the same reasons, however, environmentalists felt that regulations administered by Interior officials would result in an unholy alliance with coal operators. Their best hope for effective controls appeared to lie with the Environmental Protection Agency. The EPA had been in business for little more than a year but had already begun vigorously administering air, water, and chemical pollution controls and to clash, not only with industry, but also with other governmental agencies, including the Federal Power Commission and the Departments of Commerce and Agriculture. When the EPA stood firm, as it did with the Clean Air Act's new source performance standards, it relied on the staunch and noisy support of such prominent national organizations as the Sierra Club and the National Audubon Society. For environmentalists like Louise Dunlap, it semed absurd to entrust the Department of Interior with the responsibility of regulating its own constituency, the energy, metals, and coal producers.[9]

Faced with such a wide range of legislative options, the Ninety-second Congress failed to resolve the strip-mining question. The

[9] Louise Dunlap, coordinator, Coalition against Strip Mining, interview, Washington, D.C., February, 1974.

House did pass a bill that followed a middle path between abolition and guidelines. By a three-to-one margin, the representatives
adopted a set of uniform federal control regulations to be enforced
by the Department of Interior. The media mistakenly described that
provision as a "surprisingly tough measure," and perhaps coal people
agreed. With five national conservation groups with membership in
the hundreds of thousands actually endorsing abolition, the House
bill was not so tough. But it was certainly too tough for the Senate,
where grassroots pressure was less important. Jackson's Interior
Committee had reported out its chairman's bill for federal guidelines, and the differences between that approach and the House bill
were simply too great for resolution in the few weeks remaining
before adjournment. A major political battle, however, was clearly
brewing. As the Congress recessed for the Christmas holidays, Senate Majority Leader Mike Mansfield (D-Mont.) promised that strip-
mining controls would be a top priority for the Ninety-third Congress.

Interest-Group Coalitions Define a
National Policy for Strip Mining

"We're in a whole new ball game in Washington," announced
J. A. Overton in his keynote speech at the January, 1973, convention
of the American Mining Congress. The AMC president called for a
massive political program by America's minerals and energy producers to address the strip-mining question and a dozen other environmental issues facing them:

> The people who will make the critical decisions about mining and
> its future, both in the Executive Branch and the Congress, in
> significant numbers and in the power centers, will be new people.
> . . . I want to recommend that each and every chief officer in this
> industry become a special ambassador, each one to his own Con-
> gressional group . . . concentrate your new and added missionary
> emissary efforts to your own three representatives in the Congress
> —your two Senators and House members in whose states and
> districts you have operating facilities.[10]

[10] J. A. Overton, "The Whole New Ball Game for Mining," address delivered at the American Mining Congress Convention, January 15, 1974, and
published in *Mining Congress Journal* 60 (February, 1974), 119–121.

The "new ball game" in the Congress was a 15 percent turnover in the House of Representatives, and nearly half the Senate was new since 1966. Moreover, the House Interior Committee required fifteen new members (one-third of its membership). For the first time ever, two easterners, James Haley (D-Fla.) and John Saylor (R-Pa.), would head that committee. Furthermore, there was a new ball game down on the Mall. President Nixon, said Overton, had "virtually dismantled the senior officer corps of the Department of the Interior. Mining men must look with special quizzical interest" at two other easterners (Rogers Morton and John Whitaker) in the top Interior posts. "The mining industry leadership must seize this opportunity . . . to convey its new message. . . ."[11]

Overton's admonition certainly hit a responsive chord, for during the spring of 1973, the coal coalition mobilized the full force and range of its political wherewithal. In Washington, dozens of coal-related corporations and trade groups became active in the strip-mining conflict, and probably hundreds of others exerted the kinds of grassroots pressures called for by Overton. Five interlocked trade associations (American Mining Congress, National Coal Association, Edison Electric Institute, American Iron and Steel Institute, and the National Electric Reliability Council) headed and coordinated coal's political campaign.[12] Moreover, that same spring, market conditions in the energy business were shifting quickly toward extraordinary cooperation. Developing shortages of oil and gas had solidified the previous soft market for coal. And because of the 1970 Clean Air Act, the demand growing most quickly was for western, low-sulfur coal that could be developed quickly only by strip mining. Thus, utilities, especially western utilities, were very concerned for strip-mining development and practically dominated the Senate hearings. Just one of these groups, for example, the Western Systems Coordinating Council (WSCC), represented forty-one power systems and fourteen affiliated cities. Both the prestige of

[11] Ibid., pp. 121–122.

[12] Coal interests active in the 1971 hearings included the American Mining Congress, National Coal Association, Tennessee Valley Authority, National Independent Coal Operators Association, Surface Miners Auxiliary of West Virginia, Kentucky Surface Mining and Reclamation Association, Peabody Coal, Consolidation Coal, and Cannelton Coal Company.

its leadership and the weight of its considerable constituencies lent influence to the WSCC's opposition to rigorous strip-mining controls. Actively supporting the utilities were the steel and smelting interests. Several of the larger corporations, including U.S. Steel, American Smelting and Refining Company, Kennecott Copper, and Kaiser, had acquired huge holdings of western coal reserves. Their spokesmen were especially alarmed at particular mining control provisions that threatened to impede or even halt development of western stripping.

It was also a new ball game for environmentalists, who were growing in number and beginning to react to the same new fuel market conditions that were stimulating a united front by the coal interests. By spring, 1973, the American people were beginning to hear about and feel the impact of shortages of natural gas and heating oil. Those shortages, soon to blossom into the "energy crisis," were doing more to revive the coal business than all that industry's political activities during the previous decade. As media attention focused on coal, particularly on the incredibly thick seams in the West, conservationists, many of whom had previously paid little attention to strip mining, became increasingly alarmed. They grew fearful that coal strip mining and its associated industrial developments threatened not just the hills of Appalachia, but also the wildlife, rivers, parks, and deserts of the high plains. Ranchers and Indians, too, were becoming aware that expanded strip mining had a tremendous potential, either for environmental destruction or for windfall profits from renegotiated leases. In the East there were other reasons for concern. Community development groups in Appalachia saw increased strip mining as a threat to what good was left in the lives of mountain people, as another wave of industrial exploitation that could impose more of the poverty it had left early in the century. And for urban businessmen, the chambers of commerce, and boards of trade from Charleston, West Virginia, to New York City, a mass migration of the coal industry from east to west threatened unimaginable losses to regional economic growth.[13]

For CASM, its young lobbyists, and the conservation groups

13 Louise Dunlap, interview.

that had organized it, the new image of coal was providing a huge new constituency of strip-mining opponents. During the Ninety-third Congress, more than thirty national and regional organizations lobbied in Washington, D.C., in favor of federal control over strip mining. The Environmental Policy Center's coalition had grown in official membership to include six national and nine regional groups, with dozens of other loosely affiliated groups making contributions, organizing local pressures and letter-writing campaigns, and serving as local outlets for CASM's political literature.[14] The traditional conservationists were well represented by the Sierra Club, National Audubon Society, National Wildlife Federation, Izaak Walton League, and the Friends of the Earth; sportsmen by the Federation of Western Outdoors Clubs; Indians and ranchers by the Black Mesa Defense Fund, the Northern Plains Resources Council, and the Powder River Resources Council; community development and religious organizations by the Appalachian Peoples Service Organization and the Commission on Religion in Appalachia (a coalition, in its own right, of twenty-one national Protestant denominations and the Roman Catholic Church); and forestry interests by the American Forestry Association.[15] All these organizations were committed to strict federal regulations, and a good many supported the outright abolition of strip mining.[16]

For environmentalists, the most helpful consequence of the emerging energy crisis was that it activated the social and community development agencies of the nation's churches. As a Washington representative for the National Catholic Rural Life Conference put it: "The energy crisis . . . has brought home to all of us our dependence on limited energy resources. . . . We are being told that strip mining must be permitted to proceed at an accelerated pace in order to meet the new fuel demands. . . . If current attitudes prevail, our Nation's response will be . . . despoiled communities, valuable farm and range land lost . . . contaminated irrigation and domestic wa-

14 Ibid.
15 U.S. Congress, House, Committee on Interior and Insular Affairs, *Hearings on the Regulation of Surface Mining*, 93rd Cong., 1st sess., April, 1973; U.S. Congress, Senate, Committee on Interior and Insular Affairs, *Hearings—Regulation of Surface Mining Operations*, 93rd Cong., 1st sess., March, 1973.
16 National Audubon Society, Audubon News Release, April 20, 1972.

ter. . . ."[17] By June, 1974, this Catholic organization was actively soliciting political support by its membership for the rigorous House bill (H.R. 11500). "If we don't make ourselves heard now," read a call-for-action mailing, "the utilities and mining companies will carry the day. . . ."[18] It was of vital political importance, especially in the House of Representatives, that church groups were organizing entirely new constituencies to support strip-mining reform. One of the most active church organizations was the Christian Church (Disciples of Christ). At the behest of its Division of Homeland Ministries, the General Assembly of the Christian Church expressed concern with the "tremendous devastation to our land which had resulted from strip mining." Recalling its responsibility to exert "Christian influence in society," the General Assembly resolved that Church members "express themselves to their state legislative representatives and congressional representatives on their concerns over the economic and ecological problems of strip mining." The Assembly itself would "request the Congress . . . to enact regulatory statutes . . . and to use selective moratoriums on strip mining when necessary. . . ."[19] In an article on strip mining in *Glance*, the church reminded its flock that " 'The earth is the Lord's and the fullness thereof; the world and they that dwell therein' (Ps. 24:1). . . . All resources of the earth belong to God. Their use by man must, at all times, be governed by His laws. . . ."[20] It was one thing for opponents of federal regulation to disparage environmental zealots, but it was quite a different matter to take issue with Him.

Political involvement by the churches in the strip-mining issue extended to more than mere rhetoric. The Disciples' Homeland Ministry supplemented the rhetoric with extensive mailings of action guidelines to church members. One such guideline called on members "to support Rep. Ken Hechler's bill H.R. 1000. Ask each of your Congressmen to co-sponsor H.R. 1000 and to give you their

[17] Stephen Bossi, "Washington Farm Front," *Catholic Rural Life* 23 (March, 1974), 8.

[18] National Catholic Rural Life Conference, "Washington Memo," June, 1974 (an irregular institutional mailing).

[19] Unpublished resolution, from the office of G. A. Day, Director, Church and Community, Division of Homeland Ministries, Christian Church, Indianapolis, Ind.

[20] *Glance* 8 (September, 1973), 2.

reply." That advice was accompanied by a sample telegram and a list of appropriate Congressmen to contact.[21] Considering that the Hechler bill (H.R. 1000) was an abolition measure, it appears that the Homeland Ministry was acting well beyond the scope of the General Assembly resolution. By April, 1974, the Christian Church was coordinating its anti-strip-mining campaign with other church activist groups. A "Prepare" document was circulated to 4,000 members of Impact, the religious community's network for legislative action. The Impact guidelines were far more specific than the suggestions in the General Assembly's resolution and reflected the technical expertise that the Commission on Religion in Appalachia derived from the professional staff of CASM. The Disciples of Christ were advised to support the key legislative provisions that the environmental coalition was seeking, including (1) elimination of all highwalls, (2) regrading to an approximate original contour, (3) successful reclamation, (4) owner's consent, and (5) prohibition of mining in areas where reclamation was impossible.[22]

While the involvement of churches in the environment coalition was certainly significant, the heart of the coalition remained the national conservation groups. Of these, the National Audubon Society (NAS) was representative, although somewhat more conservative than the other CASM groups. Simply stated in its membership bulletin, the NAS policy position was as follows: "The Society's view . . . is that strip mining must be confined to areas that can be truly restored; that even in such areas effective safeguards must be established to prevent any harmful effects on surrounding areas during the mining operation, and that full reclamation of the mined area must be strictly enforced afterward. If these conditions aren't met, strip mining should be stopped."[23] Through its publications and regional chapters (300 of them), the NAS encouraged its membership to urge their congressmen to support effective control measures. In the *Audubon Leader*, NAS members learned from up-to-date information supplied by CASM which provisions were critical,

[21] Memoranda of April and May, 1973, unpublished, Christian Church, Indianapolis, Ind.
[22] Ibid., "Recommendations—Section 1," p. 2.
[23] *Audubon Leader*, January 7, 1972.

which bills to support, and which legislators were opposing the right measure. The head office encouraged local chapters to develop their own educational and political action programs using head office materials. One such program consisted of four half-minute television spots and six educational films "about the destruction that can result from strip mining." Local chapters were urged "to persuade the television station or stations in your community to show these spots as unpaid public service announcements. . . ."[24]

The National Audubon Society, through its principal publication, *Audubon* magazine, took its concerns for strip mining to more than 300,000 households and businesses. Between 1971 and 1974, several articles addressed the problem of strip mining. "Agony of the Northern Plains," the feature article in July, 1973, was a thorough and impressive indictment of western strip mining. And the readers of the appeals in *Audubon* magazine for federal strip-mining controls were a politically influential lot. A market survey showed that *Audubon* magazine subscribers were unusually well educated, highly active in business, professional, and civic organizations, and included an extraordinary proportion of corporate board chairmen, presidents, independent businessmen, and educators.[25] This kind of organized support for strip-mining regulation, reinforced by a dozen other such groups, not only had a direct effect on legislative decision making, but also helped build a broad base of public antagonism to strip mining that few politicians could ignore.

Of the two dozen bills on strip mining introduced at the beginning of the Ninety-third Congress, four had significant political support. In the Senate, Interior Committee Chairman Henry Jackson reintroduced his bill (S.425), which became, not surprisingly, the principal working document for Interior Committee markup. In the House, Kenneth Hechler once again submitted his abolition measure

24 *Audubon Leader*, March 26, 1974, January 7, April 28, 1972.
25 "National Audubon Membership Report—March, 1974." Benson and Benson, Inc., "A Profile of the *Audubon* Reader," October, 1970, a report prepared for *Audubon* magazine. The Benson and Benson survey findings, based on standard sampling techniques, showed that the average income of Audubon Society members was $23,926, that 45 percent of its members belonged to business or professional organizations, 36 percent belonged to another conservation organization, 40 percent had done postgraduate studies, and 13.5 percent were corporate board chairmen, corporate presidents, and owners of businesses.

(H.R. 1000), and at the other extreme, Representative Craig Hosmer (R-Calif.), senior minority member of the House Interior Committee, promoted a very weak measure (H.R. 12898) on behalf of the Nixon administration. H.R. 11500, the bill that eventually became the center of House debate, was introduced by Morris Udall (D-Ariz.), chairman of the Subcommittee on Environment, and Patsy Mink (D-Hawaii), chairman of the Subcommittee on Mines and Mining. The law that passed four years later was to be a thoroughly amended compromise between the Jackson and Udall-Mink bills.

By mid-1973, the differences between the environmental and coal coalitions had crystalized around four sets of issues more technically sophisticated and involuted than those of previous years. The first of these, a basic structural difference, was the ever-present issue of state versus federal preeminence. The entire spectrum of environmental interests endorsed federal standards for mining and reclamation as the bottom line of any legislation. The Udall-Mink bill authorized federal standards, and local and regional environmental groups gave it their support on the usual grounds that state laws were inadequate or inadequately enforced.[26] Moreover, citizens' groups complained of having too little input to the state regulatory process and sought greater participation in federal regulation. A U.S. Steel Corporation executive, speaking for the American Mining Congress, clearly stated industry's position: "American Mining Congress . . . will support federal surface mining legislation which is realistically designed to assist the states and the surface mining industry in conducting surface mining operations so as to have the least practicable adverse effect on other resource values . . . if the legislation recognized that because of diversity of . . . conditions in mining areas . . . the establishment of a nationwide basis of uniform standards . . . is not feasible. . . ."[27] E. R. Phelps, president of Peabody Coal and representing the National Coal Association, concurred: "The coal industry supports realistic federal legislation. . . .

---

[26] House, *Surface Mining Hearings*, 93rd Cong., 1st sess., April, 1973. For example, the Conservation Council of Virginia (p. 948); Birmingham, Alabama, League of Women Voters (p. 1142); and the Coal River Improvement Association of West Virginia (p. 1353).

[27] Ibid., p. 412.

The states should be required to establish and enforce a regulatory program based on federal reclamation criteria."[28] At a June NCA meeting, Mr. Phelps partially explained the industry's support of federal guidelines. "We want a federal law," said Phelps, "so that all companies will behave responsibly. . . . We would like it passed quickly, so we can put at least this one uncertainty behind us and get about our business."[29] Broad federal guidelines would serve coal interests in several ways. They would enhance industry stability by putting to rest public agitation for reform with a symbolic mandate while effectively continuing state regulatory preeminance.[30] They would help neutralize competitive inequities that arose from dissonant state laws. And it was good public relations for industry to support federal reform.

Since the late 1960's, the focus of coal production had been moving from Appalachia to Wyoming, and both environmental and coal interests were acutely concerned with the implications of that shift. Growing shortages of natural gas and domestic petroleum were contributing to increased coal demand in the West and Midwest, where imports were unavailable and population was rapidly expanding. That demand could be met most quickly and profitably by stripping the very thick seams of western coal with giant excavating equipment. As the EPA pressed to enforce the 1970 Clean Air Act by requiring utilities to use stack gas scrubbers, more and more utilities became interested in cheap, western, low-sulfur coal. And finally, a variety of new technologies, such as the unit train and coal gasification, were inspiring petroleum and gas interests to turn west with huge investment commitments in reserves for future energy development. Environmentalists saw the evolving east to west shift as a serious threat to the pristine air, clean water, and fragile ecosystems of the high plains. For the coal coalition, the development of western energy generated a bit of internecine friction. The larger oil, gas, and metals firms concentrated their lobbying on

[28] Senate, *Surface Mining Hearings*, 93rd Cong., 1st sess., March, 1973, p. 439.

[29] National Coal Association, "Proceedings: 56th Anniversary Convention," June, 1973, pp. 106–107.

[30] This point is thoroughly developed by Murray Edelman, *The Symbolic Uses of Politics*.

issues affecting western coal, while the older, independent coal firms that operated in Appalachia concentrated on pending rules that would affect steep-slope stripping.[31]

The debate that sprang up around this east-west problem focussed on the quality and distribution of coal reserves. On behalf of environmentalists, CASM successfully disseminated statistical data of coal reserves, claiming that 97 percent of all coal was deepmineable (see appendix C for a full account of this issue).[32] Obviously, went the argument, it would be illogical, indeed the height of folly, were national policy to allow catastrophic environmental destruction merely for the sake of developing 3 percent of the coal reserve. These CASM statistics also argued that abundant low-sulfur coal was available in eastern reserves and could be developed by deep mining, which would not aggravate air pollution. Although CASM's statistics were both inaccurate and misleading, they convinced a good many uncritical legislators and lent support to special provisions aimed at circumscribing western strip mining.

Short of prohibitionary measures, the Seiberling amendment became the principal vehicle by which environmentalists and the United Mine Workers sought to equalize the economies of eastern and western strip mining and so to curb coal's westward migration. In committee, Representative John Seiberling (D-Ohio) attached an amendment to the Udall-Mink bill that would have established a $2.50-per-ton tax on coal mined by all methods. The revenues from that tax were to sustain a fund for reclaiming abandoned strip mines.[33] However, mine operators could get credit for up to 90 percent of the taxes for expenses incurred from reclaiming strip mines, or, in the case of deep mines, could match the costs of equipment and black-lung benefits required by the Coal Mine Health and Safety Act of 1969. As the amendment itself acknowledged, its real

---

[31] Rex Chaney, National Coal Association, and Charles Cook, American Mining Congress, interviews, Washington, D.C., February, 1974.

[32] Environmental Policy Center, Coalition against Strip Mining, "Tabulation of Coal Reserves" (pamphlet), 1974.

[33] These citations to the original version of the bill refer to the committee print adopted on November 15, 1973, as basic working paper for the House Interior Committee (U.S. Congress, House, Committee on Interior and Insular Affairs, *H.R. 11500, A Bill*, 93rd Cong., 1st sess. [committee print], November, 1973). See section 301(c).

purpose was to "enable the deep coal mining industry to compete effectively with the surface coal mining industry."[34] Since the tonnage-per-acre productivity of western (thick seam) strip mining was so high, this provision would produce a huge tax burden on such operations, as their reclamation costs per acre/ton were quite low. But eastern coal operators, both deep and strip, would be able to credit nearly all the tax against the costs of health and safety regulations or reclamation (the latter being far higher per ton due to much thinner seams). As might be expected, the NCA-AMC-petroleum-gas-utility coalition adamantly opposed this idea, and even its proponents, like Morris Udall, thought it a bit unjust, since western energy would have to pay the reclamation bill for the East.

Provisions for selectively prohibiting strip mining constituted a third set of issues over which coal and environmental interests clashed. The majority of these provisions were directed toward western strip mining in particular. Most important of these was the Mansfield amendment, an extraordinary measure that delayed the Senate bill for nearly a year. After the Interior Committee had favorably reported out Senator Jackson's bill for floor debate, Senate Majority Leader Mike Mansfield (D-Mont.), inserted a provision that "all coal deposits, title to which is in the United States, in lands with respect to which the United States is not the surface owner thereof are hereby withdrawn from all forms of surface mining operations. . . ."[35] Especially for the larger energy interests, the implications of this amendment were staggering. During the nineteenth century, the federal government had sold and given away vast tracts of western lands for railroad expansion, speculation, and homesteads. Except for the railroads, the government had usually withheld the underlying mineral rights. Then, during the 1960's, the federal government leased a large portion of those mineral rights to energy developers. The Mansfield amendment would have effectively rescinded those leases. Moreover, Mansfield's restriction would have had an even wider effect because of the patchwork land ownership patterns created by federal land disposal policies. Large-scale, open-pit stripping required consolidated tracts of land for the

---

[34] Ibid., sec. 301(e).
[35] S.425, An Act, sec. 612(b), p. 91.

efficient operation of giant excavators. The amendment would have prohibited consolidating such tracts, thereby preventing the stripping of much privately owned coal as well.

Mansfield's amendment simply delighted environmentalists. CASM's Louise Dunlap called it "the first step in recognizing that . . . there are certain areas in the country that can be declared as off limits to stripping."[36] And the environmental coalition lobbied hard for other prohibitions as well. Citizens' groups, particularly from West Virginia, Tennessee, and Kentucky, wanted to prohibit strip mining on steep slopes (over twenty degrees). Farmers helped environmentalists in seeking to prohibit stripping in alluvial basins or on prime agricultural lands. Conservationists and various outdoors recreation groups wanted no strip mining in national forests or grasslands. Prohibition of strip mining in arid regions was another goal, supported by the findings of a National Academy of Sciences study.[37] And CASM members supported a provision for the designation by states of areas unsuitable for surface mining.

These prohibitionary initiatives alarmed coal men more than any other aspect of the strip-mining controversy. To Carl Bagge and the other coal spokesmen, these were growth-limiting measures favored by zealots that seriously threatened to exacerbate the energy crisis. And it was the energy crisis that became the coal coalition's principal trump throughout the legislative dispute. Bagge expressed the problem to the House Interior Committee in October: "The United States was already facing a dangerous fuel shortage. . . . Now it is careening into an energy crisis faster than ever, because Arab nations have embargoed the shipment of about 1.1 million barrels of oil per day. . . . It is inconceivable that Congress should be considering action which would stop the current production of nearly as much energy in the form of coal as the blocked Arab oil shipments represented."[38] Over and over again, congressmen heard such warnings from federal energy officials and prominent business lead-

[36] James A. Noone, "Coal Lobby Seeks House Action to Offset Senate's Tough Strip Mine Bill," *National Journal*, October 20, 1973, p. 1573.

[37] National Academy of Sciences, *Rehabilitation Potential of Western Coal Lands: A Report to the Energy Policy Project of the Ford Foundation.*

[38] Carl Bagge, quoted in Southern Coals Conference, *Commentary and Research Service* 34 (November 1, 1973), 3.

ers from utilities, steel, banking, and oil. The power producers were the most vocal defenders of expansive strip mining. Aubrey Wagner, chairman of the Tennessee Valley Authority, was especially effective in carrying the warnings of energy shortage to congressmen and state legislators throughout the East. In Owensboro, Kentucky, Wagner warned members of the Interstate Mining Compact Commission that if Jackson's bill (S.425) were not toned down, the TVA would simply not be able to serve its customers.[39] At the House Interior Committee hearings, a spokesman for the National Electric Reliability Council, representing every electric power producer in the country, testified that "any reduction in the present availability or development of additional supplies of surface mined coal would have both an immediate and a long-term adverse effect on the adequacy and reliability of the electrical energy to this nation."[40] Spokesmen for electric distributors and users, representing the National Rural Electric Cooperative Association and the American Public Power Association, agreed.[41]

Arizona's Salt River Project, one of the organizations that lobbied vigorously against stripping restrictions, exemplified the cohesiveness of diverse coal interests in their political action. The project is a huge energy complex designed to use stripped coal for meeting the burgeoning power demands of the Southwest. Its project director, Leslie Alexander, testified that "passage of a bill such as was passed by the House last year would have effectively closed down existing power plants."[42] Alexander was speaking for Kennecott Copper (Peabody Coal was prime fuel contractor), Morrison-Knudson (unit train), Bechtel (construction of generating facilities), Joy Manufacturing (electrostatic precipitator), and the joint venture financiers of the project that included five southwestern utilities.[43] On behalf of these investors, Mr. Alexander reminded the Senate that cost-benefit analysis must be the basis of strip-mining controls

---

[39] *Louisville Courier-Journal,* October 31, 1973.
[40] House, *Surface Mining Hearings,* 93rd Cong., 1st sess., April, 1973, p. 1488.
[41] Senate, *Surface Mining Hearings,* 93rd Cong., 1st sess., March, 1973, p. 630.
[42] Ibid., p. 697.
[43] Ibid., p. 698.

if long-term investment stability were to be maintained. Representatives of the Denver National and Chase Manhattan banks supported his testimony.[44]

Regulatory criteria and standards were the fourth set of issues in this legislative conflict between the coal and environmental coalitions. The criteria are the mandated conditions the legislated rules are meant to attain. Environmentalists promoted a variety of such criteria, the most essential of which were: (1) reclamation of terrain to approximate original contour, (2) no acid drainage or erosion resulting in water pollution, and (3) restoration of flora and fauna to original condition or better. For industry people, these premises for regulation were unacceptable and unreasonable. Most businessmen acknowledged that the coal industry's past reclamation record was inadequate but felt that mining coal and producing its energy justified some reasonable injury to the land. The contour reclamation should alleviate deep pits and parts of the high walls to the extent that plants could grow and erosion be minimized. Acid drainage pollution should be controlled within reason, and trees and grasses should be planted. Between these two visions was a very wide gap.

While industry generally did not object to federal authority establishing broad guidelines, they steadfastly maintained that mining and reclamation standards should be left to the discretion of the states. Peabody's Mr. Phelps felt that "federal legislation which would attempt to set out the specific reclamation requirements would not be desirable."[45] His rationale was that uniform standards would not be suited to the widely varied mining conditions across the nation. However, environmentalists were convinced that standards left to the states would be hopelessly ineffective, the product of industry manipulation. Specific technical standards became the essence of conflict as the relevant Senate and House committees concluded their hearings and turned to weeks of markup sessions.

In October, 1973, the Senate passed a radically modified version of Jackson's bill. Nearly a year later, the House passed a very different control bill, the remains of H.R. 11500. And Carl Bagge's

[44] Ibid., p. 833–840.
[45] Ibid., p. 461.

disclaimer notwithstanding, a considerable number of important changes had been made in both bills, most of which coincided with coal coalition demands. When considering the changes in the Senate bill, it is necessary to recall that even in its original form, it was a measure that coal people had accepted in principle (e.g., federal criteria by the Interior Department for regulation by the states). Industry rhetoric and media misunderstanding tended to blur this point. Nonetheless, coal interests, represented by the National Coal Association and the American Mining Congress, had still objected to several substantive provisions in that bill.

In their Senate testimony, coal spokesmen had opposed seven provisions in particular. All were favorably amended in committee deliberations. A provision for backfilling to original contour caused a problem, because in western mines there was too little overburden for backfilling the pit after thick seams of coal were removed. The amended bill exempted such situations.[46] Another industry complaint had been the provision that topsoil be segregated for replacement on top of the overburden. The industry brief argued that in continuous-cycle backfilling operations, soil segregation was costly and unnecessary, and that soil alone was not always best for reclamation. The Interior Committee amended the bill to provide for segregation of topsoil "unless replaced simultaneously as part of the mining operation and use the best available other material. . . ."[47] Industry opposed a requirement for soil compaction, and the committee qualified the rule to apply "where advisable to insure stability or to prevent leaching of toxic materials."[48] A fourth measure in the original bill required "stable and self-regenerating vegetative cover"

[46] S.425, committee print, sec. 212(b)(2); Senate, *Surface Mining Hearings*, 93rd Cong., 1st sess., March, 1973, p. 439; *S.425, An Act*, sec. 212(b)(2). This note, and the next twelve, merely document the process of change during the Senate Interior Committee's mark-up of S.425. The first citation is to the committee print of S.425 as originally introduced by Senator Jackson. The second citation references the interest group recommending change of that provision. The third citation references the amended provision as it appeared in *S.425, An Act*, the committee print reported out by the Senate Interior Committee.

[47] Sec. 212(b)(2); Senate, *Surface Mining Hearings*, 93rd Cong., 1st sess., March, 1973, p. 439; *S.425, An Act*, sec. 212(b)(4).

[48] Sec. 212(a)(3); Senate, *Surface Mining Hearings*, 93rd Cong., 1st sess., March, 1973, p. 440; *S.425, An Act*, sec. 212(b)(2).

for reclamation. An NCA witness argued that "the operator should not be required to establish vegetation if he is mining in an area where there was not vegetation prior to the mining. . . ." The Interior Committee made the necessary exemption.[49] A fifth problem with the original bill was the prohibition of stripping operations "on any land which is within one hundred feet of primary or secondary roads or lakes, streams, or tidal waters. . . ." Industry officials explained that western operations, because of their immense size, needed to "work through the creeks and farm-to-market roads" for the sake of efficiency. The committee agreed and struck the privision from their bill.[50]

The coal people did nearly as well with provisions favored by environmentalists. One such measure provided for public intervention in the permit approval process by any "person having a valid legal interest." The coal coalition claimed that this would open every permit approval to interference and obstruction by environmental action groups. The Interior Committee agreed and changed the standing to challenge to read, "any person having an interest which is or may be adversely affected."[51] Another part of the Jackson bill, section 215, provided for the designation of areas unsuitable for surface mining. Coal officials were alarmed that this mechanism would stop existing operations, and that, if used, it should take into account the amount of coal that would be excluded from the market. In the course of the markup, two amendments were added, providing that "no area shall be designated unsuitable . . . on which surface mining operations are being conducted" and that prior to making such a designation, regulators would have to determine how much coal would be affected, estimate current demand, and evaluate what impact such a designation would have "on the environment, the economy, and the supply of coal."[52]

---

[49] Sec. 212(b)(4); "Surface Mining Legislation in the Senate," *Mining Congress Journal* 59 (March, 1973), 48E; *S.425, An Act,* sec. 212(b)(3).

[50] Sec. 215(c); Senate, *Surface Mining Hearings,* 93rd Cong., 1st sess., March, 1973, p. 433; provision absent from *S.425, An Act.*

[51] Sec. 209(d); "Surface Mining Legislation in the Senate," *Mining Congress Journal* 59 (March, 1973), 48L; *S.425, An Act,* sec. 209(d).

[52] Sec. 215; Senate, *Surface Mining Hearings,* 93rd Cong., 1st sess., March, 1973, p. 440; *S.425, An Act,* sec. 216(2).

The environmental coalition made virtually no progress toward its goals in the Senate Interior Committee's markup sessions. In their testimony, environmentalists had focused on seven important objectives. As expected, federal regulatory preeminence was their fundamental concern. Section 101 (4) of the Jackson bill mandated that "the primary governmental responsibility for developing, authorizing, issuing, and enforcing regulations . . . should rest with the States." On behalf of CASM, a Sierra Club representative pleaded that the provision be changed to federal authority, preferably the Environmental Protection Agency. Jackson's committee disagreed and made no changes.[53] The National Wildlife Federation particularly supported the "return to approximate original contour of all surface and contour mining operations." Here the committee did make a change, allowing "alternate reclamation variances" for "mountain top removal" and industrial-commercial reclamation alternatives.[54] Several environmental groups sought to have the compaction provisions strengthened, but, as previously noted, the committee did the opposite.[55] For eastern environmentalists especially, a most important goal was to restrict strip mining of slopes steeper than twenty degrees. Again the Interior Committee disagreed and declined the change.[56] Several local groups, such as the Tennessee Citizens for Wilderness Planning, petitioned for a measure allowing citizen input in the process of designating areas unsuitable for stripping. Once again, the aforementioned modifications were made neutralizing the wide standing for citizen review.[57] Some of the CASM groups sought provision for more than one inspection of each mining site each month, but the once-a-month requirement was left standing.[58] And

---

[53] Sec. 101(4); Senate, *Surface Mining Hearings*, 93rd Cong., 1st sess., March, 1973, pp. 918–940; *S.425, An Act*, sec. 216(2).

[54] No variance in committee print; Senate, *Surface Mining Hearings*, 93rd Cong., 1st sess., March, 1973, p. 907; *S.425, An Act*, sec. 213(c)(2-3) added.

[55] Senate, *Surface Mining Hearings*, 93rd Cong., 1st sess., March, 1973, pp. 918–940.

[56] Ibid.; *S.425, An Act*, sec. 216, no change.

[57] Senate, *Surface Mining Hearings*, 93rd Cong., 1st sess., March, 1973, p. 994; *S.425, An Act*, sec. 216(a)(4). Citizens were given a petition right in designation review process, but the amendment noted in note 51 neutralized this gain.

[58] Sec. 213(c); Senate, *Surface Mining Hearings*, 93rd Cong., 1st sess., March, 1973, p. 995; *S.425, An Act*, sec. 213(c), no change.

on the matter of road and watercourse restrictions, environmentalists asked that the one-hundred-foot restriction be trebled. The Interior Committee removed the restriction altogether.[59]

The process of committee markup in the Senate was obviously a political disaster for the environmental coalition. The context—decisions on technical details in closed sessions—was unsuited to the political strengths and methods of environmental interests. The coal coalition, with its experts, its closely reasoned arguments of practicability, and its voluminous supporting data, was far more effective at this stage of policy making. During the spring of 1974, the story was much the same with the markup of H.R. 11500 by the House Interior Committee's Subcommittee on Mines. There the basic working document, written by Patsy Mink and Morris Udall, detailed specific operation and reclamation standards to be administered by federal authorities. It also included the Seiberling provision for equalizing by a tax the profitability of western strip mining and eastern deep mining. In general, environmentalists supported this bill, although they sought to strengthen it in several particulars. Coal people strongly opposed it and, in the House hearings, raised dozens of sharp criticisms. Once again, the subcommittee's markup sessions were unavailing for environmentalists, and the subcommittee made many important changes that corresponded to recommendations made by coal interests. To summarize briefly, the subcommittee (1) removed the Seiberling amendment, (2) neutralized the provisions for designating areas unsuitable for surface mining, (3) omitted a requirement to reclaim haul roads, (4) removed stiff qualifiers for alternate reclamation plans, (5) refused to reduce the thirty-six-month grace period for compliance, (6) diluted the prohibition on disrupting watercourses, and (7) weakened the slope requirements for backfilling.[60]

By the time the Senate and House committees reported out their bills for floor debate, environmentalists faced a decidedly up-

---

[59] Sec. 215(c); Senate, *Surface Mining Hearings*, 93rd Cong., 1st sess., March, 1973, p. 995; *S.425, An Act*, sec. 215 (provision removed altogether).
[60] The source of the original provisions of the House Bill is House, *H.R. 11500, A Bill*, 93rd Cong., 1st sess. (committee print), November, 1973. The source of the revisions made during mark-up is "Surface Mining Control and Reclamation Act of 1974," *Congressional Record—House*, July 25, 1974, pp. H7156–74.

hill battle. Compared with the original bills, what emerged after extensive revision by both committees were very modest control measures. Most environmentalists were disgusted, and, as Louise Dunlap put it for CASM, the bills were "totally unacceptable."[61] Floor debate did little to change that view, with the obvious exception of Senator Mansfield's amendment. But coal interests reacted vehemently to that provision and braced themselves for a final, massive effort to have it stricken by the conference committee. Convening in August, 1974, the conference committee met for eighty-seven hours during the next four months, under intense pressure from both coalitions to resolve favorably the significant differences between the two bills. And the Mansfield amendment remained a nearly insurmountable problem.

By October, deliberations had become painfully mired in all the rhetoric and political histrionics of the full-blown energy crisis. In the wake of the Yom Kippur War, the Arab members of OPEC had declared a boycott of oil exports to the United States. New England politicians were calling for relief from an impending winter shortage of heating oil. Independent gasoline marketers decried monopoly as they were squeezed out of business by inadequate gasoline supplies. Consumers were enraged as they helplessly watched fuel prices soar, and environmentalists feared the worst for their many energy-related goals.

And their concern did seem real as the coal coalition escalated its attack on the strip-mining bill's potential for reducing coal production and exacerbating energy shortages. For the National Coal Association, Carl Bagge warned that if the conference committee did not remove the most odious provisions, the strip-mining bill would raise electric utility fuel costs by 55 percent and necessitate the importation of 400 million additional barrels of oil per year. Picking up on President Ford's button campaign to Whip Inflation Now, (WIN) Bagge proclaimed that "the enactment of this bill would turn the President's economic program into a no-WIN war."[62] By December, public aggravation, the coal coalition's pressure, and alarming statements from Frank Zarb and other administration of-

[61] *New York Times*, May 14, 1974.
[62] National Coal Association, "Press Release," December 4, 1974.

ficials forced the conference committee to compromise on Mansfield's restriction of mining federally owned coal. Conservative Senator J. Bennett Johnston (D-La.) arranged the compromise whereby federally leased coal could be mined with the permission of the landowner and with certain machinery to prevent exorbitant royalties and unfair profiteering by landowners. Once over this hurdle, the conference members easily resolved the remaining problems. Senator Johnston concluded that "this bill is very much watered down from what the environmentalists asked for. . . ." Most congressmen shared Johnston's relief that S.425/H.R.11500 had become "a bill we can live with."[63] Within three days, both houses of Congress approved it by voice votes.

But the conference deadlock had taken its toll, and the bill arrived on President Ford's desk only four days before congressional recess. Maybe the coal interests could live with it, but they still did not wish to. In unison with the Federal Energy Administration, spokesmen for the coal coalition asked the president to veto the bill.[64] On December 30, Gerald Ford announced his decision from a ski resort in Colorado, a state that loomed large in America's coal-energy future. Throughout two Congresses, said the president, "the Administration made every effort in working with the Congress to produce a bill that would strike a delicate balance between our desire for reclamation and environmental protection and our need to increase coal production in the United States." But the Congress had unwisely settled on a bill that "would have an adverse impact on our domestic coal production which is unacceptable." President

[63] *Charleston Gazette*, December 17, 1974.

[64] That the coal interests supported President Ford's veto of the bill was obscured by a misleading report in the *New York Times* (December 18, 1974) that "a number of the nation's major companies were reported to have sent letters to President Ford urging him to sign. . . ." Bethlehem Steel was allegedly the leader of this movement. Actually, Bethlehem Steel was alone in urging Ford to sign. Bethlehem's Washington representative, John Bouchard, had worked effectively with Pennsylvania's congressional delegation to provide the 1974 bill with an exemption for hard (anthracite) coal from federal strip-mining regulation. The letter in which Bethlehem Steel had urged Ford's signature was dated December 17. On that same day, Bethlehem Steel announced its final purchase of the 420,000-ton-per-year Greenwood Stripping Corporation in northeastern Pennsylvania's anthracite region. Bethlehem's public relations department denied that the chronology was anything but a coincidence (see *Wall Street Journal*, March 3, 1975, and *New York Times*, May 8, 1975).

Ford believed that between 48 and 141 million tons of coal production would be lost to the bill's restrictions. Unemployment and dependence on oil imports would be exacerbated, and the bill's ambiguities would cause protracted regulatory disputes and litigation. With disappointment and with sympathy for the bill's proponents, the president was forced to conclude: "I find that the adverse impact of this bill on our domestic coal production is unacceptable at a time when the nation can ill afford significant losses from this critical energy resource. It would also further complicate our battle against inflation. Accordingly, I am withholding my approval from S.425."[65]

Coal's representatives were elated and celebrated the New Year by applauding President Ford's decision to veto the bill. Carl Bagge announced that "President Ford has taken a necessary step which lays the foundation for a secure and adequate energy supply for the future."[66] Ben Lusk, head of the West Virginia Surface Mining and Reclamation Association, expressed ambivalent dismay: "It's a shame that after four years of study Congress was unable to prepare a bill that would effectively protect the environment, while allowing continued coal production during these times of critical energy shortage."[67] Environmentalists did not quite believe that the president had actually vetoed what they saw as a terribly watered-down bill. Their disbelief seemed rooted in a lack of appreciation for the real political implications of Mr. Lusk's postmortem. But Lusk, on the other hand, no doubt persisted in underestimating the extent to which environmentalism was an innate response to changing social and economic conditions.[68]

The Final Inning: A Strip-Mining Policy for the Energy Crisis

After four years of hearings and debate, the statistical, economic, and technical arguments, the different prohibitions, taxes,

[65] President Gerald Ford, quoted in Southern Coals Conference, *Commentary and Research Service* 36 (January 9, 1975), 2.
[66] Ibid.
[67] *Dominion-Post* (Morgantown, W.Va.), January 1, 1975.
[68] Samuel P. Hays, "The Limits to Growth Issue: An Historical Perspective," in Chester L. Cooper, ed., *Growth in America*.

standards, and criteria for regulating strip mining had been exhaustively developed and were well known by most participants in the political contest. Federal authority to control strip mining was no longer at issue. Every operating and reclamation problem had been aired, and every banker, farmer, executive, minister, sportsman, scientist, and bureaucrat had been heard. By 1975, the policy debate had polarized—energy versus the environment. It made no difference that environmental quality and energy supply were logically interrelated parts of a larger economic and ecological system. The mass of rhetoric had succeeded in contraposing strip-mining controls and energy crisis in the public mind. It was to take two-and-a-half more years to formulate a national policy that could "balance" energy and environmental needs with respect to strip mining.

On the first day of the new congressional session, backers of strip-mining controls introduced S. 7 and H.R. 25, bills identical to the one President Ford had vetoed in December. Scarcely disconcerted, the environmental coalition was hopeful that the Ninety-fourth Congress, in light of the liberal Democratic landslide of the previous November, would enact at least as strict a measure. Joe Browder, head of the Environmental Policy Center, assured *Business Week* that environmentalists were "pretty confident that we'll have the votes for a new bill."[69] The Coalition against Strip Mining convened in Washington and reaffirmed its commitment to abolish strip mining while still preparing to support effective regulatory measures. CASM solicited all its associated groups and members to vigorously support the new legislative effort.[70] Local environmental groups advised their members to write and wire their congressmen, senators, and especially the chairmen of the House and Senate Interior committees.[71]

Once again, the coal coalition geared up its own political campaign on strip mining. Energy and related inflation were to be twin themes. Coal people had learned the extent and effectiveness of the environmental campaign and prepared for an all-out effort. At the

[69] *Business Week*, January 13, 1975.
[70] Coalition against Strip Mining, "Announcement," January, 1975 (mimeo).
[71] Newsletter, February, 1975, in files of Operation Coal, headquarters, Blacksburg, Va.

January meeting of the American Mining Congress, J. Allen Overton called for political activism by all coal interests, not merely the mining industry:

> The mining industry . . . has been carrying the case for mining to all those who influence and make the critical decisions of government. And in the process we have won some major victories. We recognize that this effort must continue. It must be a massive and an absolutely relentless effort. It must involve the entire industry— and more. It cannot be left to the American Mining Congress alone. It must continue to draw on the excellent cooperation and help of such fine performers as our friends at the U.S. Chamber, the National Coal Association and others. . . . It must continue to draw on the support of the outstanding group of corporate representatives the mining industry maintains in Washington.[72]

His comrade-in-arms, Carl Bagge, sent a letter on behalf of the National Coal Association to Senator Jackson and Representative James Haley (chairman of the House Interior Committee). The letter expressed the coalition's main theme by reiterating the production figures that the Department of Interior and the Federal Energy Administration had publicized. Based on a possible production loss of 141 million tons of coal per year, the surface-mining bill threatened the loss of 26,100 mining jobs and 20,880 additional jobs in associated industries—"47,000 jobs" became the rallying cry of the coal industry. Bagge unsuccessfully demanded full congressional hearings so that the new bill would not be considered "without weighing its enormous consequences on an America wracked by an energy crisis, inflation, and unemployment and a huge balance of payments deficit."[73]

In February, the Ford administration again introduced its own surface-mining control bill and transmitted to Congress a list of eight "critical" and nineteen "important" changes necessary if the president were to approve either S. 7 or H.R. 25. Most of the changes reflected what industry representatives had proposed during the previous legislative sessions. Ford's eight critical changes

---

[72] *Mining Congress Journal*, March, 1975, p. 51.
[73] Southern Coals Conference, *Commentary and Research Service* 36 (February 27, 1975), 2–3.

would modify the provision for citizen suits, ease restriction of stream siltation and hydrologic disturbances, clear up ambiguous terms, reduce the reclamation fund tax from $0.25 to $0.10 per ton (the remains of the $2.50-per-ton Seiberling amendment), ease standards for water impoundments, permit variances on the prohibition of stripping in national forests, and eliminate the unemployment provision.[74] Environmentalists were utterly dismayed by the president's suggestions. Louise Dunlap described them as "stupid" and "unbelievable," and Morris Udall concluded that they were "grossly deficient environmental standards."[75]

After the exhaustive hearings and markup sessions of previous years, the Senate and House Interior committees skipped full hearings, pausing only for one-day sessions to hear from government energy officials.[76] There was little opportunity for either environmentalists or coal people to exercise their usual lobbying tactics, and both concentrated on generalized publicity and letter-writing campaigns to stimulate grassroots pressures on congressmen. The coal interests belabored production loss, increasing utility rates, oil imports, job losses, and the inflationary effects of a tough control bill. The Environmental Policy Center widely distributed a booklet entitled "Facts about Coal in the United States."[77] The booklet emphasized how the shift to western coal would hurt the economy of Appalachia and reiterated its previous arguments on the low ratio of surface-mineable to deep-mineable coal, the low BTU value of western coal, the availability of low-sulfur coal in the East, and the capacity of deep mining to take up the slack of lost surface mine production. Letters, bulletins, and press releases reminded local groups of the declining fatality rates of deep mining relative to surface mining and of the high profit rates of coal producers in 1974.[78]

[74] *Congressional Record—Senate*, May 5, 1975, pp. S7447–48.

[75] Louise Dunlap, quoted in *Billings Gazette* (Mont.), February 17, 1975; Morris Udall, quoted in *Charleston Daily Mail*, February 7, 1975.

[76] U.S. Congress, Senate, Committee on Interior and Insular Affairs, *Surface Mining Briefing*, 94th Cong., 1st sess., February 1975.

[77] Environmental Policy Center, "Facts about Coal in the United States," February, 1975 (mimeo).

[78] Coalition against Strip Mining, "Bulletin," June, 1975 (mimeo).

In March, both houses of Congress adopted their strip-mining bills with only minor revisions in response to the president's recommendations. The environmental coalition had held firm, certain that it commanded enough votes to override another veto. In fact, it succeeded in getting an amendment to the House bill that entirely prohibited strip mining in alluvial valleys. With President Ford's influence waning daily, the coal coalition was unable to win further concessions from the Congress, since most of its members recognized that the bills pending were already watered down considerably from the versions environmentalists had supported back in 1972.

But while the bills moved to conference during the spring, the coal interests, cooperating with labor, hit on a new angle. For the most hilly Appalachian states with weak control statutes, the federal bills did appear to pose a threat to profits and employment. Local coal trade associations in Virginia, West Virginia, and Tennessee vigorously publicized hypothetical job losses that would result from the federal bill's provisions for reclaiming steep slopes. In Tennessee and Kentucky, nearly seventy independent strip mine operators organized the American Energy Producers Association to represent their opposition to the bills in Washington.[79] In Virginia, where the state reclamation law was perhaps the very weakest, small strip operators and truckers organized a massive protest. A caravan of six hundred coal trucks and two to three thousand miners, sponsored and financed by independent operators, descended on Washington in April to dramatize their fears of job losses. Editorials in local newspapers characterized Morris Udall, who was managing the House strip-mining bill, as "headline grabbing, stubborn . . . a good example of the many 'Little Pharaohs' that have gained unlimited power in the legislative halls of the U.S. Congress." When it came to conflicting statements about job losses, southwestern Virginians much preferred to "accept the statement of Virginia's true statesman Harry Byrd over that of Udall."[80]

In the glare of this publicity and under pressure from labor constituencies, the House-Senate conference committee struggled to resolve the differences between the two bills and to deal with Presi-

---

[79] *Louisville Courier-Journal*, May 18, 1975.
[80] *Enterprise* (Wytheville, Va.), April 10, 1975.

dent Ford's demands for twenty-seven changes. On May 5, the committee reported out a compromise bill that met eight of the president's recommendations. The committee had limited provisions for citizens' suits, siltation and water impoundment restrictions, control of hydrologic disturbances, and the prohibition on stripping alluvial valleys.[81] The House approved the measure by a vote of 293 to 115, and the Senate approved by a voice vote.

But from President Ford's perspective, the committee's changes went only part way toward meeting his concerns and ignored several others. In particular, prohibition of mining in national forests, the reclamation tax, and the provisions for surface owners' consent remained unchanged. The coal interests likewise remained unsatisfied. In a press release, Carl Bagge announced that "if Congress cannot restrain its suicidal impulses by defeating the bill, President Ford will again be the last means of safeguarding our energy future."[82] Frank Zarb, Ford's "energy czar," agreed and recommended that the president veto. Treasury Secretary William Simon and Budget Director James Lynn followed suit. And apparently Arthur Burns, chairman of the Federal Reserve Board, added the finishing touch. "Mr. President," concluded Burns, "I don't think we ought to be doing anything now to increase the imports of oil."[83] Of all Ford's advisors, only Russell Train, administrator of the Environmental Protection Agency, supported the bill, and on May 20, the president vetoed it for a second time. Dismayed but not beaten, the environmental coalition immediately set about raising support for a veto override vote in the House. But there was too much publicity in the early summer, all of which cast the administration and coal coalition as fighting for energy self-sufficiency, jobs, and reduction of inflation. As environmentalist pleas to discredit those claims fell on deaf ears, the supposedly veto-proof Congress seemed to dissolve. In June, the attempt to override failed by three votes.

For the next year and a half, the political likelihood of a federal control law seemed ever more remote. Representative Udall unflaggingly reintroduced his bill in January, 1976, but the House Rules

<hr />

[81] *Congressional Record—Senate*, May 5, 1975, pp. S7447–48.
[82] Carl Bagge, National Coal Association, "Press Release," April 30, 1975.
[83] *Pittsburgh Post-Gazette*, May 30, 1975.

Committee quickly tabled it, not wishing to waste another congressional session in a hopeless showdown with the White House. In May, the administration took the initiative by having the Department of the Interior promulgate administrative rules for strip mining federally owned coal. The federal rules generally provided for restoration of original contour but qualified that requirement with variances and a standard of, "to the maximum extent practicable." Secretary Thomas Kleppe claimed that his rules were just as strict as the bill Ford had vetoed but were improved by "a degree of flexibility that will allow us to function."[84] Environmentalists disagreed, claiming that Interior's regulations were full of loopholes and, in Udall's words, "woefully inadequate."[85] Most significantly, the Interior rules were shortly to provide the coal coalition with an important new argument—thirty-eight states and the federal government had effective rules, so why bother with federal legislation?

Jimmy Carter's presidential victory and Morris Udall's ascendence to the chairmanship of the House Interior Committee resurrected environmentalist hopes for federal regulation of strip mining. Environmental goals, including strip-mining control, were major planks in the Democratic platform. So, with the new president's blessing, Representative Udall introduced H.R. 2 on the first day of the Ninety-fifth Congress. That bill, and its companion in the Senate, were nearly identical to the bill Gerald Ford had vetoed in 1975. In Washington, the struggle over a strip-mining law had nearly become a cliche, and when Udall convened nine days of public hearings in January, he appropriately commented, "I feel that I have been here before."[86]

However, even after seven years of debate, the issue of federal regulation itself was not resolved. The Interior Committee chairman explained why still another round of hearings was needed: "Critics have argued that the need for a national bill had vanished. The bill's opponents argued that the reclamation regulations of the states have

[84] Wall Street Journal, May 12, 1976.
[85] Ibid.
[86] U.S. Congress, House, Committee on Interior and Insular Affairs, Subcommittee on Energy and the Environment, Hearings—Reclamation Practices and Environmental Problems of Surface Mining, 95th Cong., 1st sess., January–February, 1978, I, 1.

improved vastly and that environmental abuses of strip mining are ancient history."[87] And that viewpoint became obvious in the course of the hearings, as a dozen state strip-mining regulators teamed up with mine operators and utilities to describe how effective their reclamation already was. Repeating arguments from seven years earlier, the coal interests complained that a federal law was unnecessary and would only heap red tape and delay on top of smoothly functioning state regulatory relationships. And local citizens' groups from Alabama to Pennsylvania testified to the ineffectiveness of existing state regulation.[88] If anything had changed, it was that the number of interests involved in the strip-mining issue had grown even larger. In the nine days of hearings, the list of witnesses was almost endless.

The most distinctive feature of the strip-mining conflict in 1977 was the separation of issues between eastern and western interest groups. A spokesman for Atlantic Richfield's synthetic fuels division aptly expressed the concern of big western interests: "Atlantic Richfield believes there appears to be a bias in Congress in support of eastern underground mining at the expense of western surface mining because of a lack of understanding that surface mining can be accomplished in an environmentally acceptable manner, including successful land reclamation. The company is convinced that there is no need for federal surface mining legislation."[89] Independent Appalachian mine operators believed the bias to be in the opposite direction. On either side of the 100th meridian, three of four substantive issues dominated the hearing testimony and the political machinations of the next six months. Among western interest groups, the major bones of contention were alluvial valley restrictions, surface owner protection, and the rules for designating areas unsuitable for strip mining. The American Mining Congress, representing in particular the big energy developers that held federal leases to billions of tons of coal, objected strongly to the ambiguously worded constraints on strip mining in alluvial valleys. AMC spokesmen argued that, if anything, alluvial valleys, because of abundant top-

[87] Ibid.
[88] Ibid., III, 25–37, 187–230.
[89] Ibid., p. 267.

soil and proximity to water, could be better reclaimed than most other lands.[90] Environmentalists from the Northern Plains Resources Council argued in opposition that strip mining would ruin the high agricultural potential of alluvial valleys.[91] A similar provision for designating areas unsuitable for strip mining was equally alarming to coal developers. They saw it as a land-use planning device and an open-ended invitation for environmentalists to lock up the nation's energy resources. Here again, the energy crisis argument was their ace in the hole. "Because of the immediate need to expand coal production," said an oil company official, "this country does not have the luxury of being able to exclude significant coal-bearing lands from development. . . ."[92] But the National Farmers Union, which CASM organizers had carefully cultivated, rejected these coal industry pleas and recommended that "any land not fully restorable to its original agricultural use should be banned to strip mining."[93]

For western interest groups, the provision most controversial in Udall's bill required that federally leased coal could not be stripped without the consent of the surface owner. This was the remains of the old Mansfield amendment and was accompanied by a formula for determining the size of payments that a prospective coal developer could offer a surface owner. Environmentalists were committed to this measure because the formula's modest payment allowances would dissuade ranchers from giving their consent, and much of the federally owned coal would remain undeveloped. The coal interests, keenly aware of that point, argued that the consent provision would allow landowners to "arbitrarily hinder the national effort toward improving our energy availability . . . and that this provision delegates to individual landowners the custodial responsibility for federal coal. . . ."[94] A bevy of ranchers, backed by the prestigious American Farm Bureau Federation, did not mind the consent provision itself but wanted nothing to do with formulaic constraints on their bargaining power. One of the ranchers, Dan Hinnaland, told the House committee that "decisions regarding the

90 Ibid., p. 425–426.
91 Ibid., I, 177, 264–265.
92 Ibid., III, 272.
93 Ibid., II, 129.
94 Ibid., III, 274.

sale, lease or any other disposition of one's land is an individual property right and should not be legislated . . . the decision with regard to the surface should remain mine without limitations."[95] Mr. Hinnaland, the son of a Norwegian pioneer, owned 30,000 acres of Montana rangeland, underlaid by federal coal, near the future site of an energy center planned by Burlington Northern.

When Udall and his committeemen turned to hearing witnesses from the East, the issues changed but the intensity of debate did not. For the citizen groups, coal operators, and regulatory officials of the seven Appalachian coal states, variances from original contour restoration, mountaintop removal, and the complex procedure of federal regulations were the most pressing concerns. Reclamation costs and job losses were the heart and soul of coal's argument on eastern issues. The problem was the hills, especially the steeper ones in Kentucky, West Virginia, and Virginia. Most strip mining occurs on these hilly slopes where it is difficult and expensive to remove the highwall and to keep all overburden from sliding down slopes of the mining bench. On the matter of costs, the coal people, especially the smaller, independent operators, complained bitterly that the proposed rules, if uniformly applied, would put them out of business. In the past, hard data on reclamation costs had been scanty, but in the 1977 hearings, the coal people could point to the results of TVA's Massengale Mountain demonstration project. Supporting the need for variances on a site-by-site basis, TVA's chairman, Aubrey Wagner, grimly summarized the cost of the back-to-contour reclamation practiced at Massengale: ". . . the difference in cost between back-to-contour reclamation and current good reclamation practices amounts to about 40 cents for each cubic yard of overburden. This would amount to an extra $3 to $4 for each ton of coal mined from steep slope Appalachian mines (in 1973 dollars)."[96] Local labor leaders from the United Mine Workers saw the requirement for restoration to original contour as a serious threat to their jobs. Indeed, at its 1976 constitutional convention, the UMW had voted against a federal bill (which it had previously endorsed when fewer strip mines were unionized) and endorsed a preference

[95] Ibid., IV, 33.
[96] Ibid., II, 116–117.

for state-by-state strip mine regulation. Joseph Tate, head of UMW Local 2166 in Virginia, told Udall's committee that H.R. 2 "would invoke undue hardships on all United Mine Workers." Tate was convinced that he "and thousands of [his] coworkers in Virginia, and other states affected by this legislation, will join the ever-growing ranks of the unemployed."[97]

In addition to site-by-site reclamation variances, there was considerable pressure, especially from West Virginia and Kentucky, where steep hills are adjacent to deep hollows, for "mountaintop removal." This mining-reclamation technique involved taking an entire seam of coal by removing the whole mountaintop of overburden (as opposed to stripping along the transverse slope). The overburden was placed into adjacent hollows, which when filled and leveled left a plateau of ex-hollow and ex-mountain suitable for industrial, commercial, or residential development. Not only mining companies, but general economic development interests supported this technique because of the scarce and valuable flat land it created. However, for environmentalists, the idea of "mountaintop removal" was an abhorrent and shattering imposition on nature. H.R. 2 precluded mountaintop removal, since it did not restore original contour, and the technical pros and cons were argued endlessly at the hearings.

A third important concern to eastern coal interests was that Udall's bill (and also the Senate version) threatened to heap incredible bureaucratic and procedural requirements on coal operators. The complex provisions for permits, licenses, reclamation plans, maps, hearings, public notices, inspections, and reports were crucial to environmentalists determined to safeguard quality reclamation and enforcement of the law. But for small operators without the staff necessary to handle the immense paperwork, this problem boded disaster. In fact, even the larger companies, like Consolidation Coal complained of the bureaucratic burdens implicit in the federal legislation.[98]

By the close of the Udall hearings, it was evident to all that a

97 Ibid., III, 10–11.
98 U.S. Congress, House, Conference Report, Surface Mining Control and Reclamation Act of 1977, 95th Cong., 1st sess., July, 1977, H. Rept. 95-493.

federal law of some kind was certain, and lobbying on these specific issues intensified during committee markup, floor debate, and finally the conference deliberations. In its markup, the Senate Energy Committee dropped the Mansfield amendment (banning strip mining of federal coal under private land) and accepted another amendment by Wendell Ford (D-Ky.) to allow mountaintop removal and other site-by-site reclamation variances. The House Interior Committee also amended H.R. 2 to allow mountaintop removal and struck a provision for damage suits against coal operators in federal courts. In April, as pressure by coal interests on the congressional committees became intense, Carter's new Interior secretary, Cecil Andrus, suggested a series of amendments to strengthen the bills. The startling suggestions, including bans on strip mining in alluvial valleys and national forests, provided Udall and Metcalf the counterforce necessary to hold the line on further amendments. The floor debates generated more heat than light, and, with few substantive changes, both bills were approved and went to a conference committee on June 6.

The House-Senate conference committee spent two weeks adjusting differences between H.R. 2 and the considerably weaker Senate bill. The committee dropped H.R. 2's ban on stripping alluvial valley floors, accepting instead a Senate provision for regulating such mine operations. The conferees modified the House measure for surface owner consent, allowing operators and landowners to negotiate freely the price of a conveyance or, when a landowner refused to consent, to allow resolution under the jurisdiction of state law. The conference also accepted the Senate's variance to original contour where "sound engineering technology" indicates that complete regrading is too difficult. And all the conferees made an effort to simplify the bill's language and to minimize unnecessary bureaucratic procedure.[99]

In midsummer, President Carter signed into law the Surface Mining Control and Reclamation Act of 1977. In its final form, the act empowered the Department of Interior to set and enforce mining and reclamation standards and to promulgate administrative rules for the states. With the noted exceptions, strip-mined land

[99] Ibid., pp. 97–113.

would have to be reclaimed to approximate original contours, avoiding water pollution and soil erosion, with revegetation in a lasting manner to a condition as good or better than originally. Most enviromentalists were relatively satisfied with the law, and newspaper editors in and out of the coal fields hailed it as a major victory for environmentalism. Coal interests persisted in their disapproval of specific provisions and criticized the law's potential effect on energy supply but seemed grateful that the issue was settled so that expansion of coal production could proceed in an orderly, stable manner.

Compared with no law, or even with most existing state laws, the 1977 act was indeed a victory for environmentalists. However, compared with their original goals and with the bill that the House had approved in 1973, the law was not such a victory. Unlike earlier versions, it exempted small operators for nearly three years, and it allowed stripping on steep slopes, in alluvial valleys, national forests, and on prime agricultural lands. It provided variances to original contour restoration, allowed mining operations to cut through small streams and farm-to-market roads, and restricted originally proposed criteria for designating areas unsuitable to strip mining. The Mansfield amendment was gone, and the Seiberling amendment, a $2.50 per ton reclamation tax, had been pruned to $0.35.

The struggle for a federal strip-mining law was too intense, too complex, and lasted too long to be written off as a mere footnote to the legislative accomplishment of the Ninety-fifth Congress or the Carter presidency. And while our historical perspective on the seventies is still shallow, it is clear that the issues of strip mining touched on several significant changes in public values, economic structure, and the political system. When large numbers of people (the memberships of groups represented by CASM) support abolishing an entire industry, it is evident that at least some values have been changing significantly from a past in which the principle of rapid industrial growth was a national consensus. That serious politicians could continue to favor partial abolition (alluvial valleys, steep slopes, national forests) even in the face of a national energy crisis is startling. A more thorough discussion of these value changes is reserved for the conclusion, after we have looked more closely at the related environmental politics of industrial air pollution.

But it is appropriate here to consider the economic developments that made strip mining a national issue and helped stimulate the evolution of two national political coalitions. The impact of mining activities on natural environments is scarcely a recent development. Nor is energy's fundamental role in economic growth. But modern coal strip mining has grown into an immense technical system since 1945.[100] And the degree of its impact on the environment and the economy is of a new order of magnitude that constitutes a very significant historical change. By 1975, strip mining accounted for more than half America's total coal production, and coal leaders planned to double production in the next decade. We have seen how, since 1958, seven major industrial sectors became financially and technically intertwined in the present and future of coal strip mining. As coal became such a large part of the whole economic fabric, strip mining, when threatened by curtailment, became a political issue crucial to the interests of nearly the whole industrial economy. And the coal coalition, its organization, activities, and determination, was the natural political offspring of that industrial modernization. Similarly, as the scale and deployment of the draglines and power shovels grew, strip mining's effects on the natural environment impinged more profoundly on a wider and more diverse range of people. In the sixties, it touched more hikers, fishermen, farmers, conservationists, churchmen, and native Americans, whose response was to organize local and regional opposition, and, finally, a national Coalition against Strip Mining.

As the coal and environment coalitions clashed during the seventies, they rendered obsolete some traditional models of pluralism. This was no longer the disordered interaction of autonomous lobbyists picking away at legislators. The political activities of both the coal and environmental interests were highly organized, nationally

---

[100] As used here, a "technical system" means the synergism of technology and of modern corporate systems that make possible the development and deployment of technology. The environmental and economic impact of twenty-million-dollar draglines is not merely an engineering marvel, but also an organizational accomplishment made possible by a Bucyrus-Erie and a Peabody Coal.

orchestrated, and centrally coordinated. And coalition political resources, which drew on broad-based support and relied on full-time, expert staff, added incredible complexity to the issue. The political debate quickly focused on biological and geological criteria, technical standards, and elaborate engineering and cost-benefit studies that, more often than not, surpassed the capability of individual congressmen, their staffs, and even administrative bureaucrats, to absorb and sensibly evaluate. The data and implications of the Mansfield amendment, for example, were apparently beyond the ken of Congress, immobilizing it for nearly a year. The seven-year struggle behind the 1977 act is symptomatic of how industrial modernization is causing a kind of dysphagia in the democratic process.

5

Air Pollution Becomes a
National Problem:
1958-1969

FOR more than a century, industrial smoke was an American symbol of economic prosperity and social, if not human, well-being. But in 1948, that symbol began to change as a temperature inversion wrapped Donora, Pennsylvania, in a prolonged cloud of respiratory illness and death. As postwar industrial expansion accelerated, periodic air pollution crises came more frequently, and the synergism of vehicular hydrocarbons and industrial emissions made air pollution more pervasive and persistent, until it affected nearly every metropolitan area in America. In 1963, industrial flues emitted ten million tons of sulfur oxide gases and a variety of other noxious fumes.[1] From epidemiological and laboratory studies, public health authorities grew increasingly alarmed at the correlation between pollution levels and respiratory illnesses. Air pollution was becoming a national problem, spreading respiratory disease and the corrosive effects of sulfur far beyond the gates of the plant. Perhaps because industrial stacks are such visible symbols, partly because big business is a ready scapegoat, and certainly because of the contaminants yielded by its combustion, coal became the principal culprit behind the air pollution problem.

When coal is burned as an energy fuel or for industrial process, several pollutants are emitted to the atmosphere, including oxides

---

[1] U.S. Environental Protection Agency, *Report of the Hearing Panel: National Public Hearings on Power Plant Compliance with Sulfur Oxide Air Pollution Regulations*, January, 1974, p. 11.

of sulfur, oxides of nitrogen, and particulate matter. Since little is known of the adverse health effects of nitrogen oxides, sulfur oxides and particulates became the principal objects of public policy concern. Three industries in particular—electric utilities, steel, and cement—account for most coal combustion in the United States (see table 12). The electric power industry burns coal in boilers to create steam for powering turbines. The steel industry consumes the next largest share of coal, both as coke and as boiler fuel. The cement industry has been particularly dependent on coal since the development of the Portland cement process using heat recuperation from a coal-fired rotary kiln. Other manufacturers consume a declining share of coal and include a politically active subgroup, the nonferrous smelters. It was these leading coal consumers that had the most immediate interest in air pollution policy and added considerably to the breadth and strength of the coal coalition.

After 1958, federal authority became increasingly involved in the problems of air pollution, and during the next two decades, federal policy evolved through four stages of interest-group conflict over the criteria for controlling air pollution. Moreover, the struggle became increasingly polarized between coalitions of coal and environmental interest groups as participants focused on the administrative definition and implementation of those criteria. As with strip mining, the issue of federal versus state regulatory authority dominated the first phase of the political contest, from 1958 until 1967. A tradition of treating air pollution as a local nuisance lent historical precedent to industry's opposition to federal controls. Conversely, the historical inadequacy of local control fostered environmentalist support for federal authority. After Congress enacted the Air Quality Act of 1967, attention shifted to defining the precise scientific thresholds of pollutant concentrations deemed detrimental to human health. Those thresholds were to be the physical criteria upon which regulatory standards and the whole fabric of enforcement were to be based. A third stage, between 1970 and 1973, was a struggle over diluting health criteria with traditional feasibility considerations of economic and technological capability. To the extent that this conflict involved discarding those considerations that industrial capitalism demanded, it was both the logical outgrowth of the incongruent

TABLE 12
Coal Consumption in the United States (million net tons)

Year	Electric Utilities	(%)	Steel Coking	Other	(%)	Cement	(%)	Other Manufacturers	(%)
1958	152.928	(42)	76.580	7.268	(23)	8.256	(2)	117.946	(32)
1961	179.629	(48)	73.881	7.495	(22)	7.615	(2)	105.785	(28)
1966	264.202	(54)	95.892	7.117	(21)	9.149	(2)	109.936	(23)
1973	386.679	(68)	93.634	6.356	(19)			69.153*	(12)

SOURCE: U.S. Department of Energy data in National Coal Association, *Coal Facts, 1978–1979* (Washington, D.C., 1979), p. 60.
* Includes cement.

accomplishments of the 1967 act and the evolutionary precursor of a fourth stage. After mid-1973, as public awareness of the finite character of air resources matured, the conflict over criteria shifted toward a greater polarity—limited growth versus unhampered energy expansionism. What had started out as an issue of federal authority evolved rationally into a philosophical debate over the limits to industrial growth.

The politics of air pollution was at once more diffuse and more coherent than that of strip mining. Not only did industrial air pollution affect air breathers in all fifty states, but its regulation threatened the whole range of businesses that burned coal, in addition to coal producers, oil companies, and commercial banks. Because the problem and its solutions were so pervasive in their impact, there was much greater concern and political participation in both the coal and environmental coalitions. For example, cement producers did little about strip mining but became highly agitated and politically active over air pollution. And citizens' groups from Arizona to New York that knew little of the strip-mining controversy were vocal activists on air pollution. However, while air pollution was certainly a broader issue, interest groups, at least the coal coalition, were nonetheless politically organized. In the strip-mining controversy, coal producers were the principal interests liable to regulatory control. Electric utilities, oil companies, and the others had vital interests in the issue but were secondary participants. The reverse was true with air pollution, where coal producers were secondary and coal consumers were the principals. But coal's political organizations were not therefore less cohesive or active. On the contrary, constraints on industrial air pollution threatened even greater danger to the coal-producing industry's competitive viability and to the coal reserve investments of large energy developers than did regulation of strip mining. The difference merely meant that steel producers, smelters, oil companies, and utilities were, from the start, right up front with coal producers in opposing federal controls. Moreover, until 1977, air pollution control issues induced no internecine differences among coal interests in the east and the west or those in deep mining or strip mining.

This chapter examines the first two stages in the development of a national policy for air pollution. In the process, coal's political coalition evolved, the leadership of environmental activism changed, and the questions of federal versus state control and criteria crystallized and moved toward eventual resolution.

Conferences, Cooperation, and Public Health, 1958–1963

In the late 1950's, when air pollution began to emerge as an issue of national prominence, coal producers were still too disorganized politically to address themselves to environmental issues. When the Department of Health, Education, and Welfare sponsored the first National Conference on Air Pollution in 1958, coal interests were represented by only three steel companies, three utilities, and several nonferrous metal smelters.[2] And if we judge from their trade journals, coal producers seemed relatively uninterested in the air pollution issue. State and local health officials, a few members of academia, and health-oriented associations like the American Cancer Society and the National Tuberculosis and Respiratory Disease Association prompted the HEW conference. As yet, neither national conservation groups nor local citizen action groups were involved in national environmental issues like air pollution. "Ecology" was an arcane subdiscipline of biology, still a decade away from the common parlance. At this early stage, there was little sense of conflict between industry and environmental activists, primarily because the latter had little input to the conference. Also, health officials were still unclear about the ill effects of air pollutants, and industrialists had much to learn about control technologies and economic costs. Smoke, not sulfur dioxide or nitrogen dioxide, was the prime concern. Conferees enthusiastically pledged concern for air quality and the desire to cooperate in cleaning up pollution.

The conference in 1958 was highlighted by a nearly unanimous call for cooperation between industry and government in approaching air pollution problems. "Air pollution problems common to the country as a whole," said one businessman, "should be the responsibility of governmental agencies at all levels."[3] Business spokesmen

---

[2] U.S. Department of Health, Education, and Welfare, *Proceedings: National Conference on Air Pollution,* November 18–20, 1958, index of conference participants.
[3] Ibid., Conference Group C, p. 475.

were making an important point when they reasoned that "it is the joint responsibility of government and industry to sponsor and conduct research on air pollution. . . ."[4] And government officials agreed, based on their experience with local smoke. An Indianapolis official explained how "the mutual efforts of the bureau of air pollution control and industrial plant management . . . cooperation of the coal industry, industrial plants . . . railroads, and smoke control groups . . . was most important."[5] Thus, public and private leaders beginning to address the problem proceeded from the assumption that air pollution was not merely a process cost, a cost of doing business, but was also a social cost that was logically government's responsibility. And yet, with responsibility goes authority—certainly not what the industrialists, at least, had in mind. Federal dollars for research would be fine, but "problems more local in nature should be the primary responsibility of the pertinent area."[6] Clearly, the consensus of the conference was that the thrust should be "generally voluntary cleanup by industry . . . with reasonable and just . . . legislation . . . based on a sound technical foundation . . . for the recalcitrant few."[7] Local regulatory autonomy was to become the central issue at the next two conferences, vigorously supported by coal interests and local government officials alike.

Four years later, when HEW convened the second National Air Pollution Conference, the status of federal authority over air pollution had not changed. However, the problem had grown more visible, the issues better defined, and concern among environmentalists more pressing. Coal people, too, were more aware of the issue and took a more active role in the 1962 conference. The two largest coal producers, Peabody Coal and Consolidation Coal, joined the ranks of their customer allies. Representatives of the Tennessee Valley Authority and American Electric Power headed delegations of power producers from New York, Boston, Pennsylvania, and Washington, D.C. Representing the more general business perspectives were the U.S. Chamber of Commerce, the National Association of Manufacturers, and the National Coal Association. Other than a lone repre-

---

[4] Ibid., p. 478.
[5] Ibid., p. 442.
[6] Ibid., p. 475.
[7] Ibid., p. 481.

sentative of the Citizens Committee on Natural Resources, environmental activists were still conspicuously absent. Two committees
organized the themes and panel discussions for the conference. One
was the National Advisory Committee on Community Air Pollution,
with representatives from Consolidation Coal, U.S. Steel, and Gulf
Oil. The Conference Steering Committee included spokesmen for
the National Coal Association, the U.S. Chamber of Commerce, and
the National Association of Manufacturers.[8] Evidently the business
community had come to recognize the significance of air pollution
control for the future.

At this second conference, expressions of cooperation began to
blend with frank discussions of regulatory authority, and the top
priority for most participants was to assure state preeminence in
controlling air pollution. Businessmen felt strongly that any sort of
adversary relationship with government ought to be avoided. One
Bethlehem Steel executive called for close cooperation between
"offender" and regulatory agencies. To improve communications
between polluters and regulators, he suggested that businessmen
be included on air pollution committees, commissions, and boards
at every level of government.[9] Qualifying this point, Peter Short of
Lukens Steel added that he "wholeheartedly subscribe[d] to and
support[ed] the philosophy that abatement and enforcement programs, to be effective, must remain the responsibility of state and
local government." Spokesmen for Peabody Coal and Gulf Oil sec-
onded that point.[10]

It is important to distinguish between willingness to cooperate
and have federal "involvement," and the desire to have federal regulation. Some historians have characterized national legislative reforms, particularly in the Progressive era, as the product of big
business initiative.[11] But with respect to most environmental issues,

---

[8] U.S. Department of Health, Education, and Welfare, *Proceedings: National Conference on Air Pollution*, December 10–12, 1962, index of conference
participants.

[9] Ibid., pp. 283–287.

[10] Ibid., pp. 336, 38, 28.

[11] The most prominent advocate of this viewpoint is Gabriel Kolko, author
of *Railroads and Regulation, 1877–1916* and *The Triumph of Conservatism*.
In the latter, Kolko argues that "businessmen welcome and work to increase
federal intervention into their own affairs. . . ." Kolko explains that during the

businessmen, and certainly the coal coalition, consistently opposed federal regulatory preeminence.[12] And in perspective, that opposition was scarcely unique to the business community. In the case of air pollution, the Congress had previously decided, in the Clean Air Act of 1955, that air pollution was a local problem and that HEW's responsibility should be limited to supporting and assisting technical research. Local officials, anxious for their bureaucratic autonomy, their local economies, and occasionally for their local clean-up achievements, agreed. Philadelphia's director of environmental health told the conference that he favored emissions control only "at the lowest level of government." Charles Gruber, a Cincinnati air pollution engineer, and James Fitzpatrick, director of Chicago's Air Pollution Control Department, also spoke in behalf of state pre-eminence.[13]

The 1962 National Conference ended on something of a sour note when Howard K. Smith made his summary remarks. He concluded that little substantive progress had been made since the first conference, beyond industry's acknowledgement that an air pollution problem did exist. And, with surprising prescience, Smith noted that "a considerable number of delegates seemed to be vigorously attacking a dragon called 'Federal enforcement. . . .'" There had

---

Progressive era "a crucial factor was the bulwark which essentially conservative national regulation provided against state regulations that were either haphazard or . . . more responsible to radical . . . local communities (pp. 4–6). Kolko's interpretation seems inaccurate, however, with respect to both meat inspection and railroad regulation. See, for example, John Braeman, "The Square Deal in Action: A Case Study in the Growth of 'National Policy Power,'" in John Braeman et al., *Changes and Continuity in Twentieth Century America*, pt. I, pp. 35–80; and Richard Vietor, "Businessmen and the Political Economy: The Railroad Rate Controversy of 1905," *Journal of American History* 64 (June, 1977): 47–66.

[12] Walter A. Rosenbaum, *The Politics of Environmental Concern*, updated Kolko's view and applied it to the environmental movement: "In the case of pollution control," said Rosenbaum, "major corporations generally prefer the federal presence because it prevents the confusion of fifty different state regulatory systems while assuring that no major corporations will escape regulation and thereby enjoy a market advantage" (p. 81). But there is still insufficient evidence to support this view, with the possible exception of automobile manufacturers and vehicular emissions. As the 1962 conference made quite clear, the coal coalition was solidly opposed to federal regulatory authority. See also Matthew Crenson, *The Un-Politics of Air Pollution*, pp. 49, 59, and Richard Cooley, *Congress and the Environment*.

[13] Grant McConnell, *Private Power and American Democracy*, p. 398.

been "great stress on the idea that local government has the primary responsibility for air pollution control."[14] The journalist's remarks offended the National Association of Manufacturers (NAM), which claimed Smith had "dramatized the role of the Federal Government, and undercut the industry, state, and local positions." NAM alleged that his comments had "fully distorted our feeling of the conference's consensus . . . that Federal enforcement was not needed and was not wanted."[15] Obviously, expansion of federal authority was going to be a long and painful political process.

By 1963, public health groups had mounted enough pressure for federal action to convince Congress to amend the Clean Air Act. The principal advocates of legislation, the National Tuberculosis Association and the American Public Health Association, wanted nothing more than federal guidelines for the states and increased research expenditures.[16] Neither were particularly interested in national standards or federal enforcement. Several legislative proposals introduced during the Eighty-eighth Congress focused on three types of federal responsibility: (1) grants to assist states in developing control agencies, (2) increased appropriations for research, and (3) crises conferences to be convened by the HEW secretary, in which interested parties (governors, regulators, polluters) could deal with serious air pollution situations as they arose. There could scarcely be much opposition to these kinds of federal involvement, since they posed no threats to either industry or local officialdom. Indeed, the only source of friction during the 1963 legislative debate on air pollution was sparked by the political debut of two conservation groups: the Citizens Committee on Natural Resources and the National Wildlife Federation. At the Senate Public Works Committee hearings in September, both groups supported the strongest of the proposed bills (S.432) and insisted that more regulation was necessary. They called for rapid development of health criteria, emissions standards, and strict federal law enforcement.[17]

The suggestions by the conservationists, however, met with

[14] Ibid., pp. 419–420.
[15] Ibid., pp. 429–430.
[16] U.S. Congress, Senate, Committee on Public Works, *Hearings on Air Pollution Control*, 88th Cong., 1st sess., September, 1963, pp. 164, 174, 369.
[17] Ibid., pp. 176–188.

overwhelming opposition and were dismissed out-of-hand as absurd-ly and unnecessarily radical. In 1963, the coal coalition for the first time mounted a coordinated effort to assure that the clean air amend-ments would not conflict with their best interest. Members of the Senate Public Works Committee heard well-orchestrated, complete-ly consistent testimony from six of the nation's most prestigious trade associations: the National Coal Association, American Mining Con-gress, American Petroleum Institute, American Iron and Steel Insti-tute, U.S. Chamber of Commerce, and the National Association of Manufacturers.[18] R. J. Ireland, chairman of the board of Consolida-tion Coal, voiced the prime policy goal of all the coal and related business interests: "Federal Government should not enter the reg-ulatory or enforcement field, but . . . [should] provide leadership through research and technical assistance. . . ."[19] Spokesmen for all the other associations reiterated that point to qualify their "endorse-ment" of federal involvement. In support of their opposition to fed-eral regulatory standards or enforcement, the industrialists offered several arguments that were to become staples in their environmen-tal dialogue with Congress. Inevitably, coal men pointed out how much industry had already spent to control air pollution (hundreds of millions, according to American Mining Congress president J. A. Overton). Next, they declared that the existing statute (P.L. 159) was adequate and was successfully encouraging local pollution clean-up. Finally, industry representatives explained how an overall federal control plan would be too inflexible to cope with widely varying local conditions.[20]

Of these six vocal associations, only the American Iron and Steel Institute (AISI) seemed aware that health criteria were implicit in the concept of federal regulation and were, or would soon become, a major issue. According to the AISI, there was no scientific basis for environmentalist claims that there existed "a mounting danger to health." Steel's spokesman claimed that neither the surgeon gen-eral nor the American Medical Association had any evidence that air pollution caused significant harm to human health. The point was that if congressmen were to fool with national policy, they

[18] Ibid., p. iv.
[19] Ibid., p. 366.
[20] Ibid., pp. 364–368.

should not get carried away by environmentalist rhetoric, but should pay attention to "the distinction between criteria to protect health and that based on annoyance or esthetic considerations."[21]

Urban officialdom also contributed its views to the Senate hearing. Spokesmen for the American Municipal Association and the National Association of Counties supported federal research, funding grants, and even federal enforcement guidelines, as long as "nothing should be done to . . . reduce authority . . . of powers at local levels." Mayors Joseph Barr of Pittsburgh and Richard Daley of Chicago gave their qualified support to pending legislation, as long as it was absolutely clear that local authority would in no way be circumscribed.[22] Again, this position was quite reasonable for urban regulators who feared erosion of local power, had little in common with conservation and wildlife groups, were keenly concerned for the health of their local economies, and were accustomed to working with, not against, local businessmen.

The product of these polemics, the 1963 Clean Air Act, did little to clean up pollution or threaten coal interests. So innocuous was it, in fact, that its passage precipitated almost no notice in business circles for more than a year. The act reiterated the principle of local preeminence in air pollution regulation, established a system of regional conferences when state and local officials so petitioned the HEW, and provided more funding for federal research. But considering how little anyone knew about air pollution or control techniques, the 1963 act was not a bad first step. It did create some pressure on industry to begin reducing emissions and providing HEW with the time and the funding to learn the extent of the air pollution problem. The act's worst flaw was its procedural weaknesses, which rendered it so disappointingly ineffective that it actually exacerbated rather than mitigated public concern for air pollution.

Mounting Pressures for Federal Controls, 1963–1967

Until early in 1965, the coal industry press remained silent on the issue of air pollution. Finally, in the March issue of *Coal Age*,

21 Ibid., p. 282.
22 Ibid., pp. 132, 120–121.

editor Ivan Given issued a warning that "the coal industry will be one of the prime targets in the gathering push" on air pollution. He prescribed three responses to the growing challenge: "1. Participate in and encourage research; 2. Take steps to insure that legislative and governmental bodies and the public understand the basic situation . . . from the standpoints of effectiveness and reasonable cost; 3. Improve its organizational setup . . . every organization should participate, on its own behalf, as well as part of the overall group."[23] There was further evidence of the industry's growing awareness in June, at the forty-eighth annual convention of the National Coal Association. For the first time, air pollution was on the convention agenda. Vernon MacKenzie, chief of the Public Health Service's Division of Air Pollution, told the gathered coal men that "the coal industry and its biggest customer, the electric power industry, are faced with a responsibility to apply more of their resources . . . to better means of controlling pollution." MacKenzie warned coal men to expect "that standards will be developed by nonfederal regulatory agencies affecting sulfur oxide pollutants. . . ." Another convention speaker was James Fitzpatrick, Chicago's air pollution control chief. He chastised the coal industry for having spent "less than $100,000 a year nationally in developing techniques to reduce sulfur dioxide emissions. It is imperative," said Fitzpatrick, "that the coal industry invest much more money. . . ."[24] Indeed, that was one of the coal industry's most serious problems. With scarcely any large corporate units, annual production a third lower than that two decades earlier, and weak profits, the coal industry lacked either the financial or organizational wherewithal to perform research. As late as 1972, environmentalists and legislators continued to accuse coal interests of irresponsibility for not having invested in sulfur dioxide research.[25]

Political as well as technical issues were beginning to come into focus. An August editorial in *Coal Age* identified, with surprising

---

[23] *Coal Age*, March, 1965, p. 69.
[24] National Coal Association, "Proceedings: 48th Annual Convention, June, 1965."
[25] Several examples of this criticism appear in committee questions of coal industry witnesses in the 1967 Senate Public Works Committee hearings on the Air Quality Act and again in 1971, during air quality implementation hearings of the Pennsylvania Environmental Hearing Board.

foresight, the importance of standards and technical data to the process of policy formation:

> Standards are perhaps the most critical of all the items involved in pollution control . . . the big job . . . is to make sure that the time, effort, and money devoted to the task of attaining reasonable air purity are not wasted in false starts, including attempts to enforce unrealistic standards. Coal . . . must take an active part in the development of standards. And, in preparation, it must assist in the development of pollution facts and their dissemination . . . [and] see that all concerned have this information, particularly those charged with enacting legislation and developing standards.[26]

This was extremely good advice, and coal leaders should have paid earlier and closer attention to it than they did. Air pollution control, like most areas of governmental regulation, is based on performance standards aimed at achieving specific goals. These goals might be rates of profit, the fat content of ground beef, or degrees of air purity. In any case, specific standards are necessary to define enforcement activities. Slight variations in standards are extremely significant for sensitive profit margins in large-scale industrial operations. And equally important, as the editorial obliquely put it, are the criteria for those standards. In the case of air pollution, the logical criteria included levels of air contaminants detrimental to human health, capabilities of technologies available for controlling emissions, and socioeconomic costs of attaining specific air standards. Obviously, as control policy developed, the marshalling of information about such criteria would become a key element in the promulgation of standards. Eventually, it was in these crucial areas of criteria and standards that coal interests would have the money, manpower, and operational data to develop the technical input to policy formation.

In the fall of 1965, New York's Mayor John Lindsay abruptly announced his intention to ban coal from New York City. The threat of this precedent-setting action quickly extinguished whatever residual apathy coal leaders felt toward the air pollution issue. In an open letter to Lindsay, *Coal Age* editors asked if the mayor had "ascertained that overall air purity objectives are reasonable of themselves and in relation to the added costs. . . ." They also queried if

[26] *Coal Age*, August, 1965, p. 62.

"before reaching the decision to ban coal outright, . . . consideration [was] given to the possibility that it might be more practical and less costly to move first to determine reasonable standards of air quality."[27] By March, 1966, when New York's city council held hearings on the mayor's proposal for banning coal, the industry was out in force and pressed hard on the economic costs. Spokesmen for the National Coal Association, United Mine Workers, Bituminous Coal Research, and the National Coal Policy Conference all testified that a limit of coal with 1 percent sulfur content was simply not feasible.[28] Too little low-sulfur coal or residual fuel oil was available at reasonable prices, and the coal men urged patience and further study. Meanwhile, Lindsay's special task force on air pollution had already met extensively with Consolidated Edison Company officials and were saturated with Con Ed's pessimistic views on the problem.[29] Finally, Senator Robert Byrd (D-W. Va.) wrote to the mayor, admonishing him to conduct more research and to consider further the costs of substituting imported residual fuel oil for coal.[30] When the city council adopted a new air pollution ordinance in June, it was considerably modified. The ordinance established a five-year schedule for reducing sulfur emissions (applicable to fuel oil as well as coal) and accepted stack gas removal as an effective alternative to low-sulfur fuel.

Meanwhile, the controversy over Mayor Lindsay's proposal had sparked more public pressure for federal reform. Late in 1965, the Department of Health, Education, and Welfare had proposed emission standards for sulfur oxide at federal installations. In the face of "repeated strong warnings of the adverse effects of proposed HEW 'instructions,'" however, the initial regulations were quickly remanded for futher study. Government officials gave assurances that the next time around "regulations which are finally issued will be worked out in cooperation with the coal and oil industries as well as other interested parties."[31] By 1966, although coal people had managed to ward off the most serious regulatory threats, it was pain-

27 *Coal Age*, February, 1966, p. 80.
28 *Coal Age*, March, 1966, p. 26.
29 *Coal Age*, February, 1966, p. 80.
30 Ibid., p. 29.
31 *Coal Age*, October, 1965, p. 48.

fully evident that the air pollution issue was getting out of hand and that coal's political effectiveness had to improve quickly. *Coal Age* editors again warned that public pressure for air pollution reform was building and that it was vital to "prevent precipitate political action and the ensuing setback to both industry and public. This will continue to be a major coal job."[32]

When the third National Air Pollution Conference convened in 1966, both coal and environmentalist interests were well represented. Trade associations and corporate executives represented the interests of coal producers, oil companies, steel, electric utilities, and manufacturing.[33] But at this third conference, coal interests had to share the spotlight more equally with eight national and regional environmental and health groups.[34] The issues were more clearly drawn and conflict became the keynote of the conference. Now, disagreement over federal involvement in pollution control dominated the entire conference. The environmentalists had come to demand, unanimously, federal promulgation of standards, preferably backed by federal enforcement, as a minimal requirement. Articulating this view, Seymour Calvert, director of the Center for Air Environmental Studies at Penn State, argued that only federal standards and criteria could solve what had become a nationwide problem. "It is clearly a job for the Federal Government to act with restraint," said Calvert, "but act."[35] Industry and local government officials, however, held that national emission or ambient air standards should be avoided at all cost. "Congress," according to Harold Thayer of the National Association of Manufacturers, "having enacted good

[32] *Coal Age*, January, 1966, p. 7.

[33] U.S. Department of Health, Education, and Welfare, *Proceedings: Third National Conference on Air Pollution*, 1966. Coal interests participating included the National Coal Association, American Petroleum Institute, Edison Electric Institute, National Association of Manufacturers, U.S. Chamber of Commerce, Bethlehem Steel, Humble Oil, Standard Oil, Detroit Edison, American Public Power Association, and the Tennessee Valley Authority (six of the above served on the conference steering committee).

[34] Ibid. The following environmental interests participated: National Tuberculosis Association, National Audubon Society, American Public Health Association, General Federation of Women's Clubs, Citizens for Clean Air (N.Y.), New Jersey Citizens for Clean Air, West Virginia Citizens Air Pollution Council, and the Pennsylvania Thoracic Society.

[35] Seymour Calvert, Pennsylvania State University, in HEW, *Third National Conference*, p. 475.

legislation regarding air pollution, now should give it time to work." Thayer and others conceded that the federal government should contribute basic research, collect data, disseminate information, and provide technical assistance. But "we in industry hope that the legislative branch exercise restraint in the grant of police power."[36]

From the perspective of the coal industry, new federal legislation in 1967 might have had one redeeming value. That is, it offered some hope for revising the sulfur standards promulgated in 1966 by HEW for federal installations. After HEW's original proposal was postponed, "officials of three coal organizations continued to meet with federal officials to seek more reasonable SO_2 standards. . . ."[37] Although "coal at the end of the year was exerting major effort to get the terms of a succeeding [proposal] modified," HEW went ahead and again proposed limits as low as 0.25 percent sulfur content for coal burned in *new* federal installations.[38] Joseph Moody, president of the National Coal Policy Conference, saw a "clear indication that HEW wants such low-sulfur restrictions to become a nationwide standard for all fuel-burning facilities." Not only were HEW's standards way out of line with reasonable costs and available control technology, complained Moody, but

> The Clean Air Act specifically stated that state and local governments must provide leadership in the antipollution fight. I look upon this HEW regulation as a foot in the door in the federal effort to usurp the leadership with uniform nationwide federal regulations

[36] Harold Thayer, chairman of NAM's Industrial Problems Committee, in HEW, *Third National Conference*, pp. 513, 514. Industry opposition to government regulation and industry "cooperation" with government were not mutually exclusive. Business leaders repeatedly called for a cooperative approach to air pollution problems. Harold Thayer, for example, suggested an advisory committee that presaged the National Industrial Pollution Control Council formed by President Nixon three-and-a-half years later. According to Thayer, "What we will need is the kind of industry-government cooperation that we have always enjoyed in the face of national emergency. . . . I suggest that a group of top-level industry officials from the broadly representative committee with which I am associated might meet from time to time . . . with officials of the Department of Health, Education, and Welfare, the Public Health Service, the National Center for Air Pollution Control. The exchange of views to such a group would result in mutual understanding and tolerance and friendly cooperation that will lead to the development of an increasingly sound program" (p. 515).
[37] *Coal Age*, April, 1966, p. 22.
[38] *Coal Age*, February, 1967, p. 80.

as the ultimate goals. Unless this blatant power grab is checked, the state and local role in pollution control can be expected to diminish progressively until they are completely out of the picture.[39]

Perhaps the Congress, lacking the apparent political insensitivity of the Public Health Service, might be convinced to reassert the principle of state regulatory preeminence.

But in both the Congress and the executive branch, there was considerable support for federal standards of some sort. Lyndon Johnson wanted an air quality act in 1967 as part of his Great Society program. His advisors accepted the leadership of Vernon MacKenzie, who favored national emission standards for stationary sources of industrial pollution.[40] However, in the Congress, Senator Edmund Muskie, "Mr. Pollution Control" in media terms, did not care for the idea of federal emission standards, and, since he was chairman of the Subcommittee on Air and Water Pollution, his views were important. Speaking at the National Conference on Air Pollution, Muskie had made his position quite clear: "I do not favor fixed national emission standards for individual sources of pollution. We do need national ambient air quality criteria, applied as standards on a regional basis. . . ."[41] The difference between emission and ambient standards is crucial to understanding the historical development of federal policy on air pollution. In 1967, it appeared uncertain whether Senator Muskie actually understood the distinction and its implications. He thought emission standards would be "minimal rather than uniform and hence would not eliminate economic inequities of plant compliance with varying local rules." Instead, he preferred ambient air quality standards that would give "equal priority to critical areas and areas where no problem presently existed."[42] This explanation is confused, and is right for the wrong reasons. Compared with emission standards, ambient standards are minimal and would allow relocation of a company's polluting facili-

---

[39] *Coal Age*, January, 1967, p. 26.
[40] Charles O. Jones, "Satisfying the Public: Speculative Augmentation in Federal Air Pollution Policy" (unpublished paper, University of Pittsburgh, 1973), p. 8.
[41] HEW, *Third National Conference*, p. 597.
[42] Edmund Muskie, quoted in *Coal Age*, August, 1967, p. 28.

ties to a clean air area as a way of complying with standards. But emission standards are premised only on enforcement needs or best available technology, not on health criteria. Ambient standards, which would apply nationwide, would be quantitative tolerances on the at-large levels of contaminants allowable in any air region. And those tolerances had to be premised on health criteria.

In 1970, when Ralph Nader attacked Senator Muskie in his task force report entitled *Vanishing Air*, his attack was based on the notion that Muskie was soft on industry because he preferred ambient standards.[43] While this conclusion was warranted on the basis of industry preferences and superficial logic, it has not been justified by later developments, as we shall see. But, aside from his motives, Muskie probably judged accurately that emission standards were not politically feasible. Greater public concern and environmentalist support would probably have been necessary to overcome industry opposition and natural legislative inertia.[44] Moreover, Jennings Randolph (D-W.Va.) was chairman of the Senate Public Works Committee of which Muskie's air and water subcommittee was part. Senator Randolph, devoted to his state's coal industry, would probably not have approved emissions standards so adamantly opposed by his most prominent constituents. So in April, 1967, when Senator Muskie opened hearings on S. 780, the administration's bill, he did so without any intention of protecting the emissions standards.

The leadership of the coal coalition understood Muskie's position and effected a strategy first to eliminate the emission control concept and then do its best to maintain state authority and minimize the impact of federal ambient standards without overtly offending Muskie. During the seven days of hearings, the coalition presented its position with an extraordinary array of spokesmen. Representing coal producers were the National Coal Policy Conference, National Coal Association, American Mining Congress, Coke and Coal Chemicals Association, United Mine Workers, and

[43] John C. Esposito, *Vanishing Air*, pp. 269–273, 290–293.
[44] Charles O. Jones, *Clean Air: The Policies and Politics of Pollution Control*. Jones describes the process of policy formation up through 1967 as one of "gradual incrementalism." He argues that prior to 1970, public environmental concern was inadequate for sustaining anything more than small increments to previously legislated policies (P.L. 159 and the 1963 Clean Air Act).

the three largest coal-producing firms. Steel and nonferrous metals interests and their captive coal producers were represented by nine of the leading corporations. The Edison Electric Institute and five utilities spoke for the electric power producers. The American Petroleum Institute and Humble Oil (Exxon) spoke for big oil. The Pennsylvania Railroad spoke for the rail interests, and the National Association of Manufacturers and the Chamber of Commerce spoke for all the diverse manufacturing and commercial interests associated with coal.[45]

With consistency, solid data, and clearly delineated goals, the coal coalition presented an effective front. Each industrial representative pledged wholehearted support of legislation for controlling air pollution, as long as it did not include national standards, left primary authority with the states, and included three amendments offered by Senator Jennings Randolph. Witnesses repeatedly endorsed each other's positions, allowing the National Coal Policy Conference and the Edison Electric Institute to take the lead in the coordinated representation of views. Even labor cooperated, as W. A. ("Tony") Boyle, president of the United Mine Workers, echoed each of the National Coal Policy Conference's goals.

A special objective of the coalition was the retraction of the HEW's sulfur standards for federal installations. To avoid the undesirable public image of openly opposing sulfur oxide criteria, the industries called for "restudy." Edwin Phelps, president of Peabody Coal, explained the problem carefully:

> . . . the present HEW program greatly disturbs me. First of all, it is based on conclusions which I believe to be unwarranted by scientific proof. Secondly . . . the objective appears to be the establishment of an ambient air quality for sulfur dioxide of one-tenth part per million and the achievement of this standard by reducing the permissible sulfur content of the fuel which may be burned. . . . [that] would eliminate the vast majority of our coal fuel reserves. . . .[46]

[45] U.S. Congress, Senate, Committee on Public Works, Subcommittee on Air and Water Pollution, *Air Quality Act of 1967—Hearings on S. 780*, 90th Cong., 1st sess., 1967, index.

[46] Ibid., p. 2026.

With some prescience, Phelps warned of an impending energy crisis that the coal industry could prevent only if unhampered by government constraints. A Consolidation Coal executive added that not nearly enough low-sulfur coal existed to meet HEW's restrictions, and he urged more research by government on techniques to remove sulfur from stack gases. Phillip Sporn, retired chairman of American Electric Power, also dismissed the use of low-sulfur coal and offered instead the use of tall-stack dispersion of sulfur gases as a solution. Job loss and cost arguments seemed effective in opposing the HEW rules. Stuart Saunders, chairman of the board of the Pennsylvania Railroad, claimed that "it would be a serious mistake to ban fuels with more than a trace of sulfur before control technology is available." According to Saunders, "More than 17% of our 57,169 employees owe their employment to our transportation of coal. Obviously, the Pennsylvania Railroad depends heavily on a healthy coal industry."[47] NCPC's Joseph Moody, who seemed to be coordinating most of the industry testimony, summed up the coalition's concern with the HEW standards: "We do not share the belief . . . of those in the Department of Health, Education, and Welfare, who believe that the way to achieve improved air is by rigid regulatory standards coupled with a large-scale public relations campaign to create an atmosphere of fear."[48]

Nearly the entire coal community endorsed the several amendments that Senator Randolph had proposed. Those amendments would have accomplished various industry goals. Amendment No. 154, for example, would authorize state-HEW pollution conferences called only at the request of the state governors, provide that *ambient* air standards be set *by the states* within three years, and assure that any such standards would take into consideration available technology, existing air quality, and the economic feasibility of achieving prescribed standards.[49] This final group of points was especially important, as it was a preliminary effort to shift the criteria away from health considerations toward the more traditional regulatory premises of technological feasibility and cost. Still anoth-

[47] Ibid., p. 2128.
[48] Ibid., p. 2129.
[49] Ibid. Amendments reprinted in III, 1456–67.

er of the Randolph amendments sought to raise the federal research teria away from health considerations toward the more traditional commitment to $100 million a year, a provision that Nader's Raiders later described as a "raid on the federal treasury."[50] Since these measures were promoted by Chairman Randolph, approved by Representative Harley Staggers, the chairman of the House Commerce Committee, and ardently supported by coal leadership, it was more than likely that Muskie's legislation would eventually incorporate at least some of them.

In 1967, the environmental interest groups that promoted federal legislation on air pollution could hardly be called a coalition. They were geographically diffuse, relatively autonomous, and their political tactics were rudimentary by Washington standards. While the number of groups active in the federal forum had grown, few had yet developed either the technical capabilities or the manpower necessary to deal effectively with criteria, standards, the availability of technology, and cost-benefit data. Nonetheless, six national conservationist and health groups gave testimony before Muskie's committee.[51] With the exception of the Citizens Committee on Natural Resources, all the groups endorsed emission standards, either as proposed in S.780 or even more restrictive. Apparently, the Citizens Committee had the clearest notion of the complex problems of pollution control. Its spokesman explained that emission standards were useless, since they could not be related to health criteria. With Ed Muskie's hearty and perhaps confused approval, the Citizens Committee argued in favor of ambient air standards directly based on scientific health criteria.[52] These critical distinctions seemed beyond the grasp of the other environmentalists and completely lost on the other members of the subcommitte. Neither the envirnomentalists nor Muskie objected to Senator Randolph's desire for HEW to review and reissue the health criteria for sulfur oxides. Perhaps they were confident that mounting laboratory and epidemiological evi-

---

[50] Esposito, *Vanishing Air*, p. 195.

[51] Senate, *Hearings on S.780*, 90th Cong., 1st sess., 1967. These groups included the National Wildlife Federation, Izaak Walton League, Citizens Committee on Natural Resources, National Air Conservation Commission, National Center for Air Pollution, and American Public Health Association.

[52] Ibid., p. 1749.

dence on the health hazards of sulfur dioxide would result in even more stringent criteria.

About a month before the Air Quality Act became law, George Sall, representing the National Coal Association, described industry's efforts with respect to the pending legislation: "NCA and other groups in coal and oil industries set to work to convince Congress that whatever it did about controlling air pollution must be reasonable, practical, and economically feasible. . . . As a result of these activities and others, the coal industry and allies seem to be making some progress in the face of overzealous demands for instant clean air."[53] These candid remarks lend credence to the integrated and coordinated character of the coal coalition's political activity and preview major modifications in the air pollution legislation. When President Johnson signed into law the Air Quality Act, it was quite different from S.780, which his staff had proposed, and reflected most of the wishes of the coal coalition. At the heart of the new act was the provision for the states to promulgate regional ambient air quality standards and develop control plans to achieve those standards. Senator Randolph's amendment had prevailed. The switch from emissions to ambient air quality standards was equally significant and reflected Senator Muskie's preference. The coal interests were reasonably pleased with this change, as ambient standards appeared to them to be the lesser of two evils. Federal appropriations for air pollution research were increased from $65 million to $125 million. More government research obviously meant less of a burden on the coal industries and the potential for a technical fix to their air pollution problems.

The language throughout the new act reflected the industry's ardent desire for "cooperation." At every stage of control development at both state and federal levels, the act provided for industry's participation in the procedures of policy formation. Shortly after the act's passage, the National Coal Policy Conference spotlighted the best ways in which its members could participate: "Before HEW designates regions or issues criteria, it must obtain the requisite

<hr>

[53] George Sall, government relations director, National Coal Association, in *Proceedings: Diamond Anniversary Convention*, Illinois Mining Institute, Springfield, Illinois, October 12–13, 1967.

advice. It was intended that HEW obtain the best advice available. Industry members should be prepared to do all they can to
help develop sound criteria and accurate control information."[54]
Not just criteria, but also HEW's recommendations for implementation should reflect industry's knowledge and advice. In its recommendations, the HEW was to consult other federal agencies, including the Department of Commerce and the Federal Power Commission.[55] Those agencies having closer clientele relationships with
the energy business would certainly help assure that regulations
would be reasonable.

The coal coalition, Senator Randolph, and members of the
House Commerce Committee had been particularly concerned about
the sulfur oxide criteria already established by HEW. Accordingly,
Section 107(b) of the new act ordered that the previously issued
criteria should be reevaluated, and, if warranted, "there should be
no hesitancy in revising such criteria. . . ."[56] Coal people were delighted by this change but failed to notice that congressional mandate gave legitimacy to the principle of federal health criteria as
the basis of all air pollution control. In the view of industry and environmentalists alike, the 1967 Air Quality Act was coal's law, and
Coal Age acknowledged the victory. As a result of "opposition . . .
mounted by coal . . . the final version of the bill (S.780) . . . signed
by the President . . . met most of the industry's objections. The
HEW's sulfur oxide criteria were modified and specific and detailed
research . . . provided for."[57] The National Coal Policy Conference,
which had taken the lead in coordinating industry's political drive,
summarized events:

> Virtually all industry supported new legislation that would lead to
> a more effective air pollution control effort. . . . Regulations and
> reasonable enforcement procedures generally were accepted as nec-
> essary with the states to bear the prime responsibility. The legisla-

---

[54] National Coal Policy Conference, *A Guide to the Air Quality Act of
1967*, p. 5.
[55] U.S. Congress, Senate, Committee on Public Works, *Senate Report No.
403*, 90th Cong., 1st sess., 1967, p. 28.
[56] U.S. Congress, House, Committee on Interstate and Foreign Commerce, *Air Quality Act of 1967*, 90th Cong., 1st sess., October, 1967, H. Rept.
728, p. 14.
[57] *Coal Age*, February, 1968, p. 56.

tion had complete bipartisan support and was enacted without dissent in both the Senate and the House of Representatives. It reflects the Congressional determination concurred in by the Administration, industry, and many state and local authorities. . . .[58]

But all the rejoicing among industrialists, as well as the bitter complaints of the Nader task force members, failed to appreciate the significance of mandated health criteria and the extent to which this compromised legislation had furthered the upward shift in decision-making authority. Although standards and implementation procedures were still in the hands of the states, the federal government had gained, in the health criteria, the final authority for regulating air pollution. The establishment of health criteria that disregarded economic and technological feasibility was a startling precedent ill-perceived at the time and quite overshadowed the issue of federal versus state authority, leaving it merely a matter of temporary practicability. In little more than a year, coal industrialists would begin to realize just how radical the implications of federal health criteria were.[59]

The Trials of Federalism: Implementing the Air Quality Act

In the three years after Congress passed the 1967 act, HEW officials grew frustrated trying to implement the law, coal interests were increasingly alarmed by HEW activities, the public became more anxious about air pollution, and environmental interest groups expanded their memberships and matured politically. Just after the act passed, George Sall gave a political pep talk to a gathering of

[58] Senate, *Senate Report No. 403*, p. 3.
[59] Jones, *Clean Air*. Professor Jones's model of air pollution policy formation hinges on this point. He explained the 1967 act as the product of "gradual incrementalism," in contrast to the "speculative augmentation" responsible for the 1970 Clean Air Act. In historical perspective, however, that distinction is misleading, notwithstanding the sharp turnabout in public opinion after 1970. Certainly the 1970 act did considerably redirect federal air pollution policy by mandating federal ambient standards and new source performance (emissions) standards. But it did so only on the basis of the inadequate implementation of the health criteria established in 1967. Bcause those criteria excluded other traditional regulatory considerations such as cost and technical feasibility, their establishment in the 1967 act was a major "increment" in public air pollution policy. As such, it was the underpinning of still other major "increments" in the 1970 act.

coal industry leaders: "We're going to have to attack pollution control with the same kind of imagination and energy that we use to solve production problems. . . . We're going to have to exert every effort to see that logic, not emotion, is used by legislators at every level of government. . . . "[60] One focal point of those efforts was the health criteria for three coal-related pollutants: sulfur oxides, nitrogen oxides, and particulates. A subdivision of HEW, the National Air Pollution Control Administration (NAPCA), was responsible for promulgating those criteria. And as the law directed, other federal agencies were to advise NAPCA. In 1968 and 1969, NAPCA let several contracts to the Federal Power Commission. In most similar FPC studies, the utilities under its supervision provide much of the data and some of the data analysis. The Tennessee Valley Authority, a serious air polluter and politically active member of the coal coalition, also received several contracts to study sulfur oxide removal and coal-cleaning techniques.[61] It is not that these data sources were inappropriate per se, but such arrangements do reflect NAPCA's eventual dependence on industry sources for much of its decision making.

As NAPCA worked away at revising the sulfur oxide criteria and developing particulate criteria, the coal interests were publicizing and preparing studies that justified less stringent criteria. Epidemiological studies were a particularly important part of the data base for the new criteria.[62] Before the criteria were issued in 1969, coal statisticians worked vigorously, producing studies to show the lack of epidemological evidence to justify strict sulfur dioxide restrictions.[63] But the accumulation of independent research, on which NAPCA officials chose to rely, offered overwhelming evidence that sulfur oxides were a serious health threat. In the spring, 1969, NAPCA published the criteria for both sulfur oxides and particu-

[60] George Sall, speaking at the 81st Meeting of the Coal Mining Institute, Pittsburgh, Pa., December, 1967, quoted in *Coal Age*, January, 1968, p. 94.

[61] Box 15, file CP-1, NAPCA Contract Records, U.S. Environmental Protection Agency, Air and Water Programs Office, Administrative Records, Federal Records Center, Suitland, Md., accession no. 412-73-5 (hereafter cited as NAPCA Contract Records).

[62] For example, see National Air Pollution Control Administration, *Air Quality Criteria for Sulfur Oxides*, pp. 10–7 to 10–13.

[63] For example, see *Coal Age*, April, 1968, p. 75.

lates, and while some environmentalists felt that they could have been more stringent, they were far more strict than coal people had hoped.[64]

By the time the criteria appeared, NAPCA had fallen seriously behind schedule in implementing the Air Quality Act. And without the criteria, the states had made virtually no efforts to formulate ambient standards, let alone the emission regulations necessary to meet them. But the mandates of the Air Quality Act were extremely complex, and NAPCA, a fairly small administrative agency, faced a big job in preparing both the criteria and implementation guidelines for the states. In May, 1969, while the coal interests were still trying to digest the implications of the strict sulfur oxide criteria, HEW published still another important document, *Guidelines for the Development of Air Quality Standards and Implementation Plans.* Early in 1968, NAPCA had established an in-house task force to develop those guidelines for the states. The guidelines had to deal with a host of totally new implementation problems, including air basins and regions, the relationship of ambient standards to health criteria, and systems and technologies suitable for attaining those standards. For more than a year, the guidelines progressed painfully through six drafts as the task force members conscientiously tried to find reasonable ways to implement the congressional mandate. Industry apparently had almost no input to this process, nor did organized environmentalists, for that matter.[65]

In May, when NAPCA finally made public the guidelines docu-

[64] The NAPCA health criteria for sulfur oxides and particulate matter covered a range of health tolerances, the low end of which was as follows: for sulfur oxides, an annual mean level of 115 $\mu g/m^3$ and a 24-hour average level of 300 $\mu g/m^3$; for particulate matter, an annual mean level of 80 $\mu g/m^3$ (National Air Pollution Control Administration, *Air Quality Criteria for Sulfur Oxides* [Washington, D.C., 1969], and *Air Quality Criteria for Particulate Matter* [Washington, D.C., 1969]).

[65] Sidney Edelman, Chief, Environmental Health Branch (HEW), "Draft Policy Statement on Guidelines for Review of Statement on Guidelines for Review of State Ambient Air Quality Standards," May 21, 1968. Also, other drafts of guidelines and internal memoranda, all in Administrative Records, Office of Air Quality Planning and Standards, U.S. Environmental Protection Agency, Research Triangle Park, N.C. (hereafter cited as EPA Air Quality Administrative Records). That industry representatives had little input was further confirmed by an interview with Donald Walters, senior technical advisor, Office of Air Programs, EPA, June 9, 1975.

ment, coal-related businessmen were not only startled, but extremely alarmed by the contents. Just on the surface, the guidelines were so complex and thorough that they appeared to coal people to be the equivalent of federal standards and emission regulations. And indeed, it did seem that NAPCA bureaucrats had stretched to the limit their vaguely worded mandate in the 1967 act to formulate "suggestions" of control techniques and standards for the states. The American Mining Congress, representing coal producers, steel, cement manufacturers, and electric utilities, took the lead in violently attacking the HEW for having overreached its statutory authority. Ironically, the coal people were still more concerned with the matter of state versus federal authority than with the actual substance of the guidelines. AMC president J. A. Overton clearly explained industry's concern in a letter to Lee DuBridges, President Nixon's science advisor:

> Contrary to the well-conceived pattern of assignment of federal-state responsibilities as set forth in the Act and its legislative history, the "Guidelines" contain detailed instructions on the structure of the standards and methods of achieving controls. If followed, the "Guidelines"' would remove the freedom of the states in establishing air quality standards consistent with the purposes of the Act, and which in effect would institute uniform national standards which Congress explicitly rejected.
>
> The difference between the power given to the Secretary of HEW and that which has been assumed is critical and fundamental. Under the Act, states and local governments have primary responsibility for developing air quality standards and implementation plans. Under the "Guidelines," NAPCA has usurped primary responsibility. . . .[66]

To the coal people, it seemed that administrative fiat had undercut the accomplishment of their major goal in the 1967 legislative battle. Worse still, the guidelines contained an entirely new concept that appeared unjustified by the Air Quality Act and posed a serious threat to the interests of coal: the suggestion that state plans could

[66] J. A. Overton to L. A. DuBridges, July 22, 1969, Box 17, "AMC Files," NAPCA Contract Records. Also, House, *Air Quality Act of 1967*, 90th Cong., 1st sess., October, 1967, H. Rept. 728, pp. 14–17 which provided the basis for the AMC's argument.

not allow existing clean air to deteriorate significantly.[67] This concept, "no significant deterioration," was soon to become a byword of organized environmental goals, and would eventually lead to the total reorganization of federal policy for regulating air pollution. (Chapter 7 will examine more carefully the origins of this particularly important concept.)

To counter the effects of these guidelines, the American Mining Congress wrote directly to HEW Secretary Robert H. Finch, outlining the limits of federal authority and explaining how state agencies would misinterpret the guidelines. AMC then sent a copy of this letter under a different cover to the governors of all fifty states. "We request," wrote the AMC directors, "that the 'Guidelines' as they now stand be withdrawn, so that any future advice to the states may be recast. . . . When any new advice is published, we respectfully request that substantive discussions with informed industry spokesmen to be [sic] provided in advance of any such publication."[68] Although HEW did not withdraw the guidelines and state officials denied that they would be unduly influenced, NAPCA, at least, took the criticism to heart and the following year held extensive meetings with industry officials on further implementation matters.[69] Meanwhile, coal coalition leaders learned an important lesson about the politics of administrative decision making and two years later took more seriously the Environmental Protection Agency's administrative activities. They also became more interested in establishing institutional channels through which they could contribute more directly to the policy-making process.

[67] U.S. Department of Health, Education, and Welfare, *Guidelines for the Development of Air Quality Standards and Implementation Plans*, p. 7.

[68] Correspondence from the American Mining Congress to Governors, July, 1969; for examples of responses, see Governor Marvin Mandel, Maryland, to J. Middleton, NAPCA, September 10, 1969, and Georgia Air Pollution Office to NAPCA, September 2, 1969, Box 17, "AMC Files," NAPCA Contract Records.

[69] Besides the activities of the National Industrial Pollution Control Council described in chapter 2, there was, for example, a prolonged meeting at Research Triangle Park, N.C., on July 30, 1970, between NAPCA staff and various representatives of the American Mining Congress, American Smelting and Refining, Kennecott Copper, and Phelps Dodge ("Transcript of July 30 meeting," EPA Air Quality Administrative Records).

6

Administrative Politics and the Clean Air Act of 1970

"TO cope with air pollution," said Richard Nixon in February, 1970, "I propose that the Federal Government establish nationwide air quality standards. . . . We are taking these actions . . . because we know that it is now or never."[1] President Nixon's sense of crisis was probably more political than ecological. Growing numbers of environmentalists were becoming less and less patient with the federalist framework of air pollution control. Even the president recognized that it was not working very well: "Industry itself has been adopting ambitious pollution control programs, and state and local authorities have been setting and enforcing stricter anti-pollution standards. But they have not gone far enough or fast enough, nor . . . will they be able to without the strongest possible Federal backing. . . . The [Air Quality] Act has been a useful beginning. But we have learned in the past two years that it has shortcomings."[2]

Indeed it did. By distributing control responsibilities among local, state, and federal governments, the Air Quality Act seemed to have fragmented authority beyond effectiveness. The National Air Pollution Control Administration could offer only criteria and "guidance." States were to determine ambient air standards for separate control regions, but they lacked the necessary administrative and scientific expertise. Local officials were responsible for enforcing

[1] *Papers of the Presidents, Richard Nixon, 1970*, no. 37, p. 95.
[2] Ibid., number 38, pp. 102–103.

emissions controls but had no legal framework within which to do so. Not only were the lines of authority muddled; the technical and economic problems of pollution control remained totally confused, blocking the transfer of policy from paper to practice. For the next three years, national policy for controlling air pollution was to remain in a constant state of agitation, as hostile interest-group coalitions struggled to define national standards in terms of effects on human health, the natural environment, technological feasibility, and socioeconomic costs. Because of the incredibly complex nature of these issues, they were resolved in the forum of administrative rather than legislative politics. The interaction of administrative bureaucrats with well-organized, highly capable interest groups determined nearly all the crucial decisions regarding ambient standards, new-source emission standards, implementation plans, monitoring, and enforcement. Thus, the Clean Air Act, while an extraordinary piece of legislation, was only an outline—a prelude to the real political contest.

Muskie, Nixon, and the Clean Air Act

Like many other politicians, Richard Nixon was keenly aware of the growing public concern over the environment. In 1969, the spectacular oil spill in the Santa Barbara channel and the public DDT hearings in Wisconsin had helped raise public consciousness. Already, the Congress had enacted the National Environmental Policy Act, effective January 1, 1970, and Senator Edmund Muskie, with an eye on his party's presidential nomination, was proposing a new package of environmental reforms. When Commerce Secretary Maurice Stans met with the Business Advisory Council in March, environmental activism, particularly regarding air pollution, was a principal agenda item. A week later, the president established the National Industrial Pollution Control Council (NIPCC) to help businessmen cope with the atmosphere of environmental fervor.[3] Organized environmentalists were becoming intolerant of bureau-

---

[3] J. K. Horton to Maurice Stans, April 13, 1970, Box No. 1, "NIPCC— Clippings, Utilities" file, National Industrial Pollution Control Council, Administrative Records, Department of Commerce, Washington, D.C.

cratic delays, technical problems, and the apparent intransigence of industrial leaders. At the same time, environmental activists had grown in political experience, membership, and financial and professional support. In April, they organized a massive national demonstration against industrial pollution. Thousands of urbanites and students across America participated in the Earth Day protest. By May, a Gallup poll showed that the people considered air and water pollution their second most serious problem.[4] These developments, together with the inadequacy of the Air Quality Act of 1967 and early preparations for the 1972 presidential elections, set the stage for the 1970 Clean Air Act.

Early in the year, Senator Muskie's subcommittee held hearings on amending the 1967 act, particularly in regard to vehicular emissions. Oil and automotive companies dominated that testimony, and Muskie appeared to have no plans radically to revise controls for stationary sources of pollution. But several events later in the spring put considerable pressure on Muskie to maintain his image as an environmental leader. For one thing, Ralph Nader published a widely read attack on Muskie's environmental credentials. "Muskie is, of course, the chief architect of the disastrous Air Quality Act of 1967. That fact alone," wrote Nader's lieutenant, John Esposito, "would warrant his being stripped of his title as 'Mr. Pollution Control.' But the Senator's passivity since 1967 in the face of worsening air pollution problems compounds his earlier failure."[5] Then there was Nixon's sweeping proposal for thirty-seven environmental reforms that included national air quality standards, new-source emission standards, and tougher federal enforcement.[6] And finally, in mid-March and April, the House Commerce Committee held seven days of hearings at which environmentalists expressed enthusiasm for the administration's proposals. Upstaged by these events, Ed Muskie was going to have to do something extraordinary to win back the confidence and support of the environmental movement.

In deference to the intensity of public opinion, the coal coalition did not mount a frontal assault on the proposed amendments

---

[4] *New York Times*, August 30, 1970.
[5] John C. Esposito, *Vanishing Air*, p. 290.
[6] *Papers of the Presidents, Richard Nixon, 1970*, no. 37, pp. 103–106.

as they had in 1967. At the House hearings, four national trade groups calmly presented coal's views. Herbert Richey, chairman of the Natural Resources Committee of the U.S. Chamber of Commerce (and president of the Valley Camp Coal Company), offered the industry's qualified endorsement of "minimal" national standards. "We feel," said Richey, "there should be some national standards, but specific standards should be set locally." Joe Mullan, a National Coal Association spokesman, explained that by "minimal standards," Richey actually meant "goals"—something like a federal ceiling for state standards. Although both the Edison Electric Institute and the National Coal Policy Conference opposed air standards, they nonetheless would settle for "minimal" ones.[7]

In the spring of 1970, it looked as if the coal coalition could do little to influence congressional decision making on air pollution. Anyway, experience had taught coal people that the meaningful and practical decisions on air pollution were made by the bureaucrats in agencies responsible for implementing the law. During the summer, several subcouncils of Nixon's new National Industrial Pollution Control Council (NIPCC) held their first meetings, and at three in particular, air pollution was the top priority. At the meeting of the Mining and Nonferrous Metals Subcouncil in July, there was extended "discussion of present trends in Government regulatory actions in the pollution area." The problem was the relationship of emissions to ambient conditions. But the discussants, all chief executive officers of large corporations, were pessimistic about influencing congressional policy and decided instead "that the Department of Commerce may be in a position to help establish a dialogue between the industry and Government agencies, which could eliminate or forestall such problems, as well as those of technically, or economically unfeasible standards."[8] Council members also discussed steps that the American Mining Congress could take, in liaison with NIPCC, to provide data on the technical problems of pollution con-

[7] U.S. Congress, House, Committee on Interstate and Foreign Commerce, *Hearings on Air Pollution Control and Solid Waste Recycling*, 91st Cong., 2nd sess., March–April, 1970, pp. 513, 544, 648–650.

[8] Mining Subcouncil meeting, July 6, 1970, NIPCC Subcouncil meetings, minutes summaries, 1970–1972, National Industrial Pollution Control Council, Freedom of Information Files, Department of Commerce Library, Washington, D.C. (hereafter cited as NIPCC Freedom of Information Files).

trol and economic impact studies. At the vigorous prompting of Frank Milliken, Kennecott Copper's president, the NIPCC subcouncil agreed to three policy positions:

> We believe that the Administration should re-evaluate its position on national ambient air quality standards and national emission standards, and should adhere to the basic scheme of the Air Quality Act of 1967.
>
> If we are to have an amended Clean Air Act—and this appears inevitable in view of the recent House action and the work now going on in the Senate—the NIPCC and this Sub-council can serve a most valuable purpose in assuring that industry will be allowed to play its proper role in implementing the revised regulations.
>
> We would expect, too, that the government representatives on this and the parent panel [NIPCC] take early steps to assure effective liaison between the proposed Environmental Protection Agency and the representatives of Industry.[9]

Other subcouncils settled on the same course of action. The electric utilities executives discussed the "problem caused by ambient and emissions standards," and agreed that "a major hassle appears in the offing on the differences." They too concluded that the "hassle" could best be resolved, not in the Congress, but through the "interactions between NIPCC and the new EPA . . . where the sub-councils can be an important input . . . to the Council on Environmental Quality through the Commerce Secretary."[10] In August, members of the Coal Subcouncil grappled with the same question, and arrived at the same conclusions.[11]

Coal interests were hardly pleased with the bill the House approved on June 10; its measures were more stringent than the administration's original proposals. But their real problems began in August, when Senator Muskie's subcommittee met in closed sessions to mark up its bill. As the National Coal Association's Joseph Mullan later commented, "The bill that came out of the Senate was not the bill that anybody testified to."[12] In a contest of legisla-

---

[9] Ibid.

[10] Electric Utility Subcouncil meeting, July 13, 1970, NIPCC Freedom of Information Files.

[11] Coal Subcouncil meeting, August 26, 1970, NIPCC Freedom of Information Files.

[12] Quoted in James Miller, "Air Pollution," in James Rathelsburger, ed., *Nixon and the Environment*, p. 14.

tive oneupmanship with the president, Muskie and his subcommittee completely rewrote the amendments. Moreover, the high pitch of public concern over air pollution, together with the complexities of the bill's provisions, assuaged Senate opposition as the bill passed unanimously, 73 to 0. In conference, the House receded for the most part, and the Clean Air Act Amendments smoothly became law in December, 1970.

Nearly every provision of the new law foretold substantial difficulties for the coal coalition. First, the act provided that the new Environmental Protection Agency (EPA) promulgate national ambient air quality standards "for each air pollutant for which air quality criteria had been issued. . . ." These would include "primary" standards based on "such criteria and allowing an adequate margin of safety . . . requisite to protect the public health," and "secondary" standards to "protect the public welfare from any known or anticipated adverse effects associated with the presence of such air pollutants in the ambient air."[13] Here, the "margin of safety" would become a prime source of dispute among interest groups.

The second important provision, section 108, ordered up criteria for the remaining pollutants, particularly nitrogen oxides, and further authorized the administrator of the EPA to prepare new guidelines for state implementation plans: "The Administrator shall, after consultation with appropriate advisory committees and Federal departments and agencies, issue to the State and appropriate air pollution agencies, information on air pollution control techniques, which information shall include data relating to the technology and costs of emission control" (sec. 108 [b][1]). This provision soon caused an even worse commotion among coal interests than had its 1969 predecessor. To industry, the detailed guidelines appeared to be de facto national emission standards, which they had so opposed and had thought were excluded from the 1970 act.

A third major provision of the Clean Air Act, section 110, called for mandatory state implementation plans and emission standards to be approved by the EPA administrator. Rigid time schedules governed hearings, adoption, approval, and final attainment of pri-

    [13] U.S. Environmental Protection Agency, The Clean Air Act, December, 1970, P.L. 91–604, sec. 109(a)(1)(A) and sec. 109(b).

mary standards (three years after approval, or 1975). The act also required that plans be drawn up for achieving secondary standards by 1978. From the industry perspective, this section's only redeeming aspect was a provision of extensions of up to three years in special circumstances.

Standards of performance (emissions) for new stationary sources of pollution was the fourth important innovation in the act. Finally, section 111 established the preeminence of federal authority in air pollution control. The EPA was to develop a list of the large-scale industrial processes with the most serious potential for pollution and then promulgate emission standards for plants to be constructed after 1970. Besides these four large changes in air policy, the 1970 act contained a variety of important secondary provisions for citizen suits, more frequent public hearings, better monitoring, and stricter enforcement.

A most significant aspect of the amendments was the language that reaffirmed the precedent set in 1967. All the standards, and thus their administrative paraphernalia, were to be premised on physical health criteria, regardless of technological feasibility and economic cost. In that way, the Clean Air Act not only was "technology-forcing," but also assured a major political contest over the course of its administrative implementation.

The Politics of Ambient Standards, Round One: A Draw

One of the first responsibilities of the newly organized Environmental Protection Agency was to issue the ambient air standards. With unusual speed, the agency published tentative standards at the end of January, 1971 (36 *F.R.* 1502), and allowed ninety days for comments by interested parties before promulgating the official standards at the end of April. The standards, as finally adopted, are outlined in table 13.

Fifty-one environmental and civic interest groups submitted comments to the EPA.[14] Local groups from twenty-one states participated, with especially large clusters from the Southwest (New

14 Comments index, "1971 Ambient Air Standards" file, 1971 Air Pollution Files, Freedom of Information Records Office, U.S. Environmental Protection Agency, Washington, D.C. (hereafter cited as EPA 1971 Air Pollution Files).

TABLE 13
National Ambient Air Quality Standards

Pollutant	Primary	Secondary
Sulfur oxides		
annual arithmetic mean	80 µg/m³ (0.03 ppm)*	60 µg/m³ (0.02 ppm)
maximum 24-hour concentration	365 µg/m³ (0.14 ppm)	260 µg/m³ (0.10 ppm)
maximum 3-hour concentration**		1,300 µg/m³ (0.50 ppm)
Particulates		
annual arithmetic mean	75 µg/m³	60 µg/m³
maximum 25-hour concentration	260 µg/m³	150 µg/m³
Nitrogen oxides		
annual arithmetic mean		100 µg/m³ (0.05 ppm)

SOURCE: 36 Federal Register 8187, April 30, 1971.
NOTE: No primary standard is given for nitrogen oxides or for 3-hour concentration of sulfur oxides because health effects could not be accurately determined.
* µg/m³ = micrograms per cubic meter
** March 26 supplemental standard

Mexico, Arizona, Southern California) and the heavily industrial East (Ohio, Pennsylvania, Delaware). Judging from the comments, citizens in the Southwest were particularly concerned about health effects of vehicular smog and by the threat that the huge, new coal-fired power plants at Four Corners would decrease visibility and interfere with tourist demands for pristine air and "long panoramic views."[15] Because of their areas' heavy reliance on coal for electric power, steel, and manufacturing, citizens from the eastern industrial areas also seemed especially conscious of air pollution problems. In size and technical capability, participating groups ranged from the Natural Resources Defense Council and the Sierra Club to the Oak Creek (Ohio) Garden Club and the Saint Joseph (Minnesota) Rod and Gun Club.

Nearly all the environmentalist comments demanded that the EPA's proposed standards should be more rigorous. Recommendations called for allowable concentrations of sulfur dioxide to be reduced by as much as half of what the EPA proposed.[16] Environmental activists from California, Massachusetts, and Colorado complained that the proposed national standards were actually weaker than those that their own states had adopted. Local control agencies confirmed this criticism, fearing that federal preeminence would undermine their authority. Evidently, citizens' groups interpreted the act's mandate for an "adequate margin of safety" differently than both EPA officials and industrialists. A certain vagueness in the HEW criteria documents was responsible for this difference. To most environmentalists, the measurements cited in table 13 constituted the levels of pollutant concentrations that definitely harmed human health. Naturally, then, they expected that "the intent of Congress . . . to err on the side of health . . . should dictate standards substantially lower than the lowest levels known to be hazardous to less susceptible groups" (since the effects of pollution on the most susceptible groups was still unknown).[17] Many groups,

---

[15] Comments of Citizens for Clean Air, San Juan, New Mexico, March 5, 1971, EPA 1971 Air Pollution Files.

[16] Comments of Georgia Citizens for Clean Air, March 7, 1971, EPA 1971 Air Pollution Files.

[17] Comments of the Natural Resources Defense Council, March 15, 1971, p. 9, EPA 1971 Air Pollution Files.

such as the Arizona Nurses' Association, called for a shorter-term standard than the twenty-four-hour concentration to assure health safety. The Natural Resources Defense Council (NRDC), perhaps the most expert of the environmental groups commenting, recommended that "no standard should allow a concentration of any pollutant more than 75 percent of the concentration known to be harmful to the health of normal people."[18]

Aside from the specific standards, environmental interests had another objection to the EPA's proposal. It contained no clear prohibition against the degradation of already clean air. "The ambient air quality standards," according to NRDC's Richard Ayers, "should explicitly state that because of the legislative history of the Act, in air quality regions where present levels of pollutants are lower than the national standards, the present levels should constitute the federal standards of ambient air quality for those regions."[19] NRDC and other groups felt that the Clean Air Act, while not explicit on this point, had implied it and the Senate Public Works Committee had intended it.[20] This idea of nondegradation was especially important for the nonurban groups and the national conservation groups that had greater interest in maintaining the quality of more rural and primitive areas. It was the citizens' groups of New Mexico and Colorado, along with the Environmental Defense Fund, the Conservation Foundation, and the Izaak Walton League, that complained most vocally about this shortcoming in the standards document.

The quality and persuasiveness of the comments by environmentalists varied as much as did their origins and interests. Most of the local citizens' groups and many of the state organizations offered emphatic, but frequently unclear, suggestions that lacked technical justifications or adequate understanding of specific issues. Quite naturally, such lack of expertise was inherent in the part-time, volunteer nature of most of those groups. Most had no professional staff and lacked the resources and data available to permanently organ-

---

[18] Ibid.
[19] Ibid.
[20] U.S. Congress, Senate, Committee on Public Works, *National Air Quality Act of 1970*, 91st Cong., 1st sess., 1970, S. Rept. 1196, p. 11.

ized, full-time industrial interests. Nevertheless, the weight of their numbers and the degree of their concern that the air be protected probably helped considerably to reinforce the new EPA's sense of mission. More important, without an industrial constituency, the new agency had to rely completely on just such grassroots support if it were to have any political viability in Washington. And for a few of the environmental groups, the comments on standards reflected growing technical and political expertise that was impressive. Among such groups were the NRDC, the Environmental Defense Fund, the Metro Washington Coalition for Clean Air, and Stamp Out Smog in Los Angeles. These groups were learning the ropes of administrative politics and would not easily be outdone by the coal coalition.

According to Edward Tuerk, then assistant administrator of the EPA's Air Programs Office, the EPA had developed the standards internally, without any input from industry. Indeed, Tuerk felt that industry "hardly knew the Clean Air Act existed" early in 1971.[21] But in light of the previous discussions by National Industrial Pollution Control Council members, this seems like something of an overstatement. During the comment period, thirty-eight commercial and industrial organizations submitted criticisms of the proposed standards that did evince a high degree of awareness. Seven trade associations represented coal mining, oil, gas, electric utilities, and mining equipment manufacturers. Seventeen corporations that commented included eight utilities, four mining and smelting concerns, and five oil companies.[22]

For industry, the standards proposed for sulfur dioxide were the most serious threat. Businessmen knew that dependable technology necessary to achieve those standards simply did not exist at that time. But since that problem was irrelevant to the standards, they were forced instead to attack the health criteria and the epidemiological studies on which the standards were premised. The industrial interests were unanimous in their criticisms of the health criteria. For one thing, they had a very different understanding of

[21] Edward Tuerk, Office of Program Management Operations, U.S. Environmental Protection Agency, interview, Washington, D.C., May 13, 1974.
[22] "1971 Ambient Air Standards" file, EPA 1971 Air Pollution Files.

the criteria than did environmentalists, who viewed the lowest figures as an absolute ceiling for allowable concentrations of pollutants. However, industry interpreted the criteria as a range in which the lowest numbers already included an unreasonably wide "margin of safety." It was on that basis, for example, that the American Mining Congress argued that "the criteria document upon which the standards were based fails to justify the proposed primary standard. . . ." Thus, the AMC recommended that the annual average standard for sulfur dioxides should be 130 $\mu g/m^3$ rather than 80 $\mu g/m^3$.[23]

Industry representatives, however, were not offering their comments on the proposed standards in a political vacuum. A closer look at the efforts of American Smelting and Refining Company (ASARCO) is revealing. ASARCO had a double interest in the sulfur standards, as both smelter and coal producer through its subsidiary, Midland Coal Company. While making their comments through the official channels, ASARCO executives were also making coordinated efforts to modify the sulfur standards through the American Mining Congress and the National Industrial Pollution Control Council. Charles Barber, ASARCO's president, corresponded extensively with John Middleton, EPA's commissioner of air pollution control; Edward Tuerk; William Ruckelshaus, EPA administrator; and Walter Hamilton, director of NIPCC. On March 8, Middleton attended a NIPCC meeting, where he, ASARCO officials, and others discussed the costs of sulfur dioxide pollution abatement techniques. A month later, Middleton met with Hamilton to discuss the standards and the prospects of getting ASARCO's abatement cost data included in a forthcoming EPA cost study of sulfur dioxide abatement.[24] In its long and thorough comment, ASARCO argued that the maximum levels of the criteria were well below those concentrations which, even according to the evidence used in the criteria document, would be harmful to health. Why, asked ASARCO, should the standards be at all below the minimum criteria? ASARCO chal-

[23] Comments of the American Mining Congress, March 19, 1971, pp. 4–5 (ibid.).

[24] J. Middleton to C. Barber, March 22, 1971, Box No. 17, file CR-2, NAPCA Contract Records, U.S. Environmental Protection Agency, Air and Water Programs Office, Administrative Records, Federal Records Center, Suitland, Md., accession number 412-73-5 (hereafter cited as NAPCA Contract Records).

lenged the HEW epidemiological studies, presented alternate ones, and concluded that concentrations of from two to five parts per million of sulfur dioxide were not harmful.[25]

But ASARCO ran into the same problem as did the American Mining Congress. The criteria were not at issue. The problem for industry was that they could not challenge the standards on the basis of their real concern: "That the proposed . . . standards are so restrictive as to adversely affect the national welfare by limiting the availability of natural resources *at costs* [emphasis added] consistent with the needs of users of those resources." The other important comments, by the American Petroleum Institute and the Edison Electric Institute, arrived at the same conclusions.[26]

On the last day of April, the EPA announced the final version of the national ambient air quality standards. To the chagrin of both industry and environmentalists, the agency made no substantive changes in the standards originally proposed. The pressures from the coal and environmental interests had apparently balanced each other on that count. However, the EPA did concede two new points that environmental groups had suggested. It authorized a shorter-term standard for sulfur dioxide, which allowed a three-hour concentration of no more than 1,300 $\mu g/m^3$. And, of far greater importance, the EPA also inserted a new qualification into section 410.2 of the standards, which read: "The promulgation of national primary and secondary ambient air quality standards shall not be considered in any manner to allow significant deterioration of existing air quality in any portion of any state" (36 *F.R.* 8187). This statement, although less explicit than environmentalists had demanded, became a major factor in the nascent nondegradation controversy. In a departmental memorandum, John Middleton justified the absence of substantive changes in a peculiar fashion, suggesting that just holding the line was something of a victory for the coal interests. "There were several suggestions that the margin of safety be

[25] Comments of American Smelting and Refining Company, March 15, 1971, pp. 6, 9–10, EPA 1971 Air Pollution Files.
[26] Comments of the American Mining Congress, March 19, 1971, pp. 3–7; comments of the American Petroleum Institute, March 16, 1971; comments of the Edison Electric Institute, March 16, 1971; all in EPA 1971 Air Pollution Files.

increased," said the commissioner. "In our judgment, all of the recommended standards included an adequate safety margin."[27] Round one ended in a draw.

Implementation Guidelines: Round Two to the Coal Coalition

In April, 1971, while the ambient standards were still on their way to the *Federal Register*, the Environmental Protection Agency published "Implementation Plan Guidelines" for the states.[28] According to the 1970 act, these guidelines were supposed to furnish state control agencies with suggestions for control plans and data on the availability of control technologies. Interest groups following air pollution policy expected the guidelines to be an advisory document that would not materially affect the determination of state plans. But, once again, sincere EPA bureaucrats, most of whom had been with the old National Air Pollution Control Administration in 1969, had stretched their mandate from Congress to the limit and used the document as a vehicle for virtually prescribing national emission standards and control systems. At least, that was the impression received by the industrial community. A furor ensued over the scope, complexity, and specificity of the guidelines, and an anticipated three-week review period exploded in a torrent of industrial criticism and vigorous political action.

The proposed guidelines included three sections that simply appalled members of the coal coalition as well as a variety of other industrial interests. Section 420.19, which provided for "source registration," ordered that "each plan shall contain a description of the procedures that will be used for registration of significant existing sources of pollutants. . . ." (36 *F.R.* 6685). A second, and even more controversial, provision (section 420.11[a][4]) instructed states to establish a permit system for new stationary sources of pollution: "Establish and operate a statewide system under which permits would be required for the construction and operation of new sta-

[27] John Middleton, "Briefing Memo," April 14, 1971, Box No. 17, file CP-2, NAPCA Contract Records.
[28] 36 *Federal Register* 6680–6693, April 7, 1971.

tionary sources of air pollution and the construction and operation of modifications to existing sources, including authority to prevent such construction, modification, or operation. . . ." (36 *F.R.* 6682). In these two "guidelines," industry perceived a federally sponsored permit system being foisted on the states while the Clean Air Act authorized nothing of the kind. Not only would such a system force an excessive degree of authority on state regulations, but it would lay on industry the burden of proving, before construction, the reliability of a pollution control system. However, the part of the guidelines that most aggravated industrialists was appendix B, "Air Pollution Control Regulations" (36 *F.R.* 6687). This section detailed emission limitations for sulfur oxides, particulates, nitrogen oxides, abatement procedures for air pollution emergency episodes, and specific regulations for monitoring and performance testing. Most upsetting to process industries like foundries and cement producers was a subsection that called for a particulate emission limit of 0.03 grains per standard cubic foot of exhaust gas (36 *F.R.* 6692). Since the Clean Air Act required that the EPA approve all implementation plans adopted by the states, the affirmative specificity of appendix B implied that for a state plan to get approval, it would have to include all these recommendations.

In addition to these three parts, industry found objectionable EPA's failure to include socioeconomic cost considerations in the guidelines. The Clean Air Act had at least provided that cost be considered at the level of state implementation, and since industry had been forced to accept the ambient standards without cost considerations, they were determined that the guidelines for state control plans should include them.

After the guidelines were published in April, a two-phased revision occurred. First, after receiving comments from 458 interested groups, John Middleton approved a revision of the guidelines on June 28. Nearly 400 industrial firms and trade groups submitted comments on the guidelines, virtually all of them critical. Many of the comments were long technical arguments ranging up to 250 pages.[29] According to Walter Hamilton's files, NIPCC appears to

[29] EPA log and analysis, "Implementation Plan Guidelines" file, EPA 1971 Air Pollution Files.

have orchestrated this immense industry effort. Thomas Jackson, a NIPCC staffer, reported that "industry did a creditable job in commenting on the proposed implementation of the Clean Air Act."[30] Virtually the entire spectrum of the coal coalition, with the exception of commercial banking, commented on the guidelines. Coal-related comments were submitted by five coal producers, eight oil companies, seven smelters and eight foundry groups, twenty-one electric utilities, fifty-nine asphalt and cement companies and twenty trade associations, and several equipment manufacturers involved in the coal industry. Pulling together all these comments were five of industry's most impressive trade associations: American Mining Congress, National Coal Association, American Iron and Steel Institute, American Petroleum Institute, and the Edison Electric Institute. Scarcely a single provision in the entire guidelines document escaped repeated criticism by five or more commentators.[31] All the criticisms maintained that the EPA had exceeded its authority. No doubt speaking for the entire industrial community, the National Assoication of Manufacturers concluded its comment by recommending that the EPA delete the entire appendix B from the guidelines.[32]

Environmental interest groups were generally satisfied with the rigorous technical provisions of the guidelines. The principal concerns of the twenty-nine environmental organizations that commented were greater flexibility of citizen participation, shorter variances, more public disclosure of emission data, and, above all, nondegradation of air already cleaner than the primary national standards.[33]

Immensely troubled by the proposed guidelines, the business community was not about to rest its case with the formal process

[30] T. W. Jackson to W. A. Hamilton, May 21, 1971, Box No. 9, "Permit Program—Army Corps of Engineers" file; W. A. Hamilton, memorandum to NIPCC council members, December 23, 1971, Box No. 9, "Memos" file, both in National Industrial Pollution Control Council, Administrative Records, Department of Commerce, Washington, D.C. (hereafter cited as NIPCC Administrative Records). In the midst of the period for commenting on the guidelines, NIPCC also released an economic impact study that itemized billions of dollars that achieving the ambient standards would cost.

[31] "Implementation Plan Guidelines" file, EPA 1971 Air Pollution Files.

[32] Ibid., p. 33.

[33] Ibid.

of commenting to EPA bureaucrats. Late in April, the President's Council of Economic Advisers raised questions regarding the absence of economic considerations from both the standards and the implementation plan guidelines. Paul McCracken, council chairman, asked William Ruckelshaus how far "such comparison of costs and benefits has entered into the formation of proposed standards. . . ." The council was wondering "about what consideration has been given by EPA to the cost of trade-offs between alternative ways of attaining a given ambient air quality in the emission control standards [guidelines] that EPA is to suggest." Not to worry, replied Ruckelshaus. The EPA was setting up a "review and analysis system which will subject all EPA proposed standards and regulations to economic impact analysis before final promulgation."[34]

Evidently, the White House was also under pressure to do something about the relationship of costs to emissions clean-up. President Nixon's staff came up with a proposal for a sulfur emissions tax, which, in theory, would be high enough to act like a protective tariff and stimulate pollution abatement.[35] However, environmentalists feared that if the proposed tax rates were too low, the administration's scheme would actually stimulate polluting as a cheaper alternative than stack gas removal systems. Although Russell Train, chairman of the Council on Environmental Quality, and William Ruckelshaus had to defend this idea, they did so reluctantly.[36]

The coal coalition had some allies in Congress as well as in the White House. Senator John Sherman Cooper, a member of the Public Works Committee, understood that the guidelines posed a threat to the coal business in his home state of Kentucky. Senator Cooper had always been a steadfast advocate of state controls for air pollution, and now he expressed his dismay with the proposed plans to EPA Administrator Ruckelshaus:

[34] P. McCracken to W. Ruckelshaus, April 22, 1971; W. Ruckelshaus to P. McCracken, June 22, 1971, both in Box No. 17, file CR-2, NAPCA Contract Records.
[35] Council on Environmental Quality, *The President's 1971 Environmental Program*, March, 1971, pp. 5, 26–27.
[36] R. Train to J. Cobb, April 19, 1971, Box No. 17, file CR-2, NAPCA Contract Records.

> The Committee . . . specifically rejected proposals which would
> have had the Federal Government impose national emission stan-
> dards for existing sources of air pollution . . . as presently proposed.
> Appendix B, on its face . . . appears to suggest that any state sub-
> mitting an implementation plan incorporating emission standards
> which vary from those specified in Appendix B would not be ap-
> proved. . . . I would urge that if Appendix B is retained as an ex-
> ample or outline, and if specific emission levels are to be included
> in it . . . there should also be qualifying language making clear that
> the interpretation suggested by the present draft is not correct.[37]

It looked as if the summer of 1971 was going to be very warm for
William Ruckelshaus and the Environmental Protection Agency.

By June 28, 1971, the EPA had evaluated the mass of comments,
replied to suggestions from the White House and the Congress, and
prepared its revised draft of the implementation guidelines. That
revision, however, was never made public, and it is possible only
to approximate its contents on the basis of a briefing memorandum
in which John Middleton recommended the revisions to Ruckelshaus.[38] According to that memorandum, most of the changes the
EPA chose to make were in response to environmentalist demands.
Middleton and the other Air Pollution Control staff had settled on
three changes that affected coal interests:

> (b) Environmental and citizen groups urged that the States be re-
>   quired to provide for public access to emission data . . . as
>   revised, the regulations call upon states to "provide for public
>   availability" of such data.
> (c) Environmental groups, in particular, urged that EPA officials
>   establish a non-deterioration policy applicable to clear air

[37] J. S. Cooper to W. Ruckelshaus, June 11, 1971, Box No. 17, file CR-2,
NAPCA Contract Records.

[38] In a 1972 hearing, Representative Paul Rogers (D-Fla.) asked William Ruckelshaus to submit for the record "your proposed guidelines before
they went to the OMB [for further revision] . . ." (U.S. Congress, House, Subcommittee on Public Health and Environment, Clean Air Act Oversight [92nd
Cong., 2nd sess.], January, 1972, p. 479). Ruckelshaus submitted a document
entitled, "Plans for Implementation of National Ambient Air Quality Standards," which was subtitled, "Submitted to Office of Management and Budget
from EPA, June, 1971." This document, however, was not the June 28 version
that included the changes recommended by Middleton and which the EPA had
proposed in April. It contained the section numbers of the April version rather
than the section numbers of the draft that the OMB reviewed and sent back to
the EPA (those numbers are cited by Middleton in his July 19 memorandum).

areas. . . . Accordingly, the regulations have been modified to include the following statement . . . "Approval of a plan shall not be considered in any manner to allow significant deterioration of existing air quality in any portion of the state"

(e) A requirement that States develop compliance schedules for all sources has been spelled out more clearly.[39]

In response to industry's criticisms, Middleton indicated, only in vague terms, that the EPA had modified appendix B of the guidelines. Middleton seemed somewhat defensive in his description of those changes: "A great many comments were received about Appendix B . . . (Appendix B was, and still is, intended to reflect EPA's judgment as to the reasonably available means of providing for attainment of the National Standards). . . . In recognition of the apparent confusion about the nature and purpose of Appendix B, the introduction to it has been rewritten. In addition, in response to various comments, many technical changes have been made. . . ."[40] This memorandum, describing EPA's June revision of the guidelines, certainly reveals changes made on behalf of both environmentalists and industry, but scarcely suggests any overwhelming changes in its large provisions.

The June 28 revision of the guidelines never did see the light of day. It was not promulgated as scheduled, but rather was submitted to an interagency review coordinated by the Office of Management and Budget. When the guidelines finally did re-emerge in an August issue of the *Federal Register*, they were drastically different from either the April or June versions. The proposed permit system was absent, the crucial appendix B was entirely different, lacking many technical provisions and riddled with economic qualifiers, and the no-significant-deterioration clause inserted by Middleton in June was gone.[41]

Several people have speculated, and at least two investigations by Congress have tried to determine, how and why the EPA was forced to accept these crucial revisions. Richard Ayers, testifying for

[39] John Middleton, memorandum, June 28, 1971, cited in U.S. Congress, Senate, Subcommittee on Air and Water Pollution, *Oversight Hearings—Implementation of the Clean Air Act*, 92nd Cong., 2nd sess., February, 1972, pp. 47–48.
[40] Ibid.
[41] 36 *Federal Register* 15486-15506, August 14, 1971.

the Natural Resources Defense Council, blamed the "drastically weakened guidelines" on the Office of Management and Budget (OMB). James Miller, in *Nixon and the Environment*, wrote that White House aides John Ehrlichman and Peter Flanigan were responsible, according to "government sources." When Representative Paul Rogers asked EPA Administrator Ruckelshaus about the forced revision, Ruckelshaus replied, "I do not know that they submitted any recommendations to us." And when Senator Thomas Eagleton (D-Mo.) asked him the same thing, Ruckelshaus testified that "OMB did not get any final crack at the regulation. OMB is nothing more than a conduit [for] other federal agencies who want to comment on any regulations. . . . I take great exception . . . that these substantial changes in any way reflect anybody's opinion but mine on what changes should be made." His assistant, Edward Tuerk, also denied that any changes had been foisted on the EPA. The changes, said Tuerk, were made, without pressure, by the Environmental Protection Agency.[42]

But in fact, the OMB was the conduit for significant changes that were forced on the EPA, against its will. On July 19, John Middleton sent out a memorandum to several EPA executives, including Ruckelshaus' assistant, Edward Tuerk. In it, Middleton analyzed each of the five major revisions recommended to the EPA through the OMB review, identified the agency seeking the revision, and refuted each and every one.[43] The Department of Commerce was the source of all five. For example, "The Department of Commerce," quoted Middleton, "maintains that the non-deterioration provision (sec. 420-07[b]) is neither justifiable nor legally supportable." "The EPA response," according to Middleton, was that "this provision is a statement of principle (nearly identical to a statement included in the regulations setting forth the national ambient air standards). . . .

    [42] Richard Ayers, in Senate, *Implementation Hearings*, 92nd Cong., 2nd sess., February, 1972, p. 4; Miller, "Air Pollution," in *Nixon and the Environment*, p. 19; House, *Clean Air Act Oversight*, 92nd Cong., 2nd sess., January, 1972, p. 529; Senate, *Implementation Hearings*, 92nd Cong., 2nd sess., February, 1972, pp. 43–50; Edward Tuerk, interview.
    [43] J. Middleton to E. Tuerk, July 19, 1971, Box No. 17, file CR-2, NAPCA Contract Records.

The statement should be retained to keep EPA's regulations from being construed as preventing States from preserving clean air where they choose to do so." On the matter of a permit system, "The Department of Commerce and the Federal Power Commission have objections to the requirement that States set up permit systems." The EPA's response, according to Middleton, was that "the permit provision should be left intact." A third complaint, again from the Department of Commerce, was that "EPA's regulations imply that the provision of Appendix B represent the only acceptable basis of a state plan." Not so, argued Middleton. "Appendix B consists only of suggestions as guidelines. Nevertheless," allowed Middleton, "it would be relatively simple to add to the regulations a provision clearly stating that any strategy which will insure timely attainment of the national standards will be acceptable. . . ." And the story was the same with regard to a sulfur emissions tax and technological feasibility.[44]

A strong case can be made that the National Industrial Pollution Control Council was behind the Department of Commerce's imposition on the EPA's guidelines. At a NIPCC meeting in May, 1971, there was an extended discussion that "indicated widely-held and growing concern on the part of the Members that the Government and the public are underestimating the extent of the disruption . . . that is being set in motion by stringent pollution control measures being applied in unrealistically constrained time frames." The discussion "urged intense economic analyses . . . and re-examination of the scientific and technological bases on which standards, rules and regulations are being based." Attending that meeting, Secretary of Commerce Maurice Stans commented on the national ambient air standards just issued by the EPA and "emphasized the necessity for NIPCC to serve as the focal point for bringing together the information developed by industry to assist in developing achievable standards. . . ." Finally, Undersecretary of Commerce James Lynn discussed with NIPCC members the implications of the "implementation of the Clean Air Act," telling them that "industry should make economic study data on pollution impacts

[44] Ibid.

available to the Government whenever possible."[45] By June, 1971,
NIPCC had established systematic liaisons with both the EPA and
the White House, and Walter Hamilton, NIPCC's director, kept a
thorough file on the implementation guidelines and the Senate
oversight hearings.[46]

When the EPA published the official guidelines on August 14,
1971, knowledgeable environmentalists were startled and angered
by the extent and significance of the alterations. Only one of their
own suggestions had been adopted. The final revision stipulated that
"each plan shall provide for public availability of emission data reported by source owners or operators. . . ." (36 F.R. 15489). But the
number-one goal of the environmentalists had been to get a statement on the nondegradation of clean air into the guidelines. Although the EPA had agreed and even adopted such a proposal
temporarily, industrial interests and the Department of Commerce
had prevailed. An innocuous disclaimer replaced what had been the
key clause (sec. 420.2[a]) in the June revision. "Nothing in this
part," read the final version, "shall be construed in any manner to
encourage a state to prepare, adopt, or submit a plan which does
not provide for the protection and enhancement of air quality so as
to promote the public health and welfare and productive capacity"
(36 F.R. 15487). Moreover, the insertion of "productive capacity"
was meant to equate the needs of industrial growth with the maintenance of existing air quality, thereby nullifying even prior commitments to nondegradation.

Even more concrete changes in the final guidelines were the
omission of the permit system, inclusion of socioeconomic cost considerations, and the watering down of appendix B. Forty detailed
instructions for a permit system disappeared in the final guidelines,
replaced by the offhand remark that each state had the authority to
"prevent construction, modification, or operation of any stationary
source at any location where emissions . . . will prevent the attainment or maintenance of a national standard" (36 F.R. 15489). Ap-

[45] Meeting of National Industrial Pollution Control Council, May 6, 1971,
NIPCC minutes summaries, NIPCC Freedom of Information Files.
[46] W. A. Hamilton, Memorandum, December 23, 1971, Box No. 9,
"Memos" file, NIPCC Administrative Records.

pendix B, the prime target of the coal interests, was missing whole sections on particulate and sulfur emission standards. The particulate restriction of 0.03 grains per cubic foot, with which foundries and cement interests were so concerned, was gone. A table for process emissions was modified, visible emission restrictions and use of the Ringleman chart written off, and there was new emphasis on considering "background concentration," a provision favored by coal people. Finally, appendix B had a new introduction and cost qualifiers sprinkled liberally throughout. The crucial introduction now read: "The statements presented herein are not intended and should not be construed to require or encourage State agencies to adopt such emission limitations without consideration of (1) the necessity of imposing such emission limitations in order to attain and maintain a national standard, (2) the social and economic impact of such emission limitations, and (3) alternative means of providing for attainment and maintenance of national standards" (36 *F.R.* 15495).

Months later, environmentalists testified to the Senate Subcommittee on Air and Water Pollution that these final guidelines had actually weakened the Clean Air Act. The changes that the Department of Commerce had imposed closed the door on nondegradation and established the legitimacy of cost considerations. Richard Ayers, speaking for the Natural Resources Defense Council, claimed that because of the altered guidelines, the "state implementation plans . . . have mostly become little more than weak-kneed apologies for each state's present program."[47] The extraordinary revision of the EPA's implementation guidelines was the coal coalition's biggest single political accomplishment since air pollution had become a federal policy issue. Coal-related industries attained the changes through cooperation, the use of sophisticated technical and economic arguments, and by eliciting the support of the secretary of commerce and, possibly, through intervention by the White House. This guidelines incident reflects the complexity of modern policy issues, the growing concrescence of interest among diverse businessmen, and the significance of technocratic institutional linkages be-

[47] Richard Ayers, in Senate, *Implementation Hearings*, 92nd Cong., 2nd sess., February, 1972, p. 3.

tween business and government. Moreover, it further convinced environmental interest groups to pursue judicial, rather than legislative or administrative solutions.

Technological Politics: Standards for New Sources

The third phase of implementing the Clean Air Act involved emissions standards for newly constructed sources of pollution. The act authorized such standards for each major source of industrial pollution. The standards, instructed Congress, were to be based on the "best system of emission reduction which . . . has been adequately demonstrated."[48] In August, 1971, the EPA proposed new source performance standards (NSPS) for five industrial categories: fossil-fuel-fired steam generators, incinerators, cement plants, nitric acid plants, and sulfuric acid plants (36 *F.R.* 15704). Eventually there would be more than twenty sets of NSPS. At this juncture, the level of policy became extremly technical, moving completely beyond the grasp of anyone other than industrial engineers. The proposed rules involved complex equations, engineering diagrams, and prescriptions of intricate engineering techniques. As a result, only five environmental groups even participated in the comment process, and their efforts were completely ineffective.

On the other hand, NIPCC organized comments by more than two hundred industrial organizations that included forty-one regular members of the coal coalition. The National Coal Association and the American Mining Congress spearheaded comments by six steel and petroleum companies and thirty-three electric utility groups, including the nation's two largest, American Electric Power and the Tennessee Valley Authority.[49] The technical branch of EPA's Air Pollution Control Office seems to have formulated the proposed standards largely without outside input.[50] EPA staff then sifted the

---

[48] P.L. 91-604, section 111(a)(1).

[49] "New Source Standards Comment" file, EPA 1971 Air Pollution Files; W. A. Hamilton, memorandum to NIPCC council members, December 23, 1971, NIPCC Administrative Records.

[50] In July, 1971, NIPCC made a liaison arrangement with the EPA, whereby NIPCC provided thirty-one technical personnel from its member corporations to serve on informal "industrial study advisory groups" for the EPA. The EPA's senior technical advisor accepted this arrangement only

comments and isolated thirty-six specific issues, all of which had been raised by industrial commentators. When published in December, the official standards reflected sixteen modifications. Several involved "clarifications" of definitions and procedures for testing and monitoring. A provision that the EPA be notified before construction could begin was deleted, and criteria for evaluating performance testing results were significantly altered, eliminating a requirement that all values be within a 35 percent range of the average. Finally, the opacity standards for visible emissions were doubled for three source categories.[51]

It is difficult, to say the least, to evaluate how much industrial comments affected the NSPS. It is clear, however, that the technical nature of the decision-making process excluded nearly all but industry and EPA technicians from participating. OMB did conduct an interagency review, to which HEW, Commerce, Labor, Interior, and the Atomic Energy Commission contributed. But there is no evidence that their input had any effect. In fact, an EPA memorandum even indicates that the technical complexities of the rule making actually precluded congressional intercessions as well as those by other federal agencies.[52] And the five environmental groups that made comments were an insignificant factor. Only the Sierra Club and the National Resources Defense Council offered any technical recommendations, and they were relatively simplistic. The Sierra Club, for example, supported "stricter regulations for particulates, oxides of sulfur, and oxides of nitrogen," but backed their suggestions with data predicated on low-sulfur coal consumption. The Sierra Club's supportive evidence was relevant only to a small area of western coal and was generally dismissed by EPA officials.[53] The

grudgingly, as he feared that "NIPCC may come to feel that they have some vested right in implementing the Clean Air Act" (D. Walters to W. A. Hamilton, July 23, 1971, in Administrative Records, Office of Air Quality Planning and Standards, U.S. Environmental Protection Agency, Research Triangle Park, N.C.). The extent to which those technical advisors may have participated in formulating the NSPS proposal is unknown.

[51] EPA, "Changes in Standards Summarized," in "New Source Standards Comment" file in EPA 1971 Air Pollution Files.

[52] Erwin Auerbach, memorandum, October 26, 1971, Box No. 17, file CR-2, NAPCA Contract Records.

[53] Sierra Club comment, September 29, 1971, pp. 1–2, in "New Source Standards Comment" file, EPA 1971 Air Pollution Files.

Conservation Foundation, while recommending tougher standards, abnegated any influence it might have had by admitting that "we do not possess the technical competence to discuss in detail the standards themselves or the specified testing procedures: we therefore confined our comments chiefly to administrative procedures and to the general principles. . . ."[54] So much for countervailing power in the realm of technological politics.

Administrative Politics Move out to the States

At least since the 1958 national conference on air pollution, the division of regulatory authority between state and federal governments had been a major policy issue. While publicly acknowledging the need for federal involvement, the coal coalition persistently sought to limit federal authority to the bare bones. Environmental interests were equally persistent in shunning state regulation in favor of federal authority. Both groups believed that regulators at the state level were usually more susceptible to industrial influence than the expert technicians in Washington bureaucracies. For it was back home in the states, not in Washington, that industry operates its plants, employs its workmen, and disburses its payrolls. The political and economic constituencies of state politicians are less diffuse and more immediate than those of federal officials. The threat of production curtailment and layoffs is more serious. And, state control agencies do not come close to commanding the expertise and resources necessary for fending off the economic and technical criticisms of such organizations as Bethlehem Steel, Gulf Oil, and the Pennsylvania Railroad. However, it is also back home in the states where industrial emissions pollute the air and where the members of citizens and environmental groups actually live and can have firsthand contact with the officials responsible for plans to carry out the federal law. As the EPA was concluding its rule-making tasks, the arena of environmental politics shifted to state capitals. And nowhere was there a more seasoned community of environmental activists or a larger cross-section of the coal coalition than in Pennsylvania. That state is a good case in which to examine what was

[54] Conservation Foundation comment (n.d.), p. 1 (ibid.).

then thought to be the final stage of formulating policies to implement the Clean Air Act of 1970.

In Pennsylvania, as in the other states, the task of devising a plan to implement the Clean Air Act appeared monumental. The goal was to attain the national ambient air quality standards for each pollutant in various air quality regions. On that basis, the state had to determine emission standards for each of its diverse industrial operations. In Pennsylvania, that included electric power, steel, iron, coal preparation, chemicals, petrochemicals, cement, asphalt, incineration, and others. There had to be different standards for different operations ranging, for example, from a family-run foundry to U.S. Steel's biggest mill complex. Besides the standards, each state had to develop the necessary administrative machinery to inspect and monitor, maintain permit systems, and provide for hearings, variance procedures, and enforcement sanctions. Once proposed, these regulations were to be reviewed by all interested parties through public hearings, revised, and then approved by the legislature and eventually the Environmental Protection Agency. Late in the summer of 1971, the governor of Pennsylvania assigned this responsibility to the Environmental Quality Board (EQB). In reality, this nonexpert committee of eleven cabinet members, four legislators, and five "citizens," had to rely heavily on the technical staff of the Pennsylvania Department of Environmental Resources (DER) to formulate the proposed plan. In October, the EQB published a tentative plan and announced statewide hearings to be held in December.

The practical meaning of air pollution policy culminated in these rules, and for environmental and industrial interests alike, they were of paramount importance. One hundred and eighteen organizations, and many individuals as well, participated in those hearings or submitted statements and briefs. Such a turnout for a rule-making proceeding at the state level is a measure of the importance of the implementation plans and the controversy that surrounded them. Most of the groups that participated in the EQB hearings represented a different organizational level than those active in federal proceedings. The more politically effective groups that we have seen, such as the Natural Resources Defense Council and the American Mining Congress, were ill-suited to the state context. Their effectiveness was rooted in national constituencies relevant only to the federal forum. Thus, in Pennsylvania, the Group against Smog and Pollution (GASP) replaced the NRDC, and the Keystone Bituminous Coal Association took up where the AMC left off.

Fifty-eight coal-related industrial organizations took part in revising Pennsylvania's air pollution control plan. Fourteen trade associations and forty-four corporations spoke for the interests of electric power, coal mining, steel, iron, railroads, petroleum, asphalt, cement, general manufacturing, and regional commerce across the state. The group included several local businesses as well as all the state's electric utilities, four international oil companies, two giant railroad systems, and the nation's largest coal producer and two largest steel companies. Moreover, cooperating with them were spokesmen for the United Mine Workers, the United Steelworkers, and the United Papermakers and Paperworkers.[55] For a quiet town like Harrisburg, this coalition of coal interests put on a nearly overwhelming political display of opposition to the standards and regulations the EQB had proposed.

The Pennsylvania Electric Association (PEA) and the state's electric utilities coordinated the most comprehensive and vigorous opposition. These groups not only provided electricity for all Pennsylvania's residential and industrial consumers, but in doing so, consumed 30 million tons of locally mined coal each year. Since Pennsylvania's high-sulfur coal was not very competitive outside the state, the payrolls and jobs of thousands of Pennsylvania's coal miners depended on coal-fired power plants as customers. To assure that the significance of this sizeable dual constituency was not lost on state legislators or EQB members, the utilities hinged their case on grave warnings of huge electric rate hikes, fuel shortages, layoffs in mining, manufacturing, steel, and railroads, and general economic havoc.

The EQB had proposed sulfur dioxide emission standards of 1.2

---

[55] Pennsylvania Environmental Quality Board, "Public Hearings on Air Pollution Regulations" (vol. I, Philadelphia; vol. II, Harrisburg; vol. III, Pittsburgh), December, 1971; hereafter cited as EQB Hearings.

pounds per million Btu's of heat output for power plants. That was the biggest concern of the utility representatives, although the particulate standards took a close second. In their exhaustive testimonies, all the utilities made five principal points in opposing the proposed sulfur dioxide standard. First, they argued that it was technologically impossible to attain the standard. The PEA brought in outside experts to prove it. An employee of Union Electric in St. Louis gave important testimony that Union Electric's advanced limestone scrubber system was full of bugs and rarely worked. He cautioned the EQB members to "be very careful about the state of the technology."[56] A spokesman for Duquesne Light testified that the proposed standard meant a removal efficiency of 99.7 percent of the sulfur, and that, he felt, was not only technically impossible, but fiscally absurd.[57] Second, the utility people believed that EQB's standards were too high relative to the federal requirements. Third, they argued that dispersion of pollutants through high stacks was an acceptable alternative to flue gas scrubbing. Fourth, they felt that more thorough cost-benefit analysis should have been taken into account. But the fifth point, the cost of compliance, was the crux of their entire presentation. According to Allegheny Power Systems, the proposed standards would mean a 25 percent increase in operating costs for their plants in Pennsylvania. Such requirements were "unreasonable and irresponsible . . . and will cause much serious social and economic impact."[58] Duquesne Light predicted an 8.6 percent rate hike, Pennsylvania Electric Company forecast a 15.5 percent rise, and Pennsylvania Power and Light anticipated an 18 percent increase.

The Pennsylvania Electric Association commissioned the consulting firm of Gordian Associates to prepare a study entitled, "The Economic Impact on Pennsylvania Residents Due to the Proposed Sulfur Dioxide Emission Standards for Combustion Units." For the price of $45,000, this study received widespread publicity and became the center of controversy in the revision process. Because it so exemplifies tactics in environmental politics, it deserves some elab-

[56] Ibid., I, 45.
[57] Ibid., III, 388.
[58] Ibid., p. 242.

oration. The study was a statistical extrapolation of per capita costs based on two hypothetical cases of complying with EQB's proposed sulfur dioxide standards, either by stack gas removal or by substituting low-sulfur coal as the prime boiler fuel in Pennsylvania. Dr. Howard Ellis, the study's author, concluded that in the former case compliance would cost $830,842,000 in capital costs and an additional $133,687,000 for operating costs. In his other model, that of converting to low-sulfur coal, Ellis estimated an initial investment of $83,940,000, $253,414,000 annually for higher fuel costs, and $119,636,000 more each year in lost wages and taxes that would result from the 25 percent shrinkage of Pennsylvania's coal industry.[59] The day after the EQB received this gruesome report, the *Philadelphia Enquirer* reported that the "annual electric bill for an average Pennsylvania family of four could increase almost $90 if the state adopts new air pollution regulations by January 30, 1972." The newspaper also reported Dr. Ellis' grave warning of the "devastating . . . economic impact of the proposed standards on Pennsylvania residents. . . ."[60] To that, the Pennsylvania Chamber of Commerce added its estimate that by 1975, $61.7 billion would have to be spent nationally on air pollution. Robert Rauch, a Nader associate, later testified at Senator Thomas Eagleton's oversight hearings that those highly suspect cost figures were publicized in every major Pennsylvania newspaper and more than likely made a negative impact on public opinion.[61]

[59] Howard Ellis, "The Economic Impact on Pennsylvania Residents Due to the Proposed Sulfur Dioxide Emission Standards for Combustion Units," Gordian Associates, Inc., pp. I–2, II–16. In one hypothetical case, Ellis assumed compliance to the proposed restrictions by application of limestone-injection wet scrubber systems and excluded the estimated costs of controlling the resultant limestone sludge. Data on estimated maintenance costs, equipment, wages, and construction was provided confidentially by potential vendors and utility officials. In his other hypothetical case, the author estimated that all but four of the thirty-six coal-burning generating plants in Pennsylvania would have to be converted to low-sulfur fuel. That estimate was based on confidential communications with coal procurement personnel of various utilities. Prices for low-sulfur coal, after increased demand in 1975, had to be estimated including transportation rates to thirty-two plant sites. That hypothetical calculation was also based on "the judgments of several experts on coal procurement, coal resources, and coal economics" who remained unnamed in the report.

[60] "Electricity Raise Tied to Pollution," *Philadelphia Enquirer*, December 2, 1971.

[61] Senate, *Implementation Hearings*, 92nd Cong., 2nd sess., February, 1972, p. 380.

The most interesting aspect of this controversy was the way the utilities presented this data to the Environmental Quality Board. At the December 1 hearing, the report was only summarized, with emphasis on its conclusions, and EQB members were promised copies in the near future. One board member, John Elliott, criticized the report and its presentation, complaining that a nonexpert like himself could hardly evaluate it. The board's chairman did not sympathize with Elliott's point and squelched further discussion. But Elliott persisted in refusing to admit the report as evidence and asked both the Department of Environmental Resources and the governor's office to evaluate it. When they refused, he enlisted Ralph Nader's Public Interest Research Group, and through it arranged for a counterstudy by another consulting firm. Later, at the final EQB meeting, a Public Interest Research Group spokesman tried to read into the proceedings an oral summary of the counterstudy. The board, excepting Elliott and two other members, voted to exclude even a three-minute summary of that report. Victor Sussman, the DER's air pollution division chief, explained to Senator Eagleton's subcommittee that EQB members had not considered the Gordian study, because they lacked the expertise to evaluate it. He claimed that although EQB members received copies of the study during the month in which they revised upward the sulfur restrictions, they had ignored it. Robert Rauch, author of the counterstudy, strongly disagreed, and told the Senate committee that the Gordian study was "part of a pattern" emerging in environmental politics. It was "a calculated effort on the part of a number of industries to blackmail the American public."[62] Although unusually controversial, studies like that sponsored by the Pennsylvania Electric Association were becoming regular fare in environmental politics.

Pennsylvania's proposed air pollution controls also threatened a wide variety of difficult emissions problems for the state's steel industry. Steel mills use coal not only for steam-electric generation, but also to produce coke, a vital ingredient in steel-making. Integrated mills, especially those in the Johnstown and Pittsburgh areas, had both sulfur oxide and particulate emissions problems from gas heating processes, coke and sulfuric acid plants, and sinters, and

[62] Ibid., pp. 723, 373.

fugitive emissions from coke ovens, furnaces, and fuel storage facilities. Six of Pennsylvania's steel producers participated in the EQB revision proceedings. They employed thousands of workers in their mills and mines and contributed a major share of the state's gross income and nearly the entire payroll of certain industrial communities. Their political influence, especially in communities dominated by older mill facilities most threatened by the proposed controls, can hardly be understated.

A spokesman for U.S. Steel told state officials that the plan called for 98 percent removal of sulfur from coke-oven gas, a technical feat never accomplished in the United States. He recommended that 70 percent removal would be a more feasible goal. The section on particulates was just as bad, said a Bethlehem Steel representative. Arguing that the standard for particulates meant a 99.5 percent removal efficiency, he concluded that "we find that this chapter, in particular, contains more inequities and ill-considered limits than any other."[63] The smaller firms, like Alan Woods and Lukens Steel, were just as disturbed as the giants. They lacked the efficiencies of size and diversified cash flows necessary to absorb the costs of pollution clean-up. At the public hearings, steel executives enlisted the aid of local entrepreneurs to personalize the implications of rigorous pollution controls for state politicians more sympathetic to small business than large corporations. For example, the manager of the neighborhood Sears store (and Chamber of Commerce spokesman) in Coatesville, Pennsylvania, told EQB members that any threat to Lukens Steel's $61 million payroll was a threat to the whole community. "Quite frankly," said the Sears manager, "if a viable local economy is the price we have to pay for crystal clean air, then the price is far too high."[64] And while industrialists and small businessmen alike pressed the cost angle, the steelworkers and mine workers unions did their part, too. The UMW's Joseph Brennan warned EQB members that "the regulations which you are now considering, if implemented at this time . . . will bring about . . . a form of economic depression . . . worse than the environmental pollution we

[63] EQB Hearings, I, 95.
[64] Ibid.

are trying to solve."[65] Apparently air pollution was not nearly as serious an environmental problem as non-union strip mining, which the UMW had opposed since the 1960's.

In the course of the December hearings, EQB members learned that the air pollution regulations, while disastrous for steel and the utilities, would also do considerable harm to the forty thousand workers at small foundries in communities scattered throughout Pennsylvania.[66] They learned from their biggest coal producer, Consolidation, that to adopt the proposed sulfur dioxide standards "would drastically reduce the use of coal in this state and deal a vital blow to the State's economy."[67] From oil companies, they learned that refineries would go under and marginal oil production in Pennsylvania would cease. And from the Penn Central Railroad, they learned that the pollution controls might be a death blow to the nation's largest and financially troubled railroad. According to Walter Lloyd, the system's branch lines that hauled coal almost exclusively would be bankrupted by the pollution standards and would discontinue all service in their areas. Coal accounted for 13 percent of the Penn Central's freight and 15 percent of its revenues. To adopt the EQB proposals would mean that "practically all of the steam coal from Pennsylvania would be outlawed. . . ." And that, warned Lloyd, would wreak havoc with the 26,000 employees and $252 million in Penn Central revenues that underlay the entire economy of the Commonwealth of Pennsylvania.[68]

The net effect of industry's studies, briefs, and testimony was to leave the people of Pennsylvania and the members of the Environmental Quality Board with a vision of the state's entire economic system hanging in the balance of the proposed plan for implementing the Clean Air Act. In the wake of the hearings, EQB members, not to mention the governor and state legislators, quite understandably had second thoughts about the proposed standards. The firms and trade groups that testified at the hearings had plants or mines in nearly every legislative district in Pennsylvania. And the econo-

[65] Ibid., p. 196.
[66] Ibid., III, 130.
[67] Ibid., II, 89.
[68] Ibid., pp. 69–70.

mies of as many as half of the state's senatorial districts depended completely on the industries that were prophesying disaster. The revisions of the plan would bear witness to that fact.

In the face of industrial pressure of this magnitude, Pennsylvania's environmentalists could hardly hope for more rigorous revisions of the plan. Their goal seemed to be holding the ground gained in the EQB's initial proposals. To compensate for their dearth of technical expertise, the environmental activists relied on public sentiment, abundant moral indignation, and organized constituent pressures. Forty-six civic and environmental interest groups participated in the EQB hearings and revision process. The groups were geographically constituted for maximum political effectiveness: one-third from western Pennsylvania with its heavy industrial and urban concentrations around Pittsburgh and one-third from the Philadelphia metropolitan area (with the rest from rural areas). About half the groups (20) were oriented toward conservation and ecology, while nearly as many were general civic organizations (16). There was also a smattering of health (6) and church-oriented groups (4). Most were local, encompassing only a single city, county, or township. Only four were statewide (Citizens Advisory Council to the DER, the Pennsylvania Environmental Council, the Pennsylvania League of Women Voters, and the Pennsylvania Division of the American Association of University Women).

The overwhelming majority of environmentalist testimony at the hearings was nontechnical, directed more at the general problem of air pollution and social goals. Some groups bemoaned air quality, some chastised corporate negligence, others were concerned with a single local source of pollution, and all offered blanket endorsements of the principle of tough regulation. There were three aspects of the original EQB plans at which several of the better-informed environmentalists took aim. In the initial proposal, there was a provision for "alternate standards." The League of Women Voters representative and several conservation groups recognized that this was a euphemism for variance procedures that they thought were riddled with potential loopholes. Environmental spokesmen wanted the "alternate standards" provision deleted, time periods more sharply delineated, clear criteria for variances established, and ample opportunity for public participation in variance proceedings. Public disclosure of data relevant to the regulatory process was another environmentalist goal, especially for Pittsburgh's GASP and the Delaware Valley Citizens' Council, both of which had experienced disclosure problems in the past. Provision for the nondegradation of existing clean air was a third concern for nearly half the environmental groups. Since that policy had been well publicized earlier in 1971 with regard to the EPA's implementation guidelines, environmental activists wanted it stated explicitly in the state plans.

Only two or three environmental groups even attempted to deal with the technical aspects of the EQB plan. However, those few did recognize that the sulfur oxide standards were crucial. Members of Pittsburgh's GASP and the Pittsburgh chapter of the Federation of American Scientists shrewdly zeroed in on the question of "best available technology" in sulfur dioxide control. They tried to counter industry evidence that anything better than 98 percent removal efficiency was not currently possible.[69] Another organization, the Tuberculosis and Respiratory Disease Association of Philadelphia, testified effectively on the health hazards from the synergism of sulfur oxides and particulates.

It is worth noting that just two groups of environmentalists seemed in the least concerned with the economic implications of rigid controls. One, from the depressed anthracite coal region in eastern Pennsylvania, acknowledged the danger of implementing policies beyond capability: "As a citizens' organization, our first reaction is to approve stringent controls . . . but we have a bigger role . . . to determine whether or not proposed regulations are feasible and achievable . . . regulations which cannot be enforced, standards which cannot be met . . . are worse than no controls at all. . . ."[70] But few other groups shared this reasonable attitude, and the majority recommended that the EQB disregard cost and technological considerations.

After all the voices of group interest had been heard publicly, the EQB settled down to the business of revising its air pollution

[69] Ibid., III, 115–129, 530.
[70] Ibid., I, 60.

plan. That activity was shrouded by ex parte discussions and conflicting descriptions. During January, 1972, there was a series of three-cornered meetings between the Pennsylvania Department of Environmental Resources, industry, and regional EPA officials. Since no one kept any record of these discussions, their significance to the process of revision remains a matter of speculation. However, when environmentalists learned of the meetings, they angrily organized the Ad Hoc Emergency Committee for Clean Air to fight the "covert and iniquitous changes in the air pollution control regulations. . . ." The Ad Hoc Committee claimed that the secret meetings included foundry interests, the Anthracite Institute, petroleum refiners, and others, except for environmentalists. "The citizens of Pennsylvania," concluded the Ad Hoc Committee, "have been denied an effective voice in the implementation planning process by maneuvering within DER to accommodate industrial interests."[71] Although DER's Victor Sussman acknowledged the meetings with industry, he denied that they materially affected any of the changes in the standards.[72]

On January 27, 1972, the Pennsylvania Environmental Quality Board made public the official version of the state implementation plan. Environmentalists were, to say the least, dismayed. They could take solace from only two of the numerous changes. The EQB had deleted the "alternate standards" concept and replaced it with a more detailed variance provision. But Victor Sussman qualified the stricter provisions by assuring industry that "we will consider recent efforts made to comply with existing regulations in the granting of the variance" and that DER would use variance proceedings to "shed more light on 'available technology,'" which Sussman considered to be "almost a philosophical question."[73] The new plan also provided limited protection against significant deterioration of clean air: "Air quality shall be maintained at existing levels in those areas

[71] Hearing transcript, meeting of Environmental Quality Board, January 27, 1972, part 2, p. 40, Pennsylvania Environmental Quality Board, Harrisburg, Pa.

[72] Victor Sussman, in Senate, *Implementation Hearings*, 92nd Cong., 2nd sess., February, 1972, p. 723.

[73] Hearing transcript, January 27, 1972, p. 33, Pennsylvania Environmental Quality Board.

where the existing ambient air quality is better than the applicable ambient air quality standards. . . ." While that sounded pretty good to environmentalists, the very next sentence foretold a different reality: "In those areas . . . new sources shall not be established unless . . . (1) the establishment of such new sources is justifiable as a result of necessary economic or social development . . . (2) such new sources shall control the emission of air pollutants to the maximum extent consistent with the best available technology."[74]

Of far greater consequence were radical changes in the emission standards, which completely overshadowed that pair of concessions to the environmentalist cause. The EQB had collapsed under the pressure from utilities and steel companies and raised the sulfur emission standard for combustion sources by 50 percent and tripled the allowable sulfur dioxide content of by-product coke over gas. Moreover, the board doubled the standard for particulate emissions from large boiler units (power plants). The EQB's fourth major change was to broaden the definition of "process sources" to include the combustion units of manufacturers. This change pleased manufacturers, since standards for process sources were less stringent than those for combustion sources.[75]

From Pennsylvania's experience, we can generalize nothing about the course of implementing air pollution policy in the other forty-nine states. But having taken a microcosmic view, we can see more clearly the essential characteristics of environmental politics. The revisions in Pennsylvania's implementation plan perfectly reflect the strengths and weaknesses of both the coal coalition and environ-

---

[74] *Pennsylvania Bulletin* 2, no. 10 (March 4, 1972), 389.

[75] In combustion units (sec. 123.22) with ratings of 2.5 to 50 million Btu./hr., sulfur oxide emission limits were raised from 2.0 lb./10^6 Btu. to 3.0 lb./10^6 Btu. For larger combustion units, in the 2,000 10^6 Btu./hr. range or greater, the SO_2 limit was raised from 1.2 lb./10^6 Btu. to 1.8 lb./10^6 Btu. (*Pennsylvania Bulletin* [hereafter cited as *P.B.*] 1, no. 72 [October 30, 1971], 2042; and 2, no. 10 [March 4, 1972], 388). For by-product coke-oven gas (sec. 123.23), the maximum sulfur oxide content was raised from 10 grains/100 ft.^{3} to 50 grains/100 ft.^{3} (*P.B.* 1, no. 72 [October 30, 1971], 2-43; and 2, no. 10 [March 4, 1972], 338). In sec. 123.10, the limit of 0.05 lb./10^6 Btu. of particulates for large boilers was raised to 1.0 lb./10^6 Btu. (*P.B.* 1, no. 72 [October 30, 1971], 2042; and 2, no. 10 [March 4, 1972], 387). The changed definition of process sources is evident by comparing sec. 121.2 in *P.B.* 2, no. 10 (March 4, 1972), 385.

mentalists. Lacking technical expertise, local environmental interests focused on procedural changes and were relatively successful in attaining some that became important in subsequent years. But the emission standards were the crux of air pollution policy, and, since 1958, coal interests had struggled to maintain the state's authority for promulgating those standards. When the coal coalition finally did confront the state and rigorous emission proposal, it exerted every bit of prestige, technical expertise, and economic leverage it commanded to alter the crucial sulfur and particulate standards. Here we see the reasons for industry's consistent preference for state preeminence. The Department of Environmental Resources, let alone the EQB, simply lacked the material resources necessary either to evaluate or to refute the contentions of industry. There was just no one around who could deal with the cost study by Gordian Associates. It was the same with the technological issue, where the state's control authority saw the question as nearly "philosophical." However, by themselves, expert advantage and mounds of data did not account for the EQB revision. The politically crucial lever used by the coal coalition was the threat to jobs and electric rates. When dozens of Pennsylvania's most respectable corporate executives testified to impending economic disaster, the environmental interests group lost. In Washington, the job-cost lever was merely helpful. But Pennsylvania was where the miners actually mine, where the foundrymen pour their molds, where the smoldering blast furnaces meant prosperity, and where the homeowner paid his monthly electric bill. And in every legislative and senatorial district where industry ran its mills and mines, the threat to wages and jobs, not air, was the politician's most serious problem.

The Clean Air Act allowed the states nine months (until February, 1972) to come up with plans for implementing the national ambient air quality standards. Few other states did as well as Pennsylvania. Many of the states exceeded the deadline, and of those that were completed, most were less adequate than Pennsylvania's. Although environmental interest groups in Pennsylvania had suffered considerable losses, there were scarcely any other states in which even half as many environmental groups had been active. The 1970 act gave the Environmental Protection Agency four months in which to approve or disapprove the state plans. Thus, as June, 1972 approached, William Ruckelshaus was preparing to make the final decision that would set in motion the actual, physical process of cleaning up industrial air pollution. He had no way of knowing that two extraordinary circumstances, both of which had been evolving for years, were about to come to the surface and create a new context of national controversy.

7

Growth, Energy, and Air Pollution: America's Bicentennial Crisis

LATE in the spring, 1972, a Sierra Club attorney walked into the federal district court building in Washington, D.C., and filed suit for an injunction and a declaratory judgment to bar William Ruckelshaus from approving state implementation plans that allowed clean air to deteriorate significantly. Three weeks later, in June, Judge Julius Pratt held that "the Clean Air Act of 1970 is based in important part on a policy of non-degradation of existing clean air. . . ." Therefore, concluded Judge Pratt, "in permitting the states to submit plans which allowed the pollution level of clean air to rise to the secondary standard level of pollution, is contrary to the legislative policy of the Act."[1] The EPA administrator could approve none of the state plans, and "no significant deterioration" quickly became *the* point of conflict in air pollution politics. It took Congress five years to resolve this issue because the concept of no significant deterioration (NSD) contraposed two very much larger social issues: limits to growth and the energy crisis. These same two issues that had muddled the strip-mining controversy completely confounded air pollution policy. It is no coincidence that President Carter signed into law the Clean Air Act Amendments of 1977 only weeks after approving the Federal Surface Mining and Control Act.

To appreciate air pollution politics after 1972, it is worth a brief and superficial digression to consider the historical roots of both the

[1] *Sierra Club* vs. *Ruckelshaus*, 344 F. Supp. 253, 256 (D.D.C. 1972).

energy crisis and the idea of limiting industrial growth. Although energy policies antedating World War I are not irrelevant, let us at least consider several statistical trends that began in the 1950's to foretell the fuel dislocations that culminated in 1973–1974. First, coal production dropped to nearly half its post–World War II level and had still not fully recovered by 1975. While oil and natural gas production increased steadily, new explorations, drilling, and discovery of reserves began dropping off after 1955. By 1968, total reserves of both gas and petroleum were declining. Third, the United States began importing more and more crude petroleum and fuel oil after 1958, imports amounting to nearly 23 percent of national consumption by 1973. Then, during the first four months of 1972, most major oil refineries appeared to operate at about 3 percent below their normal capacity, so that by the summer, gasoline inventories were unusually low. By rebuilding those gasoline inventories during the fall, those refineries allowed supplies of winter fuel and heating oil to lag. As a result, there was a shortage of heating oil in New England by January, 1973. Since refiners had to restock low fuel-oil inventories, they lagged in gasoline, and by July, 1973, Americans experienced lines at gas stations.[2] At about that time, the public began learning that those spot shortages were possibly part of a larger, more consequential energy problem, all of which had been developing several months before the Yom Kippur War. Both Presidents Gerald Ford and Jimmy Carter reacted vigorously to the "energy crisis," making it the preeminent issue of public concern since 1974.

Resistance to expanding industrialism has even deeper historical roots, dating at least to the late eighteenth century. More recently, the 1950's began to witness the blossoming of conservation groups devoted to national parks as a way of preserving unique natural areas from the intrusions of industrialism. Echo Park, Dinosaur Monument, and the Redwoods were the objects of heated political contests during that decade. By the 1960's, wilderness areas, wild rivers, marshes, seashores, and the disposition of Alaska lands had become national controversies. Moreover, citizens' groups in urban

[2] Fred Allvine and James Patterson, *Highway Robbery: An Analysis of the Gasoline Crisis.*

areas, such as Tampa, Southern California, and Long Island, began to promote zoning restrictions, land banks, and tax schemes that would discourage or halt urban growth and suburban sprawl. And in academic circles, a few economists, demographers, agronomists, and ecologists began to consider the future implications of unrestrained economic growth and possible alternatives. While hardly a popular controversy, the idea of limiting growth became more widely disseminated and a subject of heated academic debate late in 1972 after the publication of a startling book, *Limits to Growth*.

This book, sponsored by the Club of Rome and based on an MIT computer simulation, predicted that "if the present growth trends . . . continue unchanged, the limits to growth on this planet will be reached sometime within the next one hundred years." However, Dennis Meadows and the other authors held out the promise that "it is possible to alter these growth trends and to establish a condition of ecological and economic stability."[3] As other scholars, including E. F. Schumacher, Herman Daly, and Paul Erlich added their visions of economic equilibrium, traditional economists and most industrial and financial managers joined the debate in adamant disagreement. And while the limits-to-growth debate grew vociferous and the shortages of heating oil more serious, Judge Pratt's decision was working its way toward affirmation by the Supreme Court in June, 1973. A month after the Supreme Court's decision in *Sierra Club* vs. *Ruckelshaus*, the Senate held a special hearing on the problem of no significant deterioration. Carl Bagge, president of the National Coal Association, spoke for the entire coal coalition and admirably summed up why air pollution policy, particularly the NSD concept, became the leading edge in the conflict between energy crisis solutions and the notion of limits to growth: "The nondegradation decision has thrown the nation into an unforeseen, and we believe unintended, instant no-growth policy. The lack of legal definition of what constitutes 'significant' deterioration of air quality means that no industry can build any plant which emits any air pollutants whatever unless it is willing to gamble on the ultimate definition of 'significant.' . . ."[4]

[3] Dennis L. Meadows et al., *The Limits to Growth*, p. 29.
[4] U.S. Congress, Senate, Committee on Public Works, Subcommittee on Air and Water Pollution, *Hearings on Nondegradation Policy of the Clean Air Act*, 93rd Cong., 1st sess., July, 1973, p. 119.

We shall first examine the process by which the NSD concept evolved, and then look at how the demands of energy crisis clashed with growth-limiting values as the Congress struggled to enact the Clean Air Act Amendments of 1977.

No Significant Deterioration: A New Departure in Air Pollution Policy?

Business opponents of no-significant-deterioration policy did not acknowledge that the concept had any substantive roots in either statutory policy or administrative intent prior to 1972. As Carl Bagge put it, the entire question was rhetorical, created by rabid preservationists and amplified into reality "because a federal judge once decided two words in the preamble of the Clean Air Act prohibit the 'significant deterioration' of air that is cleaner than the most rigid federal standards now in effect."[5] But this was not entirely so. Bagge and others from the coal-energy community were quick to forget the Environmental Protection Agency's 1971 implementation guidelines and, before that, the plans that the National Air Pollution Control Administration had issued in 1969. The NSD concept was implicit in the 1967 Air Quality Act and in the goals of many of those who had labored on behalf of federal air pollution controls.

It should be recalled that by 1963 support for a national policy on air pollution derived from two quite different sources. Originally, physical health groups, interested in respiratory and heart disorders associated with urban air pollution, were the impulse behind federal action. But they were soon joined by conservation organizations that approached the air pollution problem from another historical tradition. At the Senate hearings in 1963, the Citizens Committee on Natural Resources and the National Wildlife Federation were among the few interests calling for a firmer federal hand in air pollution. Neither of these two groups was oriented toward urban-industrial affairs, but rather toward the natural environment. Many of their members, people devoted to protecting the remnants of undeveloped nature, were philosophically descended from nineteenth-century preservationists who had fought for national parks and were first organized under the leadership of John Muir. The values some mod-

---

[5] Carl Bagge, quoted in *Coal Mining and Processing*, December, 1975.

ern conservationists brought to air pollution politics contained something of those expressed by Muir in his eloquent defense of Hetch Hetchy Valley (in the Yosemite):

> Hetch Hetchy Valley . . . is a grand landscape garden, one of Nature's rarest and most precious mountain temples . . . the sublime rocks of its walls seem to glow with life . . . while birds, bees, and butterflies help the river and waterfalls to stir all the air into music. . . .
>
> Sad to say, this most precious and sublime feature . . . one of the greatest of all our natural resources for the uplifting joy and peace and health of the people, is in danger of being dammed and made into a reservoir to help supply San Francisco with water and light. . . . Nature's sublime wonderlands . . . however well guarded . . . have always been subject to attack by despoiling gain-seekers and mischief-makers of every degree from Satan to Senators, eagerly trying to make everything immediately and selfishly commercial. . . . These temple destroyers, devotees of ravaging commercialism, seem to have a perfect contempt for Nature. . . .[6]

Most certainly, cleaning up polluted urban air was the principal goal of the 1967 act. But it is hardly surprising, since conservationists from the Muir tradition actively lobbied for the law, that it was also intended to guard clean air from the "devotees of ravaging commercialism."

As stated in its preamble, the purpose of the Air Quality Act was "to protect and enhance the quality of the Nation's air resources so as to promote the public health and welfare and the productive capacity of its population."[7] In *Sierra Club* vs. *Ruckelshaus*, Judge Pratt interpreted this phrase to mean that Congress intended not only to clean up ("enhance") polluted air, but also to maintain ("protect") the existing quality of clean air. The judge also noted that the Senate report accompanying the 1967 act further stated that "the Air Quality Act . . . serves notice . . . that there will be no haven for polluters anywhere in the country."[8] At first, the industrial community appreciated the significance of clean air areas, but not that the law in any way protected them. Early in 1968, the Na-

---

[6] John Muir, *The Yosemite*, pp. 255–256.
[7] 42 U.S.C. Sec. 1857-18571 (Supp. V, 1970).
[8] U.S. Congress, Senate, Committee on Public Works, *Senate Report No. 403*, 90th Cong., 1st sess., p. 2.

tional Coal Policy Conference distributed to its members *A Guide to the Air Quality Act of 1967*. In it, the NCPC emphasized the importance of "including in a control region only those areas absolutely necessary. . . ." Apparently, the NCPC felt that to do so would "permit a wider choice in location of new power plants outside of the area where the pollution problem is in fact serious."[9] The booklet explained that "this would permit plant location to be a meaningful alternative to substitution of fuels or other controls." This was precisely what environmentalists feared and what National Air Pollution Control Administration officials anticipated. However, the NCPC also recognized that "any State . . . may set more stringent standards for stationary sources in order to achieve a higher level of ambient air quality. . . ."[10]

Charged by Congress with implemnting the act, the National Air Pollution Control Administration set about its work early in 1968. NAPCA officials established an in-house task force to develop guidelines for state regulatory authorities. In a May discussion paper, Sidney Edelman, a member of the task force and chief of NAPCA's Environmental Health Branch, addressed himself to the problem of significant deterioration. "Not only is air quality to be 'enhanced,'" Edelman wrote, "but it is to be *protected*, obviously against a loss of quality or degradation."[11] According to his logic, "standard setting activity by the State is called for even if the level of air quality in the region is better than that which the criteria would require. . . ." For precedent, Edelman recalled that the Federal Water Pollution Control Administration (FWPCA) had adopted a nondegradation policy to implement the 1965 Water Quality Act. That provision stated that "in order to 'enhance the quality of the water,' standards shall include a provision to assure that present water quality will not be degraded."[12] Accordingly, Edelman rec-

[9] National Coal Policy Conference, *A Guide to the Air Quality Act of 1967*, pp. 11, 18.
[10] Sidney Edelman, Chief, Environmental Health Branch (HEW), "Draft Policy Statement on Guidelines for Review of State Ambient Air Quality Standards," May 21, 1968, p. 2, Administrative Records, Office of Air Quality Planning and Standards, U.S. Environmental Protection Agency, Research Triangle Park, N.C. (hereafter cited as EPA Air Quality Administrative Records).
[11] Ibid., p. 8.
[12] Ibid., p. 9.

ommended the following policy in his suggestions for the first draft of NAPCA's guidelines:

> To the extent that it [air quality] is better than the criteria with respect to other pollutants, the protection of the public welfare would call for the maintenance of such better air quality to the extent possible. In my view, an adaptation of the FWPCA policy which would protect the existing air quality in a region which is better than that called for by the air quality criteria should be established to serve the purposes of the Clean Air Act.[13]

Edelman made no mention of the FWPCA policy qualification that clean water qualities might be lowered where "such change is justifiable as a result of necessary economic or social development. . . ."[14] Until 1977, opponents of no significant deterioration continued to argue that the Sierra Club's manipulation of extraneous verbiage in the preamble of the 1970 Clean Air Act was solely responsible for the issue. But Edelman's paper confirms that NSD was fundamental to administrative interpretation of the 1967 Air Quality Act and had logical precedent in an even earlier policy for water pollution control.

NAPCA officials responsible for drafting the implementation guidelines were well aware of the difficulties in defining just what amount of deterioration was "significant." They recognized too the growth-limiting potential of an NSD requirement. For more than a year, they labored through a half-dozen drafts of the guidelines, repeatedly changing and debating the provision for maintaining clean air. In their earliest draft of October, 1968, they had emphasized, but did not go beyond, the need to "protect" the air against a loss of quality.[15] However, the next revision reflected second thoughts and included a provision to guard against NSD limits: "If the calculated air quality is appreciably less than the proposed standard, the implementation plan regulations will be considered unduly restrictive. States will be advised and some relaxing of the regulations may be made."[16] But in the third draft, which circulated in

[13] Ibid., p. 10.
[14] Ibid.
[15] "Draft of Guidelines, October 10, 1968," p. 3, EPA Air Quality Administrative Records.
[16] "Draft of Guidelines, October 29, 1968," pp. 1, 5, EPA Air Quality Administrative Records.

December, the deputy chief of abatement programs criticized the "inference that a policy of degradation is permissible."[17] In January, 1969, a fourth draft drew similar comments from the Bureau of Abatement and Control, where an official recommended that "a nondegradation statement is needed. . . ."[18] In the next to final draft (February, 1969), the issue was addressed, but without "degradation" or "deterioration" language: "Where air quality is already satisfactory . . . steps to protect and preserve it will be necessary . . . In any event, air quality standards that would permit a significant rise in pollution levels . . . would not be consistent with the intent of the Air Quality Act."[19] Throughout the spring of 1969, John Middleton, the commissioner of NAPCA, traveled about the country making speeches to explain the emerging policies for controlling air pollution. In Phoenix, for example, Middleton cautioned against "employing air quality criteria as a license to pollute the air up to a given level." In June, when he addressed air pollution regulators in Pennsylvania, Middleton explained rather bluntly that the act prohibited fouling up clean air.[20] If the business community had any contact with NAPCA officials at all or listened to Middleton's speeches, they should not have been so surprised in midyear when the Department of Health, Education, and Welfare published its *Guidelines for the Development of Air Quality Standards and Implementation Plans.* In it, the government stated its position quite clearly: "Air quality standards which, even if fully implemented, would result in significant deterioration of air quality in any substantial portion of an air quality control region clearly would conflict with this expressed purpose of the law."[21] While they may not have understood before, industrial interests fully appreciated the implications of this ruling.

[17] Dean S. Mathews, deputy chief, Abatement Program (NAPCA), Memorandum, December 30, 1968, EPA Air Quality Administrative Records.

[18] Marginal notations on "Draft of Guidelines, January 28, 1969" from Bureau of Abatement and Control, EPA Air Quality Administrative Records.

[19] "Draft of Guidelines, February 19, 1969," EPA Air Quality Administrative Records.

[20] John T. Middleton, Commissioner, NAPCA, "Air Conservation in 1969: Who Will Make the Decisions?" a paper delivered at the air pollution briefing in Phoenix, Arizona, February 4, 1969; idem, "Public Policy and Air Pollution Control," a paper presented at the Penjerdel Regional Conference, Swarthmore, Pennsylvania, June 11, 1969, pp. 4–5.

[21] U.S. Department of Health, Education, and Welfare, NAPCA, *Guidelines for the Development of Air Quality Standards and Implementation Plans.*

In its fifty-state protest of the guidelines, the American Mining Congress highlighted this clause as among the worst of HEW's abuses.[22]

As Senate and House committees began considering how to revise the Air Quality Act, the spotlight continued to shine on health problems and dirty air. Nonetheless, several national conservation groups turned out for the hearings in 1970 and continued to lobby vigorously throughout that year for tougher national policy. Once again, precise "no significant deterioration" language did not appear in the 1970 amendments, but the new act did retain the "protect and enhance" language used in the old Air Quality Act.[23] Moreover, the intent of that language was made clear during the public hearings. Robert Finch, secretary of Health, Education, and Welfare, testified before the House Commerce Committee that "one of the express purposes of the Clean Air Act is 'to protect and enhance' the quality of the Nation's air resources. Accordingly, it has been and will continue to be our view that implementation plans that would permit significant deterioration of air quality in any area would be in conflict with this provision of the Act."[24] Senator Edmund Muskie's subcommittee gave careful consideration to the same point. Senator John S. Cooper from Kentucky wanted clarification of this point and asked an HEW spokesman "if the region or an area had a certain air quality which might be higher than other areas of the country. . . . It could not be degraded; is that correct?" Undersecretary John G. Veneman responded, "Yes . . . we did not want deterioration of the air in those areas that may be below what the standard is at the present time."[25] Not surprisingly, the Senate report that accompanied the Clean Air Act explicitly stated that "the Secretary [HEW] should not approve any implementation plan which does not pro-

[22] AMC correspondence to Governors, July, 1969, Box No. 17, file CP-1, p. 6, NAPCA Contracts Records, U.S. Environmental Protection Agency, Air and Water Programs Office, Administrative Records, Federal Records Office, Suitland, Md., accession no. 412-73-5 (hereafter cited as NAPCA Contract Records).

[23] P.L. 91-604, 84 Stat. 1676, 42 U.S.C. Sec. 1857-18571.

[24] U.S. Congress, House, Committee on Interstate and Foreign Commerce, *Hearings on Air Pollution Control and Solid Waste Recycling*, 91st Cong., 2nd sess., March 5, 16–20, April 14, 1970, p. 297.

[25] U.S. Congress, Senate, Committee on Public Works, Subcommittee on Air and Water Pollution, *Hearings on Air Pollution*, 91st Cong., 2nd sess., 1970, pp. 132–133, 159.

vide . . . for the continued maintenance of . . . areas where current air pollution levels are already equal to, or better than, the air quality goals. . . ."[26] However, a major argument in industry's *amicus curiae* brief in the appeal of *Sierra Club* vs. *Ruckelshaus* was that no NSD provision was explicit in the Clean Air Act itself.[27]

It is conceivable that nothing of substance might ever have come of "protect and enhance" had not the coal coalition and the Department of Commerce pressed the removal of the NSD clause from the EPA's 1971 implementation guidelines. As discussed in chapter 6, when the EPA promulgated tentative ambient air quality standards in January, 1971, environmental interests vigorously sought the inclusion of an NSD provision. EPA officials had been preoccupied with ambient air standards to clean up dirty air and had made no mention of NSD. However, they willingly included the NSD qualifier when they revised the standards in April. Likewise, when they put out their proposed guidelines, they again omitted mention of deterioration. Persistently, environmental groups again urged that the EPA include the NSD clause in the guidelines. In June, Middleton agreed to do so. The fact that the well-established, national conservation groups were so carefully watching over the NSD concept at this early date indicates their concern, not for dirty air, but for clean air. Then in July, industrial interests intervened through the good offices of Maurice Stans, the OMB review, and possibly the White House, and forced the EPA to omit the NSD rule from the official guidelines published in August. Until then, NSD had remained only a bit of principle on paper. But when environmental activists angrily learned how Middleton's decision was revoked, they filed suit in the courts to force the issue. Once in the courts, "no significant deterioration" would either evaporate altogether or would have to become a practical reality.

When the Supreme Court affirmed *Sierra Club* vs. *Ruckelshaus* without opinion in 1973, the decision brought a storm of protest from the industrial community. Coal-related interests were the most

---

[26] U.S. Congress, Senate, Committee on Public Works, *National Air Quality Act of 1970*, 91st Cong., 2nd sess., 1970, S. Rept. 1196, p. 11.
[27] Senate, Nondegradation Hearings, 93rd Cong., 1st sess., July, 1973, pp. 279–281.

vocal critics because, as Carl Bagge put it, the decision "will stop the contruction of any new fossil fuel power plants in most of the United States. . . . It will also wash out any prospect of producing synthetic natural gas or petroleum . . . killing our best chances of meeting the energy crisis from our domestic reserves."[28] Spokesmen for the Edison Electric Institute and the National Rural Electric Cooperative Association joined Edwin Phelps, president of Peabody Coal, in calling on Congress to amend the Clean Air Act and alleviate this problem. Because NSD threatened economic growth, it was far too serious a measure to leave to administrative rule making, especially when the EPA had already shown its support for the idea.

While the wheels of the legislative mill began creaking slowly into action, the Environmental Protection Agency had to comply with Judge Pratt's ruling and develop a set of NSD regulations so that state implementation plans could be revised, approved, and put into action. EPA officials applied themselves furiously and in just a month proposed four alternative schemes for preventing significant deterioration. As usual, the EPA held hearings and elicited comments on the various plans. Both the Sierra Club and the Natural Resources Defense Council rejected all the EPA approaches and offered their own plans. The Sierra Club suggested that air quality deterioration be defined in terms of the concentration of air pollution averaged over a one-kilometer sphere, the center of which would be an emission source. EPA people rejected this proposal out-of-hand, both because it defined significant deterioration arbitrarily and because it "would impose severe growth restrictions" for which the Sierra Club has presented no rationale. . . ."[29] Under the NRDC proposal, "the total emissions in clean areas, plus a five percent increase, were to be divided by the total population in clean areas to arrive at the allowed per capita emissions."[30] That too was unsuitable, since it would determine plant site according to population considerations instead of location of natural resources.

In December, 1974, the Environmental Protection Agency se-

[28] Carl Bagge, quoted in *Pittsburgh Post-Gazette*, June 12, 1973.
[29] U.S. Environmental Protection Agency, *Technical Support Document— EPA Regulations for Preventing the Significant Deterioration of Air Quality* (EPA-450/2-75-001), pp. 10–11.
[30] Ibid., pp. 14–15.

lected the least offensive of its alternatives and made it official.[31] The NSD regulations applied to new industrial emissions in air regions that were cleaner than the pollution levels defined by the secondary ambient air quality standards. Since neither the Congress nor the Courts had defined *significant*, the EPA did its best to shift responsibility to state and local governments by arguing that any definition had to be predicated on social, economic, and environmental factors that vary from one area to another. What it did do was to identify "classes" of different allowable increments to the existing levels of suspended particulates and sulfur oxides. These increments were very small, as little as 3 percent of the secondary sulfur standard for a Class I area.[32] Initially, the EPA identified three classifications of air quality areas, but it would be up to the states and federal land managers to make the choices. Class I applied to areas in which practically any change in air quality would be considered significant. Class II were to be areas in which deterioration that normally accompanied moderate, well-controlled growth would be less than significant. Class III applied to all other areas in which deterioration up to the national primary standards would be allowed.[33] As one might expect, the EPA rules satisfied neither coal nor environmental interests, and both promptly filed court suits and renewed their appeals that Congress resolve the issue by statute.

There were a number of good reasons why coal interests so adamantly opposed the NSD concept, and among them, frustration and a total lack of sympathy for limits-to-growth thinking ranked high. The coal industry had been down for a very long time, taking second place to government-sponsored nuclear power, government-

[31] 39 *Federal Register* 42513, December 5, 1974.

[32] Ibid., p. 42515. The increments that were allowed above baseline concentrations are as follows:

Pollutant	Class I	Class II
Particulate matter		
annual geometric mean	5 $\mu g/m^3$	10 $\mu g/m^3$
24-hr. maximum	10 $\mu g/m^3$	30 $\mu g/m^3$
Sulfur dioxide		
annual arithmetic mean	2 $\mu g/m^3$	15 $\mu g/m^3$
24-hr. maximum	5 $\mu g/m^3$	100 $\mu g/m^3$
3-hr. maximum	25 $\mu g/m^3$	700 $\mu g/m^3$

[33] Ibid., p. 42514.

subsidized petroleum imports, and government-regulated natural gas. In 1975, for the first time in more than two decades, the prospects for coal were looking up. Coal was to be "America's Ace in the Hole."[34] All the studies by banks, the National Petroleum Council, and the Federal Energy Agency, agreed that coal seemed to be the only viable energy fuel on which the United States could build.[35] Environmentalists were successfully blocking construction of nuclear power plants, and the capital costs of nuclear-generated electricity were rising out of sight. Reserves of natural gas were down to less than seven years, and scarcely any gas had been available for new customers since 1973. Since the United States had become dependent on imported petroleum for nearly 50 percent of its supply, OPEC, the cartel of foreign producers, had been able to raise prices more than 400 percent. And since most energy authorities believed that solar power was hopeless in the immediate future, it looked as if coal would have to carry America's industrial growth at least into the twenty-first century.

Of course, there were several potential impediments to the coal revolution about which coal leaders worried. Financial forecasts indicated that too little capital would be available for the massive coal-energy investments needed in the next decade. Environmentalists constantly warned that, particularly in the West, water resources were inadequate for significant energy expansion, either for reclaiming strip mines and cooling power plants, or as process feedstock for coal gasification and liquefaction. Then, too, there were the various problems that the push for federal strip-mining controls threatened. But "no significant deterioration" raised the most serious problem, the spectre of limits to growth. Perceptively, coal people recognized that NSD was not merely a clean air measure. Indeed, many saw it as a cloak for something far more pernicious. "I am not at all sure," wrote Keith Doig, a Shell Oil vice-president, "of the sincerity of some of the proponents [of NSD]—in fact, it appears

---

[34] This is the title of a widely marketed film made for the National Coal Association; it became the slogan for the NCA in its published materials after 1975.

[35] For example, see National Petroleum Council, *U.S. Energy Outlook: A Summary Report*, pp. 4–6; Federal Energy Administration, Project Independence Blueprint Final Task Force Report, *Project Independence*.

that genuine concern for our environment is being used by others to achieve quite different objectives." Doig warned Shell stockholders that "some 79 percent of all the electrical generation capacity now planned for the next decade could not be built" if the Congress upheld the EPA regulations for NSD.[36] Coal people could deal with substantive problems like water resources and capital. But just when the energy crisis had given coal a new lease on the future, it seemed inconceivable that a responsible government could allow air pollution controls to thwart coal's solution to the energy crisis. As Gary Knight put it on behalf of the U.S. Chamber of Commerce, NSD would "mandate undeveloped areas [of the U.S.] into eternal poverty."[37]

The coal coalition and the larger business community were not alone in pressuring Congress to dispose of NSD. President Gerald Ford and the newly organized Federal Energy Administration (FEA) objected strongly to the NSD notion. The administration's solution to the energy crisis was Project Independence, a grand plan for reducing dependence on oil imports from OPEC by building up the coal industry and stimulating the development of a huge new synthetic-fuels industry to gasify and liquefy coal. Late in 1973, various administration spokesmen began publicly criticizing a variety of "overly-strict" air pollution controls, including, and most especially, no significant deterioration. Dr. Betsy Ancker-Johnson, assistant secretary of commerce for science and technology, denounced as "unnecessarily stringent" air quality standards that called for degrees of purity not justified by the concomitant socioeconomic costs.[38] John Love, the president's energy czar, complained that "outside of the major cities, there is much overkill in the state emission limitations."[39] These were practical people, not unlike most businessmen, who had come to accept the need to mitigate the health hazards that industrial pollution had caused. But, basically,

[36] Keith Doig, quoted in Shell Oil Company, *Shell Shareholder News*, November, 1975, p. 2.

[37] Gary Knight, U.S. Chamber of Commerce, quoted in *Wall Street Journal*, June 8, 1976.

[38] Quoted in Southern Coals Conference, *Commentary and Research Service* 34 (October, 1973), 2.

[39] Quoted in Southern Coals Conference, *Commentary and Research Service* 34 (September, 1973) 2.

they believed in the principle of continued industrial growth and could neither understand nor sympathize with those who shared Muir's values or, worse, rejected the growth premise of industrial capitalism. And in still more practical terms, they did not believe that NSD and Project Independence could coexist. In March, 1975, the FEA released the required environmental impact statement on the administration's Energy Independence Act. That report devoted special attention to the problem of NSD: "The significant deterioration regulations could have a major inhibiting effect on the location of new power plants and new energy resource development projects. . . . The regulations could preclude the siting of such facilities in areas zoned for minimal, or even moderate amounts of deterioration [i.e., Class I and Class II]."[40] Thus, the Ford administration could no more accept the existing constraints on energy development than could the coal community, and under these various pressures, the Senate Public Works Committee and the House Commerce Committee once again took up the problems of federal air pollution controls.

The Clean Air Act Amendments of 1977

Technically, Senator Muskie's hearings in 1975 were for "oversight" of the 1970 Clean Air Act rather than for consideration of a particular amendment. Simply put, the energy crisis had overtaken environmentalism, and Congress had to resolve the conflict between these two public issues. Jennings Randolph, chairman of the Public Works Committee, made an introductory remark that put the problem of federal environmental policy in precisely this perspective: "We are beginning today against a background of growing concern for the economic conditions within our country and also the problem of adequate energy supplies. . . . I have a personal regret . . . that there are those who would use this situation . . . to weaken the pollution programs that have been enacted into law by Congress in

---

[40] Federal Energy Administration, *Draft Environmental Impact Statement: Energy Independence Act of 1975 and Related Tax Proposals* (DES 75-2), quoted in U.S. Congress, Senate, Committee on Public Works, Subcommittee on Environmental Pollution, *Implementation of the Clean Air Act—1975*, 94th Cong., 1st sess., April, 1975, p. 664.

the name of securing a plentiful energy supply. . . ."[41] But there was a deeper conflict that soon became evident. For the coal coalition, the larger business community, and the Ford administration, the energy crisis and its proposed solution, Project Independence, symbolized the values of industrial prosperity and continued economic growth. For many environmentalists, and particularly the activist staff of larger conservation groups, the Clean Air Act's constraints, especially NSD, symbolized the primacy of natural values and the rejection of industrial growth as a worthwhile national goal. Because the issues symbolized these larger value differences, the controversy was to be intense and prolonged and compromise to be reached only with the greatest difficulty. Moreover, the technical complexities of the issues and the weight of countervailing documentation added to the obstacles.

But it was the incredible diversity of pluralist interests gathering around clusters of issues that made this political contest among the most intricate and thoroughly lobbied since the Taft-Hartley Act in 1947. Russell Train, administrator of the EPA, offered the first testimony in the long battle. Because he did not share the Ford administration's desire to emasculate the Clean Air Act, he straddled the issue in a way that made the political problems intelligible. First, he based his testimony on the energy crisis and the problems it caused. "The Clean Air Act must take account of these problems," said Train. "This is not a time to dismantle the Act, but rather a time to provide necessary flexibility to deal with the problems at hand. . . ."[42] "Flexibility" translated into coping with three problems. First, something had to be done about the majority of metropolitan areas that would not have achieved the ambient standards by the June (1975) deadline. Second, it was evident that because automobile manufacturers were trying to improve fuel efficiency, they could not also comply with the act's deadlines for cleaning up vehicular emissions. Third, and most important, the Congress had to resolve the no-significant-deterioration controversy. Literally hundreds of interest groups were concerned with at least one of these

---

[41] Senate, *Implementation of the Clean Air Act—1975*, 94th Cong., 1st sess., March, April, 1975, p. 134.
[42] Ibid., pp. 140–152.

three problems. Conservation groups and energy developers cared most about NSD. Automobile manufacturers, city pollution regulators, retail, wholesale, and parking lot interests cared about vehicular emissions.[43] And established manufacturers, energy suppliers, and urban environmentalists eventually focused on "nonattainment" of primary standards. For Congress, this was more than three separate struggles. It was to mean Machiavellian alliances, partisan frictions, log-rolling, and compromising among the politicians who represented the conflicting interests in each of the three areas of contention.

Unlike the Congress, President Ford and his administration had a clear vision of the changes needed. When Interior Secretary Rogers Morton presented the administration's proposed changes, it was evident that he shared none of Russell Train's qualms about dismantling the act. The very first point in his testimony was that "since coal conversion is the keystone of an effective energy program . . . we have problems resulting from court decisions with respect to significant air quality deterioration." Once the NSD delay was resolved, then other changes could be made. "We intend," said Morton, "to develop an intermediate program to meet our energy needs . . . using more coal and assuring that the clean air standards which power plants have to meet are reasonable." Evidently, both NSD and the standards would have to go. Finally, Morton announced that it was necessary to delay compliance schedules for power plants "in relatively isolated locations," but not past January 1, 1985.[44] Environmentalists in the audience no doubt waited breathlessly to hear what Frank Zarb would have to add on behalf of the Federal Energy Administration. Zarb was already recognized as the administration's most outspoken critic of environmental constraints and growth-threatening measures. He laid out in more precise detail just what the administration wanted of Senator Muskie's committee. First, he wanted the law amended to allow the use of "intermittent controls" by power plants instead of requiring scrubbers. That meant

---

[43] The political contest over automobile emissions was intensely fought and was a major aspect of the whole policy controversy. However, it is beyond the scope of this study, and is treated only peripherally when it impinged on the coal-related issues of NSD and "nonattainment."

[44] Ibid., pp. 280–281.

dispersion instead of clean-up. Second, he asked for variances to allow manufacturers and power plants to convert from oil to gas to coal. Third, he recommended "that the Clean Air Act be amended to provide a five year suspension of automobile standards" along with staggering increases in the allowable concentrations of pollutants in automobile emissions. Finally, Zarb got to the most serious problem. He explained that "the litigation on the significant deterioration issue was initiated in 1972—at a time when the country lacked a unified national policy on energy." Apparently suggesting that by 1975 there was such a policy, Zarb argued that there was a need to construct "large, coal-fired power plants in the short term, and synthetic fuel facilities in the longer term." The problem was that "the significant deterioration regulations could have a major inhibiting effect on the location of new energy projects." So the bottom line of the administration's shopping list was a request for "Congress to provide that the Clean Air Act does not require or authorize EPA to establish standards more restrictive than primary and secondary ambient air quality standards."[45]

It would be needlessly redundant to catalogue the legions of witnesses who testified at Muskie's hearings, especially since the hearings were only a preliminary investigation of interest-group wishes and no bill other than the administration's was actually before the committee. However, to appreciate subsequent events, it is necessary to identify the precise objectives of industrial and environmental interests that related to coal-energy development. Surprisingly, environmentalists, even in the face of the energy crisis, were by no means on the defensive. Although only two environmental organizations testified at the hearings, they were the most professional and technically skilled of the lot. The Natural Resources Defense Council addressed only two issues: ambient standards and vehicular emissions. David Hawkins, NRDC's spokesman, took the EPA to task for having promulgated criteria for only four of sixteen pollutants originally proposed in 1969. Moreover, Hawkins argued that scientists had since discovered that those four criteria were inadequate to protect human health. Accordingly, he not only recommended continued tough enforcement for noncompliance areas,

[45] Ibid., pp. 320–347.

but that the criteria and associated standards be made more rigorous.[46] Even more startling was Richard Lahn's testimony on behalf of the Sierra Club. While virtually the entire business community and the Ford administration were demanding that Congress revoke the NSD regulations, the Sierra Club devoted its entire statement to criticizing the weaknesses of the EPA's existing NSD regulations and recommended an entirely different and far more rigorous scheme. Lahn defended the concept of no significant deterioration by reminding the senators that sixteen states had filed *amicus curiae* briefs on behalf of the Sierra Club's position. Moreover, besides most conservation groups, NSD had the support of the National League of Cities and the U.S. Conference of Mayors. While these groups were not exactly concerned with pristine air, they did have a very good reason for favoring NSD. Since electric utilities and large manufacturers were unable to expand their facilities in urban areas without using the most advanced and expensive scrubber equipment, they preferred to move to the relatively unpolluted countryside as a compliance alternative. Urban mayors and eastern industrial states recognized this as a serious economic threat and said so in their brief to the Supreme Court:

> The health of the economies of urban-industrial regions is dependent upon industrial continuation and growth. It is in the best economic interest of these regions that sources remain in them and utilize the emission controls necessary. . . . The requirement of no-significant deterioration prevents rural regions from allowing lenient emission controls that are so much less expensive that an industry will have a financial incentive to relocate . . . no-significant deterioration removes the possibility of economic coercion between competing regions. . . .[47]

This alliance of strange bedfellows was just one of the many peculiar political twists in what was becoming a maze of air pollution policy. The Sierra Club's chief complaints with the existing NSD rules were that the increments presently allowed by the EPA were far too large and covered only two pollutants, not six. Lahn introduced a dramatically different scheme that would lump together all

[46] Ibid., pt. 2, pp. 1600–13.
[47] Ibid., pt. 1, p. 852.

areas where air was cleaner than the national standards and would set a rigorous allowable increment for all major pollutants. This plan, he argued, would not seriously affect growth, assuming use of the best available control technologies. He dismissed industry's fears and problems as nothing more than "the natural tendency of some leaders of industry and government agencies to become emotional when told that the old way of doing things isn't good enough." According to the Sierra Club spokesman, such fears should simply "be discounted."[48]

Notwithstanding Lahn's opinion, industry leaders had despaired of the old way of doing things and were all in favor of making drastic changes in the existing federal programs for controlling air pollution. Spokesmen for the coal coalition felt that even Gerald Ford's proposals were inadequate, and, with amazing consistency, they proposed an entirely new conceptual approach to air pollution. Petroleum, steel, mining, smelting, and electric utility interests all suggested what amounted to four basic changes. First, there should be no emission standards stricter than those necessary to achieve the primary ambient air standards, and, intermittent controls should be accepted as an alternative to scrubbers. Second, compliance deadlines should be postponed for at least five years to meet the contingencies of energy crisis. Third, state implementation plans and their entire system of emissions standards should be scrapped. Instead, when it was necessary to meet the primary ambient air standards, the EPA should determine emission standards solely on the basis of commercially available, fully proven control technologies. Fourth, and most emphatically, the government should completely forget about the concept of no significant deterioration.[49] Nearly every industry recommendation was based on industry's view of the energy crisis, inflation, and the impact of existing regulations on continued economic growth and future energy development. Where the regulations did not absolutely threaten growth, coal spokesmen argued that the excessive costs of compliance were contributing to de facto limits on growth by draining huge amounts of capital (or

48 Ibid., p. 910.
49 Ibid. See pt. 1, pp. 840–848, 1056–1600, and pt. 2, pp. 1621–41, and 1792–99.

consumer spending power where the costs were passed on) away from growth investments. Paul Geist, executive vice-president for New Mexico Public Service, made this final point decisively when he described the Four Corners Power Project. Not only was his company spending "$3,000 to $4,000 per acre to reclaim surface-mined land which can be purchased for $25 to $50 per acre," but even while NSD had yet to be implemented, his utility had already "committed to spend more per kilowatt on a scrubber system than we paid per kilowatt of power plant less than 8 years ago."[50]

By April, 1975, when the fourteen days of hearings were over, it seemed as if years of conflict and the pressures of energy crisis had driven both environmentalists and the coal coalition to extreme positions that lacked continuity with the past. Moreover, it was clear that Congress would be hard-pressed to bridge the immense gap that separated energy development and growth-limiting environmentalism. In June, Senator Muskie's subcommittee began working on a bill. After five months and twenty-four markup sessions, it reported S. 3219 to the full Public Works Committee, which spent another three months and twenty-four markup sessions making further revisions. In the House, Representative Paul Rogers' committee began working on its bill later and spent even longer. For both committees, the two largest bones of contention were no significant deterioration and automobile emissions. In managing his bill, Senator Muskie's biggest problems were Lloyd Bentsen (D-Tex.) and Gary Hart (D-Colo.), whose views on automobile emissions were diametrically opposed. Bentsen was determined to give the Big Three an extension and raise the allowable emission levels, whereas Hart wanted even tougher standards than already existed. In the full committee, Howard Baker (R-Tenn.) was the senior minority member with the unenviable task of pressing the administration's proposals without much help from either James Buckley (C-N.Y.) or Pete Domenici (R-N. Mex.). Representative Rogers had somewhat more difficulty holding his bill together in the very large House Commerce Committee chaired by Harley O. Staggers (D-W. Va.). The automobile industry's two leading advocates, John Dingell (D-Mich.) and James Broyhill (R-N.C.) were committee members and

[50] Ibid., pt. 1, p. 866.

were determined to give Detroit a five-year extension. During the markup, several of the most closely contended amendments related to NSD. Although pro-Detroit and anti-NSD people voted together for the most part, nearly all the amendments failed by narrow margins.[51]

While Congressional committees labored over the amendments, the coal coalition attacked no significant deterioration in court, hired consulting firms to forecast the economic consequences of NSD, and generally publicized the impending threat to economic growth and energy independence. On January 2, 1975, the American Petroleum Institute, on behalf of nine of its largest members, filed suit against the Environmental Protection Agency to block implementation of the NSD rules. All eight corporate petitioners were mining or developing coal, and all held extensive coal reserves. Several were leading developers of synthetic fuels processes, and one, Union Oil, was deeply involved in oil shale development.[52] Much of the case was argued on the findings of two immense studies API had commissioned. One study concluded that accurately monitoring air pollution in the small quantities necessary to implement or enforce NSD regulations was impossible.[53] The other study, conducted by geologists at Kent State University, attacked the concept of "buffer zones" apparently implied in the EPA's implementation program for NSD. This study's devastating maps showed that the NSD regulations could inhibit the development of as much as 86 percent of West Virginia's coal and significant although lesser amounts in other Appalachian coal states.[54] According to the API brief, "In the West,

---

[51] *Not Man Apart*, analysis of the House Commerce Committee voting on H.R. 10498, May, 1976, p. 9.

[52] American Petroleum Institute, "Brief for Petitioners," United States Court of Appeals for the District of Columbia Circuit, No. 75-1665. Besides API, the petitioners were Standard Oil (Ohio), Atlantic Richfield, Continental Oil, Exxon, Gulf Oil, Mobil, Shell Oil, Texaco, and Union Oil of California.

[53] Greenfield, Attaway & Tyler, Inc., *An Examination of the Accuracy and Adequacy of Air Quality Models and Monitoring Data for Use in Assessing the Impact of EPA Significant Deterioration Regulations on Energy Development (EF75-58R)*, August 8, 1975.

[54] John T. Anderson et al., *Reserve and Resource Data on Coal, Uranium, and Oil Shale in the States of North Dakota, South Dakota, Montana, Wyoming, Colorado, Utah, Michigan, Ohio, Kentucky, Tennessee, and West Virginia*, April 19, 1975. Also, summary report on same, May 12, 1975.

with its extensive deposits of oil shale and uranium in addition to coal, the inhibitive effects of the regulations would be even more severe." The "inhibition" zones for Class I areas would lock up 61 billion tons of Montana coal, 34 billion tons in Wyoming, and 100 percent of the extractable shale-oil deposits in Colorado and Utah. From this, the API concluded that "in addition to the implications of the regulations for our national energy supplies, the inhibitive effects of the Class I and shadow zones raise serious concern for the economic survival of the rural areas of the Nation."[55]

Before long, the alarming conclusions of these studies began appearing outside the court, circulated among western Congressmen, state and local trade associations, and newspapers in the coal fields.[56] In Missouri, for example, the state Chamber of Commerce issued a pessimistic press release and an ominous map of Missouri based on API materials. Glen Scott, the Chamber's executive vice-president, announced that half the state, "the area south of the Missouri River . . . will face a virtual stalemate in future growth if this amendment passes."[57] The Missouri Department of Natural Resources immediately took the whole NSD issue under study. Electric utilities were also at work on the costs of NSD. The Electric Utility Clean Air Coordinating Committee hired the National Economic Research Associates (NERA) to see how the costs of NSD would affect consumers. Under the direction of Dr. Lewis Perl, NERA completed studies in December, 1975, and April, 1976. They showed that if NSD were implemented, it would cost Texas consumers $2,625 per household over the next fifteen years. Consumers in the rest of the nation, except the Northeast, would have to pay anywhere from $228 (Mid-Atlantic) to $2,115 (South Central) extra for NSD.[58] Like the other studies, these reports by NERA re-

[55] API, "Brief for Petitioners" (No. 75-1665), pp. 10–11.

[56] See for example, Holmes Alexander, "The Clean Air Act," *Martinsburg Journal*, January 28, 1976.

[57] Missouri Chamber of Commerce and Missouri Oil Council, "News Release," April 6, 1976, p. 2.

[58] Lewis Perl, National Economic Research Associates, "An Analysis of the Costs to the Electric Utility Industry of House and Senate Significant Deterioration Proposals," December 12, 1975. Also, idem, "Estimated Costs for the Electric Utility Industry of Nonsignificant Deterioration Amendments Currently Considered by the United States Senate," April 16, 1976.

ceived wide circulation in the media.[59] Industry apparently hoped that such reports would have some effect on public and congressional attitudes toward no significant deterioration. Indeed, it had cause to be concerned after a 1975 poll by the Opinion Research Corporation had "showed that 94 percent of the American people opposed a policy of dispersing air pollution into areas which still have clean air and favor keeping clean air areas as clean as they are now."[60]

By the end of 1975, as word of the Senate committee markup activities started leaking out, coal leaders became even more worried. Carl Bagge, in a speech to a gathering of coal operators, made quite clear that the National Coal Association, along with the utilities, oil companies, and other coal interests, was in real danger:

> Congress has turned a deaf ear on all of the Administration's pleas . . . both the Senate and House subcommittees have added injury to injury by writing a hazy environmental slogan into their bills. You have heard the slogan before . . . it's called no-significant deterioration and it has already caused the coal and electric utility industries more harm than any other single interpretation of the Clean Air Act. . . . This decision can and, no doubt, will be used to halt development across the land . . . but instead of removing this obstacle to energy development, the House and Senate subcommittees have amplified its impact by writing it into the law. . . .[61]

Bagge concluded his speech by calling on all coal people to take immediate action and "get involved in this personally."

He was right about the congressional committees. In February, 1976, the Senate Public Works Committee reported out a tough bill that would allow automobile manufacturers only a one-year delay and that approved NSD regulations almost identical to the EPA's. In May, the House Commerce Committee reported its bill with somewhat weaker NSD provisions and a two-year delay for Detroit. Floor debate in both houses lasted for several months. Throughout the summer, literally scores of amendments were offered and voted

---

[59] See, for example, *Journal of Commerce*, April 26, 1976, and *Dominion-Post* (Morgantown, W. Va.), April 23, 1976.

[60] U.S. Congress, House, Committee on Interstate and Foreign Commerce, *House Report No. 94-1175*, 94th Cong., 2nd sess., May 15, 1976, p. 117.

[61] Carl Bagge, "Let's Set aside the Slogans," reprinted in Southern Coals Conference, *Commentary and Research Service* 37 (January 15, 1976), 162.

on. A veteran staff member of the Public Works Committee described the lobbying as "the most overwhelming campaign I've seen in the ten years I've worked on Capitol Hill."[62] Nearly all the lobbying and all the debate clustered around the two crucial issues of NSD and auto emissions. Muskie and Rogers, floor managers of the two bills, were nearly exhausted by the time their bills passed in August and September, respectively.

At the end of May, President Gerald Ford made a personal appeal to Jennings Randolph and Harley Staggers (chairmen of the Senate Public Works and House Commerce committees) expressing his "serious reservations concerning the amendments dealing with auto emissions standards and prevention of significant deterioration." The president had previously asked that the "Congress clarify their intent by eliminating significant deterioration provisions," but now it had nearly gone and done the opposite. So as the floor debate began, Ford warned party leaders of the potential harm involved in their actions: "In view of the potentially disastrous effects on unemployment and on energy development . . . I believe the most appropriate course of action would be to amend the Act to preclude application of all significant deterioration provisions. . . ."[63] He also recommended that they vote for the pending Dingell-Broyhill amendment on auto emissions. Muskie's bill included a tougher NSD provision than did the House bill, and it was in the Senate, on August 3, that the NSD issue came to a head after days of debate. Already several Republican Senators, including minority leader Hugh Scott (Pa.) and Jake Garn (Utah) had unsuccessfully tried to amend the crucial section, but the amendment most likely to succeed was one introduced by Democrat Frank Moss (Utah) to delay NSD rules for a year so the situation could be studied further. This modest-sounding proposal was intended to separate NSD from the package of clean air amendments, leaving it with a far narrower base of support in the future. Senators defending the Moss amendment spoke repeatedly and at length on the disastrous effects of NSD on energy supply, inflation, and economic growth. The bill's de-

---

[62] Quoted in National Wildlife Federation, *Conservation Report*, no. 13 (May 7, 1976), p. 162.
[63] *Congressional Record*, June 3, 1976, p. S8447.

fenders cited recent studies showing that NSD would not harm growth and argued that the rules had already been in effect (an exaggeration) for eighteen months and the economy was still functioning. When the vote came, only thirty Senators voted with Moss, and the amendment failed. Environmentalists considered its defeat the biggest environmental victory of the Ninety-fourth Congress. The vote for the amendment had come from southern conservative democrats, western energy states with multiple national parks, Appalachian coal states, and supporters of the Dingell-Broyhill amendment for auto emissions. But a majority of eastern, central, and Pacific state senators prevailed.[64]

A month later, the House rejected an amendment by William Chappell (D-Fla.) to strike the NSD provision from its bill. Although the vote was fairly close, its outcome reflected majority satisfaction with the already compromised NSD provisions in H.R. 10498. However, a few days later, the House adopted the Dingell-Broyhill amendment to freeze existing emissions standards for automobiles and to delay the compliance deadline until 1982. Thus, late in September, the conference committee faced the task of resolving sharp differences in the two bills on the two most controversial issues. The result was that the conferees from the Senate backed away on the automobile emissions, and the House members accepted most of the Senate's provisions for no significant deterioration.

By the first of October, it appeared as if the struggle in Congress was over, although the coal interests continued to hope that President Ford would veto the bill as he had twice before with the strip-mining bills. But the two Senators from Utah, Frank Moss and Jake Garn, refused to give up. Their state encompassed a larger percentage of federally owned land than any other state in the lower forty-eight, and zones of inhibition nearly covered Utah. Moreover, just three months earlier, Southern California Edison had conceded defeat in its battle to build the largest coal-fired power plant ever conceived. For nearly thirteen years, the California utility had planned to build a 3,000-megawatt plant costing nearly 4 billion dollars on the Kaiparowits Plateau of Utah. It would have consumed

[64] National Wildlife Federation, *Conservation Report*, no. 22 (August 6, 1976), p. 268.

60,000 tons per day of Utah coal and been the biggest stimulus to the Utah economy since the arrival of Brigham Young. In the words of a bitter utility executive, environmentalists were responsible "for beating the project to death" for the sake of protecting Utah's air from significant deterioration.[65] So in the closing days of the Ninety-fourth Congress, Moss and Garn filibustered, threatening to block final passage of other legislation if the Clean Air Act amendments were not set aside. With less than a day left before recess, congressional leaders agreed to table the bill indefinitely, saving Gerald Ford from having to make a veto decision.[66]

The accession of Jimmy Carter to the presidency meant, among other things, that Edmund Muskie and Paul Rogers would not have to work against a hostile administration. During his campaign, Carter had strongly endorsed most environmental goals, specifically mentioning amendments to the Clean Air Act. Thus, in 1977, there was to be neither a veto threat nor agitated Energy and Interior officials testifying against no significant deterioration. But there was plenty of political excitement over the development of a new major policy issue. Section 110 of the old 1970 act authorized the EPA to prevent any new industrial sources of pollution from being constructed in any air region that had not achieved compliance with the ambient air quality standards. Prior to the mid-1975 compliance deadline, this point had been moot, and even then, EPA gave most urban areas the maximum extension of two years. However, this meant that after June, 1977, the Environmental Protection Agency faced the problem of what to do about seventy-four major cities that had yet to comply with the standards for at least one pollutant. Realizing the implications of this provision in the existing law, environmentalists pressed the EPA to enforce "nonattainment" meas-

---

[65] See, for example, Jack McLellen, "Kaiparowits, Southern Utah at the Crossroads," Sierra Club Bulletin, August, 1975, pp. 6–7, 25–27; Wall Street Journal, September 7, 1976, and October 20, 1977; High Country News, April 23, 1976.

[66] It should be noted that, by and large, the news media erroneously attributed the demise of the Clean Air Act Amendments of 1976 to the intense lobbying of the automobile industry. Certainly, Detroit had been adamant, even threatened to curtail production, but the Dingell-Broyhill amendment alleviated their worst concerns. It was the coal coalition's opposition to no significant deterioration, with its potential for constraining energy development, that resulted in Congress' failure to amend the Clean Air Act in 1976.

ures. The House bill in 1976 had anticipated the emerging problem and sought to provide a construction variance in dirty cities "to allow reasonable economic growth."[67] The Senate filibuster had thus killed not just the NSD mandate, but also the variance on "nonattainment." So in December, 1976, the EPA was obliged to promulgate an interpretative ruling that set in force "offset" requirements. Simply put, the EPA rules meant that for a new industrial plant (or major modifications) to locate in a still-polluted city, it not only would have to use "best available control technology" (BACT), but also would have to arrange for an "offset" reduction of existing emissions, equal to or greater than its projected addition, from some other source in the city.[68] In other words, nonattainment (or "offset") did for industrial areas what NSD did for undeveloped areas— threatened to limit industrial growth and economic prosperity. The new policy caused an uproar in the business community and among urban government officials.

In February, 1977, when Edmund Muskie convened his subcommittee for its fifty-seventh day of hearings on the Clean Air Act, its members faced three major issues rather than two, and the universe of affected interest groups had suddenly expanded by at least one-third. Between the Senate and House hearings, literally hundreds of organized interests either testified or submitted statements. It seemed that either NSD, nonattainment, or vehicular emissions threatened not merely the basic coal-energy industries, but also shopping centers, automobile dealers, stone crushers, hotels and motels, building contractors, food marketers, paper makers, painters, retailers, druggists, truckers, and realtors. Among the groups were thirty-nine national trade associations, nine national environmental groups, three industrial unions and the AFL-CIO, countless corporations, regulators, local government officials, commercial groups, and in a rare congressional appearance, the Business Roundtable.

Apparently, the Business Roundtable, a new industry organization with 176 members who were chief executive officers of major

[67] U.S. Congress, House, Committee on Interstate and Foreign Commerce, *Clean Air Act Amendments of 1976,* 94th Cong., 2nd sess., May 14, 1976, H. Rept. 94-1175, pp. 177–181, 346–347.
[68] 41 *Federal Register* 55525, December 21, 1976.

corporations, replaced the old NIPCC as the coordinating agent of the energy industry's political position. Speaking for the Business Roundtable, Frank Milliken, president of Kennecott Copper, told Representative Rogers' committee what was in store for it during the next few days of hearings:

> You will hear testimony from corporations and trade associations representing the basic American industries--oil, chemicals, paper products, electric power, mining, and steel. These industries, together with the automobile industry, are the most heavily involved in compliance with the entire spectrum of federal environmental regulation. . . . Each of these industries will present information designed to assist the subcommittee in its deliberations on amendment of the Clean Air Act.[69]

Before the larger presentation began, Milliken summarized the two overwhelming concerns of the energy-intensive industrial community: "We are convinced that the two major stationary source issues encompassed in H.R. 4151 [are] those dealing with nondeterioration and nonattainment. . . ." Milliken concluded that "it would be ironic if the enactment of more stringent, and unnecessary, environmental regulations in the cause of improving the quality of life ultimately served to reduce the quality of life by deterring other, equally important economic and social goals."[70] Never before had such a large segment of the industrial community so thoroughly and formally coordinated a public presentation on any political issue before the Congress. Under the aegis of the Business Roundtable and in response to impending limits to growth, an even larger political coalition, an "energy coalition," had superseded the coal coalition.

During the hearings, the energy coalition's strategy was to present evidence that documented the technical and economic problems that NSD and nonattainment policies threatened and to ask that the two policies not be mandated by statute immediately, but be set aside temporarily for further study and consideration. Surprisingly, few congressmen on either the Senate Public Works or House Commerce committees seemed in the least receptive to this

---

[69] U.S. Congress, House, Committee on Interstate and Foreign Commerce, Subcommittee on Health and Environment, *Clean Air Act Amendments of 1977*, 95th Cong., 1st sess., April, 1977, pt. 2, p. 1081.
[70] Ibid., p. 1083.

apparently reasonable proposal. And the evidence that the industrialists presented was enough to devastate even the most ardent environmentalist. For example, a Texaco executive, representing the American Petroleum Institute, testified that "constraint on growth in the petroleum industry and in the other basic industries in our economy is far more serious than is generally recognized." He made the extraordinary point that for Amoco and Gulf Oil, NSD and nonattainment actually overlapped in one situation. Those two firms were involved in the 5,000-acre Rio Blanco oil shale experimental tract in Colorado. At that location, the air was very clean in terms of sulfur oxides and particulates and was thereby eligible for a Class II NSD designation. However, it was a noncompliance area with respect to hydrocarbons and oxidants and was also eligible for nonattainment constraints. It would not be easy to build an experimental oil shale refinery.[71] A panel of utility officials, coordinated by the Edison Electric Institute, presented the usual massive studies (authored by Lewis Perl of NERA) that showed the cost per household ($26) of the proposed NSD regulations to be higher than the cost of the existing EPA rules criticized the year before. Congressman Rogers rejected out-of-hand the assumptions of the new NERA study and curtly dismissed Dr. Perl and the other Edison Electric Institute witnesses.[72]

The centerpiece of the American Mining Congress's statement characterized NSD and nonattainment as "two concepts that . . . actually relate to growth/no-growth issues." The AMC argued that "federal regulation of growth in this context should be confined to providing procedural guidelines that will assist the states to arrive at rational judgments. . . ."[73] On its surface, this statement does not appear unique, but it said something very important. By this point in 1977, the debate had moved beyond particularistic concerns for environmental quality. It had come to focus more explicitly on economic growth. Indeed, the AMC was no longer even arguing limiting growth, but was merely asking that regulation of growth be left

[71] Ibid., p. 1204.
[72] Ibid., pp. 1570–71.
[73] U.S. Congress, Senate, Committee on Public Works, Subcommittee on Environmental Pollution, *Clean Air Act Amendments of 1977*, 95th Cong., 1st sess., February, 1977, pt. 2, p. 506.

to local authority. In a sense, it was as if twenty years had brought the conflict between the energy industry and environmentalists full circle, once again arguing federal versus state authority, but on a different issue—that of limiting growth rather than of actually cleaning up the environment.

Although nine national environmental organizations made statements at the hearings, their efforts seemed nearly superfluous. The intricacies of the crucial provisions had been carefully worked out over nearly three years, and environmentalists could find little to criticize in the committee bills. However, throughout the spring markup sessions, lobbying by the energy interests remained intense, and the congressmen gradually relented and made a number of important changes. In both the Senate and House committees, the nonattainment restrictions were rewritten. Generally, states were given the opportunity to develop new implementation plans and compliance schedules for the air regions that had yet to achieve the ambient standards. For the new plans, the deadline was extended until 1982 (or until 1987 for certain pollutants). New plants could be constructed without the "offset" reduction, although the additional net pollution by 1982 would have to be less than the ambient standards. Another new provision allowed fossil-fuel power plants a compliance extension until 1987 in instances where they would use "experimental" clean-up technology. While these changes alleviated the most immediate no-growth fears of urban industrialists, they were backed with rigorous penalties for polluters who did not meet the revised compliance requirements on schedule.[74] Both committees wrote several loopholes into their NSD provisions to allow "flexibility" for siting power plants and energy centers. For example, at the behest of Senator Dale Bumpers (D-Ark.), Muskie's committee raised the acreage minimum for national parks requiring mandatory class I designation from five to six thousand acres. As Bumpers explained to Utah's exasperated Jake Garn, the change exempted Hot Springs National Park, which was actually "not a park" as much

[74] U.S. Congress, Senate, Committee on Environment and Public Works, *Clean Air Act Amendments of 1977*, 95th Cong., 1st sess., May 10, 1977, S. Rept. 95-127, pp. 54–55, 143–149; also, U.S. Congress, House, Committee on Interstate and Foreign Commerce, *Clean Air Act Amendments of 1977*, 95th Cong., 1st sess., May, 1977, H. Rept. 95-294, pp. 13–15, 207–217.

as a resort city, for otherwise "it would be caught up in absolutely no growth . . . which would literally destroy any future hopes" the locals might have had.[75] The House committee not only raised the NSD increments but agreed to a major change, the Breaux amendment (John Breaux, D-La.). It provided a waiver of the class I increments for sulfur oxides for eighteen days during the year. That was precisely the variance the four-billion-dollar Intermountain Power Project needed, and had asked for, if it were to be built in south central Utah.[76]

During floor debate, both the House and the Senate agreed to extend the compliance deadline on automobile emission standards for two years, until 1980. In the Senate, there were any number of challenges to NSD, most of which were promoted by Utah's Senator Garn. After several of his proposals to eliminate NSD failed, Senator Ted Stevens, an Alaska Republican, substituted the Breaux amendment for Jake Garn's final amendment. Because that amendment had already passed the House and had more organized support, Stevens, concerned for economic growth in his own huge state, hoped it might slip by. However, President Carter intervened with a strongly worded letter opposing the Senate's adoption of the Breaux amendment, and it was defeated by a 61 to 33 margin.[77] Late in July, the House-Senate conference committee met to resolve the final differences between the two bills. By then, the House and Senate were largely in agreement on both nonattainment and automobile emissions. No significant deterioration, as always, remained the outstanding controversy. The Senate version established a size of 6,000 acres,

[75] *Congressional Record,* June 9, 1977, S9242.

[76] The Intermountain Power Project was a consortium of municipalities and utilities that planned a 3,000-megawatt, coal-fired power project in south-central Utah, nine miles west of the Capital Reef National Park. Proposed changes in the House Bill would have changed that park's NSD designation to class I. The project, planned for compliance with class II NSD rules, would then have exceeded the class I standards several days each year, when there was a temperature inversion, on several mountain peaks in the park. Project spokesmen appealed to Congress for a waiver on the grounds that they were already committed to spend $580 million on pollution control equipment and had received the necessary air pollution permits. After five months of committee discussions and floor debate, the Congress agreed to the waiver. See, House, *Clean Air Act Amendments of 1977,* 95th Cong., 1st sess., May, 1977, H. Rept. 95-294, pp. 1572–75.

[77] *Congressional Record,* June 9, 1977, pp. S9271, S9278.

in contrast to the House bill's 25,000 acres, as the minimum for national parks that would be designated "mandatory" Class I NSD areas. The conference adopted the Senate's acreage designation as well as its tougher Class I increments. In return, however, the Senate conferees agreed to adopt the Class II increments and the waiver provision, the Breaux amendment, that were in the House bill.[78] Having resolved that problem, the conference quickly reported out the final bill, and in August, Jimmy Carter signed it into law. Of course, the politics were far from over and would continue as the EPA and the states moved forward to implement the new law. But the passage of the 1977 Clean Air Act Amendments, along with the strip-mining law a month earlier, marked the culmination of two decades of political conflict over coal-related environmental policy.

[78] U.S. Congress, House, "*Conference Report to Accompany H.R. 6161*," 95th Cong., 1st sess., August 3, 1977, H. Rept. 95-564.

8

Coal and the Public Interest

THE national environmental policies adopted in the summer of 1977 were the results of a modernizing process that began in the 1840's. It was during that decade that coal started replacing renewable energy resources—wind, water, and wood—as the basic fuel for industry. That change in energy source stimulated the process efficiencies, geographic flexibility, and energy intensity necessary for the factory system to expand and marked the beginning of the end of preindustrial social and economic patterns.[1] Until then, work, production, and community had been tied to the land, bound by the limits of dispersed solar energy, and largely consistent with the rhythms of nature. So in perspective, it is understandable and fitting that coal, the essence of industrial growth and antithesis of traditional society, became the object of an environmental reform movement and the subject of intense political conflict that culminated in challenging some of the premises of industrial growth. Moreover, it is certainly not a coincidence that political activity to mitigate stationary-source air pollution and the ill effects of coal strip mining began near the end of the 1950's, a decade of unprecedented industrial growth and modernization. Nor is it surprising that a growing

[1] Henry Adams, *The Education of Henry Adams,* chap. 33, "A Dynamic Theory of History," and chap. 34, "A Law of Acceleration," pp. 474–498; Alfred Chandler, *The Visible Hand: Managerial Revolution in American Business,* pp. 76–77; Philip Scarpino, "A Quest for Order—Energy as a Factor in Change Over Time" (unpublished paper, University of Missouri at Columbia, 1978).

coalition of energy industrialists contested environmentalists every step of the way, finally attaining compromise national policies in the context of energy crisis.

By accelerating the modernizing process, World War II escalated the intensity of coal's impact on the natural environment. Postwar elaboration of new technologies made coal mining and combustion more environmentally offensive to a greater number of people. Before 1941, strip mining coal was a marginal sort of business endeavor, suited only to isolated pockets of very shallow coal seams. But during the 1950's, manufacturers were able to produce ever larger and more energy-intensive strip-mining equipment that made stripping profitable at greater depths and thus over a far wider area. At the same time, some coal operators, by merger or reinvestment, were able to attract the capital and build the management necessary to expand the scope of their strip-mining operations. As strip mining began to affect more people by more serious environmental damage, those most affected, the sportsmen and conservationists, began to react. The technology of coal-fired generation of electricity underwent a similar modernizing process. The economies of scale and the availability of new metals and boiler designs encouraged ever-larger generating units. Bigger generating units meant more centralized energy production by bigger utility companies and, with it, more concentrated emissions of air pollutants. The beginnings of an "all-electric" promotion during the 1950's meant not only that the volume of stationary-source air pollution increased, but also that it became more intensely concentrated in urban-industrial areas. This modernizing tendency of the power industry focused emissions problems, which, when combined with increasing vehicular hydrocarbons and periodic temperature inversions, caused health experts and conservationists to become concerned.

As the social costs of coal development multiplied, they stimulated a variety of political initiatives and reactions. Among the earliest was the modernizing-reformist response by health experts who wished to investigate the problem scientifically and to search for a technical solution. The groups that called for the first national air pollution conference in 1958 were heart and lung disease organizations, state and city health officials, and professionals in the surgeon general's office and the Department of Health, Education, and

Welfare. The solution as they saw it was for the federal government to finance more research on the health effects of air pollution and on the development of pollution control technology. During the next two decades, this professional involvement continued to grow and expanded into an ever-larger bureaucratic system of health and air pollution expertise. Since strip mining, at least in the early 1960's, did not seem to threaten human health, it did not stimulate a parallel modernizing response by professionals, with the possible exception of fishery biologists alarmed by acid mine drainage.

Amateur conservationists took an entirely different view of coal-related environmental problems, looking for solutions not from technology, but from government intervention. During the 1950's, organized groups like the Sierra Club began to shift their attention from park creation and wilderness protection to the growing physical impact of industrialism upon the natural environment. This too was initially a modernizing response to fix faulty market mechanisms. By 1961, conservationists and sportsmen in Pennsylvania were demanding that the state force entrepreneurs to clean up their mining operations. Since free enterprise obviously failed to provide the incentive necessary to guarantee that all production costs be internalized, the government should act as the agent of the consumer and force producers, in this case strip miners, to mitigate the environmental side effects of their endeavors. With respect to air pollution, conservationists initially asked industrialists voluntarily to internalize the social costs of cleaning up. But voluntarism was inconsistent with competition and with management's obligations to maximize profit, and conservationists quickly shifted to asking government to force clean-up on industry. In 1970, when the immense costs and technological problems of emissions control appeared to have halted progress, environmentalists moved a step further and began seeking policies that demanded control of pollution regardless of cost.

Backed by the public's enhanced awareness and concern for environmental problems after 1970, some environmental activists began pursuing legislative and administrative policies that reflected a desire to curb industrial growth rather than correct its abuses. Such initiatives, which included efforts to ban strip mining and to enforce absolute standards for nondeterioration, scarcely reflected a national consensus or even unanimity among environmentalists. Nevertheless, they did command increasingly widespread support among national conservation organizations and in the opinion polls. An expanding body of intellectual literature on the limits to growth, the accumulated frustration with the plodding progress of environmental reform, and the American people's increasing preoccupation with leisure activities provided the basis for this new direction in environmental activism and public policy.

A third kind of response, that of energy industrialists, was to resist government intervention, hasty and inefficient alterations, and commitment of capital to nonproductive ends. Indeed, this was not an illogical business response. When the problem first arose in the late 1950's, business leaders, like most others, assumed that government was responsible, in large measure, for paying the social costs of mitigating pollution. Moreover, if there were to be some limited regulation of the incorrigible few, it should be at the state and local levels to assure flexible implementation. Most corporate managers were quite willing to contribute to the research effort and to use technological solutions when they were proven effective and commercially feasible. Reasonable costs for clean-up and reclamation could easily be passed on to consumers. But reclamation beyond returning the land to useful purposes and pollution control beyond safeguarding human health seemed unreasonable and impractical and was rejected out-of-hand.

The more pragmatic corporate managers did not seriously oppose environmentalism until 1969 when HEW published health criteria that seemed to go beyond what was necessary to assure human health. Even then, members of the coal coalition did not become truly agitated until 1971, when the strip-mining bills introduced by Senators Nelson and McGovern and the EPA's implementation guidelines threatened to usurp managerial prerogatives, to demand solutions to unsolved technical problems, and to impose serious costs and constraints on growth. From then on, for businessmen and environmentalists alike, the rhetoric increased, the political conflict intensified, and the values grew more polarized.

The principal objective of this study has been to examine the form and substance of interaction between business and government during a twenty-year evolution of public environmental policy. Of course, any attempt to draw generalized conclusions risks oversimplification, since at the outset neither business nor government is itself a coherent entity. At best they are interacting systems of individuals and organizations with only limited consistency in the behavior of their parts. To this extent, the notion of a coal coalition is a somewhat artificial construct, useful for organizing data and generating a perspective but problematic in that it obscures internal frictions and risks overstatement. Certainly there were some differences in the policy preferences between eastern and western coal producers or between electric utilities and oil companies, just as there were among environmental activists who embraced different notions of limiting growth, of health criteria, or of reclamation standards.

Those qualifications notwithstanding, it is nonetheless evident that the traditional pluralist model of fragmented units competing independently in the marketplace of public policy does not accurately characterize the recent history of coal-related, environmental politics. Two reasons for the inadequacy of that model stand out. By the late 1950's, the process of industrial modernization had begun to forge a new series of financial and technological linkages among coal-related firms. Those interdependencies led naturally to new organizational relationships within and among trade associations and semiofficial advisory councils. Thus, by the end of the 1960's, a growing structural framework lent itself to a broader based, interindustry political system. Moreover, at least until 1977, neither the ideological premises nor the practical effects of environmental reform posed significant, persistent sources of dissension among the majority of coal coalition members. Very few businessmen accepted the rationale for cost-inefficient, technologically impractical regulations. Fewer still bought the notion of limiting economic growth. And, once the policy debate over reclamation and air pollution reached the federal level, the reform provisions at issue rarely implied any wholesale, income-redistributive effects among coalition members (although each clause might have a greater or lesser effect on particular firms in different circumstances). Thus unified political purpose and interlinked organizational system led to relatively concerted and sustained political behavior by a very large sector of American industry.

This pattern of interest-group organization suggests several interesting implications for the American political process. A greater and more diverse number of businessmen became involved in making public policy. For example, as late as 1972, professional papers on even the technical aspects of strip mining or air pollution drew little attention at the trade associations' national conventions. But by 1977, whole sessions of those conventions were devoted to the impact of new environmental regulations and the consequences of pending policy issues. Likewise during the 1970's, large corporations devoted more and more staff resources to public policy issues, while the chief executive officers of smaller firms began testifying more frequently before Congress and submitting technical position papers to federal regulators. From the business perspective, this politicization is a healthy sign suggesting greater participation by an informed electorate. As Irving Shapiro, chairman of the Business Roundtable put it, "a lot of business people don't understand the political system. It's only in recent years that businessmen have come to recognize that there's a job to be done and you can't do it sitting in your office."[2] On the other hand, consumer advocates and populists see the new political activism of business, especially its cohesiveness as in the case of the coal coalition, as a threat to democratic decision-making.

The accumulation and coordination of political influence by a large sector of business involved a number of trade-offs. This problem was particularly evident in 1973–1974 when the Mansfield and Seiberling amendments to the strip-mining legislation threatened to pull the coalition apart along east-west lines. Likewise, in 1977, the pressures and contradictions between no significant deterioration and nonattainment raised some barriers between industrial interests concentrated in developed areas and those expanding into the more pristine, rural areas of the West. In both instances, trade groups like the National Coal Association and the Edison Electric Institute had to blur their policy positions somewhat in order to avoid alienating individual members. For the Business Roundtable, which tried to distill the disparate coal as well as automobile manufacturer interests into a single, coherent policy position, the only acceptable solu-

[2] Irving Shapiro, quoted in *Business Week*, December 20, 1976, p. 63.

tion was to recommend further study of NSD and nonattainment. Thus, the need for internal consensus seemed to impose a ceiling on the effectiveness and range of coordinated political action by business.

In rhetoric and substance, the environmental politics of coal reflected both adversary and cooperative relationships between business and government. In one instance, J. A. Overton spoke of working with new congressmen and EPA officials; at another point, Carl Bagge called for fighting those who would impose the undesirable rules and regulations. As the coal coalition, the environmental issues, and the regulatory apparatus evolved, the business-government relationship displayed an ambivalence that had also characterized the politics of reform during both the Progressive era and the New Deal. At times it appeared as if the technical complexities of the issues were leading to a new, more positive relationship between business and government. In 1974, Walter Hamilton, director of the National Industrial Pollution Control Council, described his organization as "the next and logical extension of the new concept of business-government partnership. . . ."[3] But by 1979, many former NIPCC members were fighting the Environmental Protection Agency tooth and nail over the implementation of the Clean Air Act Amendments and the Surface Mining Control Act. Notwithstanding the steady trend toward greater governmental involvement in business affairs, it seems that deep-seated traditions in American law, politics, and ideology dictate a continued ambivalence.

Besides its effects on political organization, the modernizing process has significantly altered the arena of political debate as well as the forum of decision making. After 1967, the technical complexity of environmental policy issues increasingly escalated beyond the grasp of nonexperts while discretionary authority accumulated in administrative agencies. The quantity of strippable versus deepmineable coal reserves, the availability of effective scrubber technology, and the capital and consumer costs of a given emission standard are examples of key issues in the political debate about

[3] W. A. Hamilton to S. T. Small, April 28, 1970, Box No. 9, "Memos," file, National Industrial Pollution Control Council, Administrative Records, Department of Commerce, Washington, D.C.

which most congressmen, staffers, affected businessmen, and environmentalists—let alone the press or the general public—knew little. The hearing record for the very committees determining policy bears frequent witness to this problem. In floor debate, even such congressional experts as Senator Muskie occasionally appeared at a loss when dealing with issues raised by difficult air pollution data. And at the state level, this problem amplified a hundredfold and was painfully evident, for example, in the proceedings of Pennsylvania's Environmental Quality Board.

As a result, the details of public statute were frequently resolved in debate among a handful of experts. While this situation is hardly unique to environmental issues, it nevertheless has diminished the efficacy of an informed electorate, or even its representatives, to govern on behalf of the greatest good. Moreover, the importance of complex data to the policy debate has afforded unique political leverage to those who command the resources to provide elaborate cost studies and technical briefs. This in turn has made amateur lobbyists and grassroots participants even less effective and has stimulated still more complex political coalitions that can afford the necessary consultants and staff experts.

The growing complexity of the policy issues also contributed to shifting more and more discretionary authority from the legislature to administrative agencies and to the courts. In the case of Pennsylvania's regulation of strip mining, the law eventually became something akin to a guideline. Under William Guckert's pragmatic command, regulation proceeded as a bargaining process in which day-to-day decisions bore little resemblance to the statutes. At the national level, a similar situation developed after 1967 when the Congress, in the Air Quality Act, delegated authority for national health criteria, determination of air quality regions, and implementation guidelines to the National Air Pollution Control Administration. Likewise, the 1970 Clean Air Act authorized the EPA to promulgate national air quality standards, new-source performance standards, and vehicular emission standards, and to determine, in its guidelines and approval procedures, the appropriate technologies and enforcement systems states and corporations might use. More recently, the 1977 Surface Mining Reclamation Act, itself a lengthy and detailed document, has led to an immensely complicated and discretionary set of administrative rules that coal producers believe has vastly exceeded the intent of Congress.

A related development has been the expansion of court dockets for the adjudication of administrative rulings. The best example of this phenomenon was the case of *Sierra Club* vs. *Ruckelshaus*, in which the Court's interpretation of a three-word phrase that appeared in, but then was removed from, the EPA's 1971 implementation guidelines, eventually resulted in a fundamentally new concept for regulating air pollution and in major revisions in the Clean Air Act. Such judicial interpretation is hardly new, but the scope and volume of the new discretion has recently reached proportions that affect the institutional organization of the political system itself.

By the mid-1970's, administrative decision-making (and to a lesser extent judicial) had become the crucial focus of far greater political activity than two decades earlier. From this study, which has emphasized how administrative politics have shaped environmental policy, it is fairly obvious that amateurs have been severely limited in the influence they can exert on administrative rulemaking. The procedure is too technical and bureaucratically complicated. Moreover, the forum of agency decision-making is even less public than is the legislature. When EPA specialists met with industry engineers in 1971 to discuss sulfur oxide control techniques, there was certainly no countervailing interaction with environmentalists. Nor should there necessarily be. The point here is simply that more and more decisions involving true policy issues result from a technocratic institutional arrangement of informal, business-government interaction. And, as government continues to expand its involvement in highly complex business affairs, the democratic political process will continue to evolve in that direction.

The law, as J. W. Hurst characterized it for the nineteenth century, allowed for the free release of energy and, one might add, for the free release of environmental pollutants as well.[4] Even when coal's environmental impact was acknowledged as a significant social cost, few attributed full responsibility for clean-up to either business

[4] J. Willard Hurst, *Law and the Conditions of Freedom in the Nineteenth-Century United States.*

or government. During the past twenty years, that ideological perspective has changed considerably, and with it the law. The two bills enacted during Jimmy Carter's first year as president articulate a national policy of balancing preindustrial values against the force of industrial modernization. Neither the strip-mining act nor the clean air amendments will stop economic growth or energy development. However, both go a long way toward qualifying the merits of free-wheeling energy use. Both laws reflect a desire to mitigate and internalize, as far as practicable, the social costs of energy production.

The Surface Mining Control and Reclamation Act of 1977 purports to prohibit strip mining where reclamation to original environmental quality is not feasible or possible. Where it is, the law appears to require that the environment be fully restored. Likewise, the Clean Air Act Amendments made a sincere effort to assure that ambient air quality standards, regardless of expense, be attained everywhere by 1987. It protects air quality in natural environments to a degree many think impossible and restricts new construction in developed areas that have failed to attain the national goals. Before the year 2000, more than $100 billion of natural wealth will likely be spent on compliance with these mandates. If these two national policies do accurately mirror social values, then there has been a very considerable change in those values since the Eisenhower era.

However, final judgment should perhaps be withheld. During 1978–1979, a bitter political struggle that involves utilities, coal producers, congressmen, miners, and federal regulators has been raging over the promulgation of new-source performance standards for sulfur oxides. The states have just begun the intensely political process of reformulating their NSD classifications. Coal operators and state governments are suing the federal Office of Surface Mining over its reclamation rules and enforcement procedure, while polluted cities are resisting the constraints of the nonattainment provisions. All of which only suggests that the two 1977 acts merely marked the beginning of yet another round in the environmental politics of coal.

Appendix A

Technical Aspects of Coal Surface Mining

"SURFACE mining" describes several methods for removing coal from the ground by first removing all the earth and rock lying above the coal seam. The percentage of coal produced by surface methods, as opposed to deep or underground removal, has increased steadily since World War II. By 1975, approximately one-half the 640 million tons of coal produced was mined by surface removal methods. There have been four essential differences between surface and deep mining that have accounted for the rapid growth of surface mining. First, at least for small and medium-sized mines, the initial capitalization and development lead-time has been smaller for surface than for deep mines. Thus, it has been easier for a firm to enter the coal industry via surface mining. Second, surface mining has been more efficient, in terms of the amount of coal that can be removed from a given seam, than has deep mining. A surface mining operation can generally remove as much as 80 or 90 percent of the coal in the ground. A third difference has been the role of labor and the safety requirements. The majority of deep miners, unlike surface miners, are unionized, and work in a deep mine has always been extremely dangerous. Since 1970, federal health and safety requirements for deep mining have added tremendously to its costs and contributed to declining productivity. The fourth and most crucial difference has been the environmental damage caused by surface mining. Until the 1970's, surface-mine operators took little care or expense to control environmental damage from the mining operation or in reclaiming the land they mined. Altogether, these four considerations have made surface mining more efficient economically than deep mining by a factor of as much as four.

Surface-removal methods fall generally into three categories: area mining, contour mining, and auger mining. *Area mining* is applied to relatively flat terrain where one or more horizontal coal seams lie within about 150 feet or less of the surface. After an area has been cleared of trees and drilled and blasted to loosen the rock, an excavator removes a swath of the "overburden" (material lying above the coal seam). A few state laws require that this process include segregating the topsoil from the other overburden material. Once bared, the coal is removed by smaller equipment (typically shovels or front-end loaders) and carted out the end of the pit by truck. Successive parallel cuts are made, and the overburden removed from each swath is placed in heaps ("spoil banks") in the previous cut so that the process of refilling the pit is continuous. Area mining is the most efficient surface-mining technique and is particularly appropriate for the flat and gently rolling terrain and relatively thick, near-surface coal seams in the West and Midwest.

Contour mining is the process of removing coal from along the edge of a slope, traversing the contour of the slope with reference to the coal seam, for perhaps miles. The expression *strip mining* derives from the ugly, snake-like scars this mining method left in the Appalachian hills. A cut is made into the slope at a point where the ratio of overburden depth to the seam thickness maximizes the amount of coal to be profitably removed (see figure A.1). Until recently, the overburden was cast down slope, thus opening a bench transverse to the contour, from which coal could be removed by truck and hauled away along the previously opened bench. Regulations in some states have necessitated variations of this process to alleviate some of the environmental damage. In Pennsylvania, for example, the "modified block cut" became necessary to comply with Pennsylvania's prohibition against leaving highwalls and disturbing downslope areas. In this method, only the overburden from the first cut is cast downslope. The overburden from each succeeding, transversely adjacent cut, is refilled by truck or loader in the bench of the previous cut (see figure A.2). This technique has been applied

FIGURE A.1

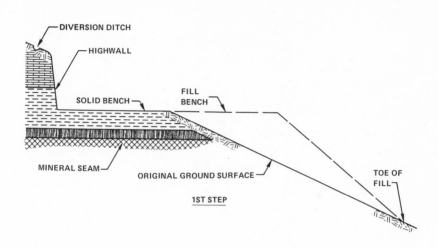

DIVERSION DITCH

HIGHWALL

SOLID BENCH

FILL BENCH

MINERAL SEAM

ORIGINAL GROUND SURFACE

TOE OF FILL

1ST STEP

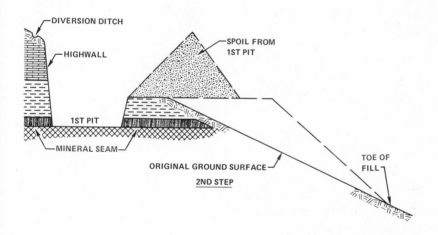

DIVERSION DITCH

HIGHWALL

SPOIL FROM 1ST PIT

1ST PIT

MINERAL SEAM

ORIGINAL GROUND SURFACE

TOE OF FILL

2ND STEP

FIGURE A.2

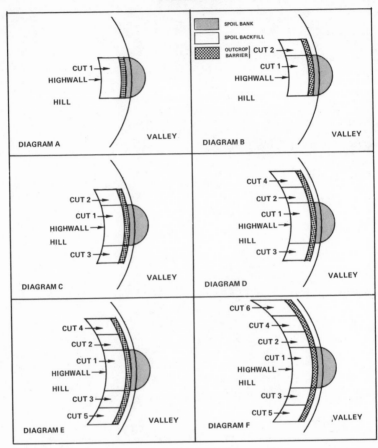

MODIFIED BLOCK CUT

successfully and economically to slopes of up to twenty degrees.[1] There are other variations for less damaging, steep-slope mining, such as "boxcut" and "low-wall barrier," which are also improvements on the old-style, contour cut-and-run practices, but they still create erosion and slides and leave a highwall behind.

Auger mining is usually ancillary to contour mining. This pro-

[1] Lee Saperstein and Edwin Secor, "Improved Reclamation Potential with the Block Method of Contour Stripping," a paper presented at the Research and Applied Technology Symposium on Mine Land Reclamation, March, 1973, Pittsburgh, Pa.

cess involves boring horizontally into a coal seam where its edge is exposed at the highwall where the contour operation ceased. Large augers, as much as six feet in diameter, can penetrate two or three hundred feet into a hill, forcing the remaining coal back out of the hole like wood shavings produced by a drill bit. Augering accounts for only a fraction of total surface-mine production, but it is important because it adds considerably to the resource efficiency of the contour-mining process. Its principal environmental problem is acid water discharge, but that can be reasonably mitigated by inserting a plug of non-acidic overburden material to seal off the mouth of the auger hole.

A multitude of environmental problems derive from coal surface mining, and prior to the 1960's most were written off as unavoidable side effects of a necessary industrial process. Generally, there are three kinds of problems: the creation of a pit (or bench), the destruction of vegetation in the mining area, and the pollution of adjacent surface waters and underground aquifers. The water problems have been the most serious and difficult to mitigate. The Department of Interior has catalogued thousands of miles of eastern streams that have been biologically ruined by acid mine drainage from coal mining. This chemical form of water pollution is produced by the leaching and oxidation that occurs when sulfur-bearing rock formations are exposed to air and water in the mining process. Most coal, especially in the eastern and midwestern fields, is riddled with both organic and inorganic sulfur. Aquatic biota are particularly susceptible to destruction by sulfates and sulfides released into water courses. And, in addition to creating the acid condition, coal surface mining creates physical water pollution by erosion and sedimentation from mining operations and inadequately reclaimed slopes.

The Environmental Protection Agency has identified five groups of procedures for avoiding water pollution from strip mining: methods for handling pollution-forming materials, waste-water control, controlled mining procedures, water infiltration control, and erosion control.[2] Carefully designed mining methods can themselves be deterrents to water damage. For example, one recent improvement in

[2] Environmental Protection Agency, *Processes, Procedures, and Methods to Control Pollution from Mining Activities*, 1973.

contour mining leaves behind a mineral barrier as a deterrent to downslope drainage and leaching (see figure A.3). Segregation of acidic and inert overburden, with burial of the acidic materials at the base of the highwall, is another method for reducing acid drainage. Drainage and runoff channels on the final reclamation contour can also be used effectively. And, finally, where water pollution is unavoidable, the water can be treated before release by such techniques as settling ponds, lime acid neutralization, and regulated discharges to receiving streams to help assimilation. Some western coal fields have a particularly difficult water problem that became a heated issue in the debates over federal strip-mining controls. There are some formations in Wyoming and North Dakota where the thick coal steam is itself the aquifer. Obviously, removal of the coal upsets the underground hydrography, and in a land where water has always been a scarce and valued commodity, such disruption has been a major concern to environmentalists and water users.

A second large problem created by strip mining is the pit from which coal and overburden have been removed. To what extent should it be refilled? Or, in contour mining, to what extent should the highwall be reduced? Simply put, environmentalists have sought the maximum reclamation of "approximate original contour," whereas mine operators have favored varying degrees of partial regrading. The problem on steep slopes is keeping the overburden from moving downhill both during and after the mining operation. In open-pit mining, especially in the West where the coal seams removed can be very thick (as much as 120 feet in some places), the problem is having enough overburden to recreate an original contour. And, in both cases, restoring the original contour is expensive. There are some alternatives to original contour restoration recognized by some state laws and the 1977 federal law. In West Virginia, some stripping operations have permitted "mountain top removal," where what was a hill becomes a plateau intended for housing, commercial, or recreational development. As one might expect, environmentalists have been particularly leery of the utility of such projects. Another variation, widely used in many states, has been to leave the final cut in an area mine unfilled so that it becomes a lake, ostensibly for recreational purposes. However, it must be clear to the reader that until 1977, with the enactment of the federal law, only one state,

Pennsylvania, required reclaiming strip mines to "approximate original contour." Elsewhere, partial refilling and partial highwall regrading was the rule for more than three decades.

Revegetating disturbed areas is the third important aspect of surface mine reclamation. Prior to the 1970's, few states required much in the way of assuring successful revegetation, but it should be noted that many mine operators have partially revegetated their lands on a voluntary basis for years. Those efforts have had a mixed degree of success. While some states have required minimal replant-

FIGURE A.3

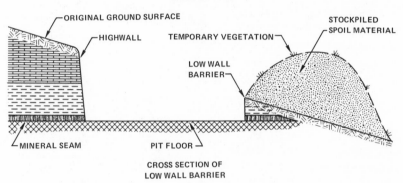

CROSS SECTION OF
LOW WALL BARRIER

ing, none have provided for long-run follow-up to guarantee that the planting would continue to thrive. Even where the soil has been segregated, it has been difficult to grow worthwhile vegetation because of the damage done the soil's nutrient value, the rock mixed into the soil, and the soil's pollution by sulfide and metallic materials. The surface-mining industry purports to have done substantial research in developing natural and hybrid trees and shrubs that grow in reclaimed areas. Moreover, they have defended their reclamation efforts, identifying model tracts of healthy woodlands, game areas, and even productive grazing and crop sites. In sharp contrast, environmentalists have claimed that few reclaimed areas to date have recovered properly, since the soil takes hundreds of years to redevelop healthy properties. Once again, the West presents special problems for revegetation. Not only is the average annual rainfall less in the West than in the Appalachian fields, but the precipitation is irregular, creating extreme conditions of flood or drought.[3] Such conditions, combined with generally thinner topsoil, result in more fragile ecosystems that are far more difficult to rehabilitate after the trauma of strip mining.

All these reclamation problems and dozens of still more technical matters have made for a very complex political environment in which the controversy over federal surface-mining regulation was waged. Understandably, command and manipulation of technical data became an essential lever for influencing policy.

[3] National Academy of Sciences, *Rehabilitation Potential of Western Coal Lands*, a report to the Energy Policy Project of the Ford Foundation. For a summary of the historical problems of environmental damage from strip mining, see U.S. Department of the Interior, *Strip Mining and Our Environment*.

Appendix B

Stationary Source Air Pollution: The Technical Issues

ALTHOUGH coal contributed to only 20 percent of America's total energy consumption in 1970, it provided more than half the fuel energy for generating electricity.[1] And coal's share of the electric generating market has continued to grow during the 1970's. Large amounts of coal are also used in the primary metals industries, both as coke and for generating electricity and process heat.[2] The combustion of coal, especially by these two industries, generates the bulk of all air pollution from stationary sources. Particulates, nitrogen oxides, and sulfur oxides are the three most serious contaminants released by coal combustion.

Particulates are pieces of ash that result from incomplete combustion. Relatively large particulates called "fly ash" constitute smoke, most of which was brought under control by local ordinances that resulted from antismoke crusades between the 1890's and early 1950's. However, microscopic particles, as small as 500-millionths of a meter in diameter continued to be emitted outside California until after the passage of the 1970 Clean Air Act.[3] During the 1960's, scientists determined that particulates not only pose a serious health

[1] U.S. Department of the Interior, Bureau of Mines, *Minerals Yearbook, 1971*.

[2] Office of Science and Technology, *Patterns of Energy Consumption in the United States*.

[3] U.S. Department of Health, Education, and Welfare, *Air Quality Criteria for Particulate Matter*, p. 12–2.

hazard, but also contribute to various ill effects on photosynthesis, vegetation, fabricated materials, and the visual aesthetics of the environment.

Oxides of nitrogen, particularly nitric oxide (NO) and nitrogen dioxide (NO_2), are a second group of pollutants emitted when coal is burned. They are thought to have indirect health effects as agents of photochemical smog. Moreover, a considerable body of laboratory and epidemiological evidence suggests that exposure to high NO_2 concentrations can increase airway resistance and possibly produce pulmonary edema and aggravate acute bronchitis.[4] However, because evidence on nitrogen oxide health effects has remained incomplete, it did not crystallize into a clear policy issue until 1977 and has thus been treated only peripherally in this study.

The third and most serious coal pollutant is sulfur oxide gas. The sulfur content of coal generally ranges from 0.5 percent to as much as 5 percent of the coal. When coal is burned, the sulfur content yields gaseous emissions containing twenty-five to thirty parts of sulfur dioxide (SO_2) to one part of sulfur trioxide (SO_3).[5] In the atmosphere, SO_2 is partly converted to more SO_3, and that sulfur trioxide is further converted to suspended sulfuric acid in the presence of moisture. For the most part, the health problem of sulfur oxides relate to irritation of human respiratory systems. These health hazards are further aggravated by synergism between sulfur oxides and particulates.[6] Laboratory studies have linked sulfur oxide concentrations to respiratory problems, and epidemiologic evidence has correlated sulfur oxide concentrations with morbidity rates. Because of its seriousness, the sulfur emissions problem has been the most heated issue in the development of federal policies for controlling air pollution.

Emission control has stimulated a whole new field of technology and a new set of economic realities for industrial processes that pollute. More efficient combustion, fabric filters (called "baghouses"), and electrostatic precipitators are the three principal methods for

---

[4] U.S. Environmental Protection Agency, *Air Quality Criteria for Nitrogen Oxides*, pp. 11–3 through 11–8.
[5] U.S. Department of Health, Education, and Welfare, *Air Quality Criteria for Sulfur Oxides*, p. 10–2.
[6] Ibid., p. 10–7.

controlling particulate emissions. The widest use of fabric filters has been in the steel and foundry industries, where this thirty-year-old technology has become capable of removal efficiencies greater than 99 percent.[7] The electrostatic precipitator is the primary particulate control device for electric utilities, where removal efficiencies higher than 99 percent are attainable only at very high costs and energy expenditures.[8]

The most serious stationary pollution problem has been the sulfur emissions, and coal-fired power plants are their principal source. Sulfur oxide emissions from such plants increased from 10 million tons in 1963 to 16 million tons by 1972.[9] Although the total amount of SO_2 in the nation's air had dropped by 27 percent by 1976, the concentration of SO_2 in 106 urban counties where the majority of Americans live still exceeded the health tolerance levels mandated in the 1970 act.[10] To date, there have been two general options for controlling sulfur emissions. Sulfur oxide emissions can be substantially circumvented by burning coal with a low sulfur content. Or, sulfur oxides can be removed after combustion by treating emissions with flue gas desulfurization (FGD) devices, commonly called "stack gas scrubbers." There is a third alternative that has been favored by coal-consuming industries. Most notably, the Edison Electric Institute, American Electric Power, and the TVA have endorsed using tall stacks and "intermittent control" techniques to disperse and dilute, rather than remove, sulfur emissions.[11] However, regulators and environmentalists have persistently opposed

[7] Battelle Memorial Institute, *A Systems Analysis Study of the Integrated Iron and Steel Industry*, pp. VI–20 through VI–23.

[8] Ibid., pp. VI–2 through VI–11.

[9] U.S. Environmental Protection Agency, *Report of the Hearing Panel: National Public Hearings on Power Plant Compliance with Sulfur Oxide Air Pollution Regulations*, p. 11.

[10] Environmental Protection Agency findings, reported in *Wall Street Journal*, February 24, 1978.

[11] See, for example, Phillip Sporn, retired president, American Electric Power, "Pioneering with High Stacks on the OVEC and AEP Systems," in *The Tall Stack for Air Pollution Control*. For TVA support of tall stack alternatives, see testimony of L. Seeber, in EPA, "Hearings on Power Plant Compliance, Transcript, Public Hearing and Conference on Status of Compliance with Sulfur Oxide Emission Regulations by Power Plants," p. 2343. See also Aubrey Wagner, chairman of the board, Tennessee Valley Authority, in Southern Coals Conference, *Commentary and Research Service* 35 (June 13, 1974), 13.

these methods that industrialists prefer as nothing more than temporary solutions.

The solution of burning low-sulfur coal has raised a number of problems. Most easily accessible low-sulfur coal is buried under the western plains, far from the largest coal markets. For many potential users, transportation costs have been prohibitive. Furthermore, billions of dollars of capital and long lead times for opening new mines have thus far inhibited sustantial increases in the supply of low-sulfur coal. And environmentalists have been loath to encourage rapid development of western low-sulfur coal, since that would mean rapid expansion of strip mining in the West. Finally, certain federal standards, for "no-significant deterioration" (NSD) and "best available control technology" (BACT), necessitate cleaning the emissions even from coal with the lowest sulfur content.

Flue gas desulfurization (FGD), the remaining feasible alternative, can be achieved by five or six chemical treatment processes.[12] Of those, only the processes that use wet lime and limestone have had much application to date or are planned for widespread development in the immediate future. Lime scrubbing involves bringing the flue gases in contact with a lime slurry, wherein the sulfur oxides and lime combine chemically in a sludge waste. There are a few more expensive systems that recover elemental sulfur as a by-product. In 1973, the EPA estimated that "63,000 megawatts [of coal-fired electric capacity] are expected to need substantial reductions [of sulfur emissions] either through the use of low-sulfur coal or FGD."[13] But by the 1975 deadline for achieving federal air quality standards, only 5,000 megawatts capacity of FGD equipment had even been scheduled.[14] Besides the technical issues over the workability of FGD equipment (refer to appendix C), stack gas scrubbers have three serious disadvantages. First, they are very expensive and can contribute as much as 20 or 30 percent to the cost of gene-

[12] Sulfur Oxide Control Technology Assessment Panel (SOCTAP), *Final Report on Projected Utilization of Stack Gas Cleaning Systems*, April, 1973. This study considered six systems: wet lime/limestone, magnesium oxide scrubbing, catalytic oxidation, Wellman-Lord sodium process, double alkali systems, and dry limestone injection.

[13] EPA, *Hearings on Power Plant Compliance*, p. 14.

[14] Ibid., pp. 21–26.

rating electricity. Secondly, FGD systems use significant amounts of energy to operate (as much as 15 percent of the power plant's capacity), and thereby stimulate greater coal consumption and more emissions. And finally, most FGD devices create a considerable sludge waste product. In fact, American Electric Power, opposing mandatory use of FGD, estimated that the number of scrubbers required by the EPA would generate enough sludge to cover the District of Columbia to a depth of five feet (a vision that AEP executives relished).[15]

[15] Russell Train, speech to the New York Board of Trade, reprinted in *Oil Daily*, June 17, 1974. See also SOCTAP, *Final Report*, p. 54.

Appendix C

The Politics of Information: Two Issues

SINCE 1968, two issues involving technical information not only obscured, but at times also dominated the political debate over federal policies to control air pollution and strip mining. Any consideration of air pollution invariably sparked disputes among industrialists, environmentalists, and regulators over the question of "best available control technology" (BACT). This issue derived from the congressional mandate in the 1967 Air Quality Act that ambient air quality standards were to be based on human health criteria rather than on costs of clean-up or the technology available to do the job. The 1970 Clean Air Act reasserted this principle for federal air quality standards. However, businessmen refused to accept health criteria as the premises for pollution standards, and when the EPA promulgated the standards in 1971, the business community argued that the technology necessary for attaining those standards did not exist. Moreover, the 1970 act also called for federal emission standards for particular *new* sources of pollution. And, those new-source performance standards were to reflect the "degree of emission limitation achievable through the application of the best system of emission reduction which . . . has been adequately demonstrated" (P.L. 91–604, Sec. 111[a] [1]). Thus, whoever established what was the best available control technology would also determine the emission standards. Although there were disagreements over what was the BACT for baghouses and precipitators, the most heated disagreement focused on stack gas scrubbers for removing sulfur. Only a handful of scrubbers had ever been used at commercial power plants, and industrial leadership was convinced that they were not only impractical, but simply did not work. Environmentalists, on the other hand, were committed to scrubbers for cleaning up air pollution, since the only viable alternative was to burn low-sulfur coal, and that would mean more strip mining in the West. EPA regulators had to believe that scrubbers would work, or they would be left with no basis for determining the standards for new sources. In the years after 1971, disagreement over the state of scrubber technology caused nearly total delay in implementing the pollution controls necessary to achieve the 1975 deadline for attaining clean air.

In 1974, the EPA held national hearings intended to determine just what was the state of BACT with respect to scrubbers. Most electric utilities that testified acknowledged that scrubbers, *when operating properly*, could reduce sulfur oxide emissions by 85 to 95 percent.[1] But the majority of businessmen had refused to initiate plans to install such systems because operational difficulties crippled the efficiency of most existing scrubber systems. The EPA had also organized an interagency assessment committee (SOCTAP) representing the EPA, the Department of Commerce, the Federal Power Commission, and the Council on Environmental Quality. While the SOCTAP findings recognized the welter of mechanical problems with scrubbers, it nonetheless concluded: "We have examined the status of stack gas cleaning technology in the United States and Japan and have concluded that sulfur dioxide removal from stack gases is technologically feasible in commercialized installations. We have concluded that the technological feasibility should not now be considered a decisive element in the utilization of these systems. . . ."[2]

After the EPA issued the SOCTAP report, the BACT controversy died down, although electric power officials continued to grumble over having to invest in scrubbers. Although far behind schedule,

[1] U.S. Environmental Protection Agency, *Report of the Hearing Panel: National Public Hearings on Power Plant Compliance with Sulfur Oxide Air Pollution Regulations*, p. 3.

[2] Sulfur Oxide Control Technology Assessment Panel, *Final Report on Projected Utilization of Stack Gas Cleaning Systems*, p. 1.

the Clean Air Act was forcing the continued development of the necessary scrubber technology; twenty-one generating units had operational scrubbers by mid-1975. By 1983, seventy-five more units were planned for installation.[3]

In 1976, the BACT controversy arose again and became a central issue in the debate over the 1977 Clean Air Amendments. This time, the BACT concept cut two ways for industrial polluters. On the one hand, industry failed to block a provision that ordered new sources in clean air areas to utilize the current BACT even where lower control performance would comply with the standards. But, on the other hand, the coal interests did succeed in getting a three-year waiver from attaining air standards if they utilized newly available, unproven control technology.[4] It remains to be seen how administrative politics will define BACT during the next few years as the 1977 act is implemented.

In the realm of strip-mining regulation, the distribution and quality of coal reserves was the informational issue on which the political debate focused. As regulaton of strip mining became a federal issue after 1971, three questions about coal reserves became crucial in the struggle over a federal law: the availability of surface-mineable as opposed to deep-mineable coal reserves, the reserve quantities of low-sulfur as opposed to high-sulfur coal, and the relative distribution of those reserves between the East and the West. Environmental groups that opposed strip mining sought to convince congressmen that coal reserves which could be deep mined were far more abundant than those suitable for strip mining. They argued that it was illogical for the nation's environment to suffer at all from . strip mining when far more coal was available for deep mining. The coal interests, especially the larger oil companies, utilities, and railroads with huge vested interests in strippable reserves, wanted to expand strip mining rapidly in the rich western coal fields. Especially after 1973, when "energy crisis" became a Washington buzz word, coal developers argued that rapid expansion of strip mining

[3] McGraw-Hill Company, *1976 Keystone Coal Industry Manual*, pp. 276–277.

[4] U.S. Congress, Senate, Committee on Environment and Public Works, *Clean Air Act Amendments of 1977*, 95th Cong., 1st sess., May, 1977, S. Rept. 95-127, pp. 151–154, 159–161.

was vital to America's well-being. Furthermore, they argued that most low-sulfur coal was in the West, and that large-scale stripping of those reserves was necessary for meeting air pollution standards. Many environmental groups, especially concerned for the fragile ecosystems in the western plains, argued that eastern coal fields had even more abundant reserves of low-sulfur coal. Their corollary to this argument was that local markets were closer to Appalachia and that the mining jobs were more sorely needed in that region.

According to the U.S. Geological Survey, the "identified coal resources" of the United States are nearly 1,600 billion tons. Of this amount, nearly 118 billion tons were designated as strippable resources.[5] These aggregate figures were generally accepted by the coal industry and environmentalists alike. The difference emerged not over "resources," but over "reserves." Reserves described the amount of coal recoverable by mining techniques either already in existence or likely to be available in the foreseeable future.[6] The Bureau of Mines estimated there to be 45 billion tons of strippable reserves, a downward adjustment from the 118 billion figure due to depletion from previous production, topographic limitations, natural and manmade impediments, a recovery factor of 80 percent, and other lessor factors.[7] The coal industry had vigorously promoted this 45 billion figure, emphasizing its easy availability in amounts adequate to meet national coal demand for more than ninety years.

From 1972 until 1977, Congress considered a score of bills for federal surface-mining regulation. Dozens of technical provisions were debated in terms of how they would affect the nation's energy supply, air pollution clean-up, industrial migration to the West, and restoration of lands previously ruined by strip mining. All these issues hinged on the character and distribution of coal reserves. And it was the environmental interests and not the coal industry that succeeded in manipulating the data and publicizing it in a way that served their objectives.

The Environmental Policy Center's Coalition against Strip Min-

[5] U.S. Department of Interior, Bureau of Mines, *Demonstrated Coal Reserve Base of the United States on January 1, 1974*, p. 1.
[6] U.S. Department of Interior, *Strippable Reserves of Bituminous Coal and Lignite in the United States*, p. 4.
[7] Ibid., p. 13.

ing (CASM) represented twenty major environmental organizations and dozens of smaller groups as their Washington lobby on behalf of strong federal regulation of strip mining. The CASM staff, particularly Louise Dunlap and John McCormick, compiled coal-reserve data that revealed a 34:1 ratio of deep-mineable to strippable coal reserves and a 30:1 ratio of deep-mineable to strippable low-sulfur coal reserves.[8] These findings were widely publicized across the nation and particularly in Washington, where they convinced a number of congressmen. In the course of political debate since 1973, many senators and representatives used the 34:1 ratio to defend their support of stringent regulations, especially constraints that pertained to western strip mining. Moreover, several newspapers picked up CASM's ratio and used it as the basis for editorial support of rigorous strip-mining regulations.

For some reason, the National Coal Association apparently never discovered the extraordinary errors in the CASM's data that tremendously skewed the ratio in favor of the environmentalist arguments. Perhaps the coal coalition's problem was that its membership had conflicting interests on the east-west division of coal development. Nonetheless, the CASM's 34:1 ratio was based on two huge flaws in the data. Their figure for deep *reserves* was derived by subtracting strippable *reserves* from total coal *resources*. That meant that their deep-reserve figure was too large by 73 billion tons of strippable resources. Then, the other part of this error was the comparison of strippable *reserves* (45 billion tons) to all deep mineable *resources*. This further exaggerated their ratio by a factor of 43 percent. When corrected for both problems, the more realistic ratio is 18:1 for all coal reserves and 17:1 for low-sulfur reserves. The second large problem with the CASM figures was that the reserve data on which the ratios were based included sub-bituminous and lignite reserves as part of the deep-mineable reserve. However, because of the low energy value and high water content of those coals, it will scarcely ever be either economically or technically feasible to deep-mine such coal. Inclusion of those reserves was most misleading. When the CASM data are again corrected for that error, the politically

---

[8] Environmental Policy Center, Coalition against Strip Mining, "Tabulation of Coal Reserves" (pamphlet), 1974, pp. 1–6.

volatile ratios shrink even further, to as little as 8:1 for deep-mineable versus strippable and 3.5:1 for low-sulfur deep-mineable versus strippable.

Both the BACT and the coal-reserve data issues are prime examples of the technical complexities that have become interwoven in political decision-making. Because mastery and manipulation of such information has become so important to the political struggle, the expert resources of interest groups has become more significant, and balance among them, a tenet for pluralism, less likely.

Appendix D

Who's Who in Coal

Table D. 1   Forty Largest Corporate Coal Producers, 1976
Table D. 2   Forty Largest Coal Reserve Holders, 1976
Table D. 3   Petroleum/Gas Interests in the Coal Industry
Table D. 4   Membership and Activities of Coal Interests Most Involved
in Federal Environmental Policy Making

TABLE D. 1
Forty Largest Corporate Coal Producers, 1976

Rank	Fortune 500 Rank	Parent Company	Coal Subsidiary	Tonnage (million)
1	336	Newmont Mining Group	Peabody Coal	73,050
2	16	Continental Oil	Consolidation Coal	54,919
3	211	Amax Group (20% owned, Standard Oil of Calif.)		21,839
4	20	Occidental Petroleum	Island Creek Coal	19,421
5	137	Pittston Group		18,554
6		Pacific Power & Light	Pacific Power & Light Decker Coal (50%) Bridger Coal	18,370
7	12	U.S. Steel		17,115
8	28	Bethlehem Steel	Bethlehem Mines	13,555
9	45	Ashland Oil–Hunt Oil	Arch Mineral Group	13,467
10		Gulf Resources & Chemical	C&K Coal R&F Coal Stahlman Coal	9,885
11		North American Coal		9,594
12	76	Standard Oil of Ohio	Old Ben Coal	9,257
13		American Electric Power	Central Appalachian Coal	8,265
14	375	Penn-Virginia Corp.	Westmoreland Coal	7,900

Table D. 1 (continued)

Rank	Fortune 500 Rank	Parent Company	Coal Subsidiary	Tonnage
15	296	Eastern Gas & Fuel	Eastern Associated Coal	7,840
16	7	Gulf Oil	Pittsburgh & Midway Coal	7,294
17		Peter Kieweit Group	Decker Coal (50%)	7,137
			Big Horn Coal	
			Redbud Coal	
18	98	General Dynamics	Freeman-United Coal	6,510
19		Texas Utilities	Industrial Generating	6,500
20		Montana Power	Western Energy	6,407
21	8	General Electric	Utah International	6,073
22		Houston Natural Gas	Zeigler Coal	4,584
23		Falcon-Seaboard	Falcon Coal	4,506
24		Alabama By-Products		3,997
25		Rochester & Pittsburgh Coal		3,942
26	264	St. Joe Minerals	A. T. Massey Coal	3,821
27		Quaker State Oil	Valley Camp Coal	3,683
28		Montana-Dakota Utilities	Knife River Mining	3,595
29	449	MAPCO, Inc.	Webster County Coal	3,208
30	81	Republic Steel		3,158
31		Bates Manufacturing		3,016
32	1	Exxon	Monterey Coal	2,866
			Carter Coal	
33		Jones & Laughlin Steel	Gateway Coal	2,695
34	134	Lykes Resources	Youngstown Coal	2,531
			Olga Coal	
			Buckeye Coal	
35	203	ASARCO	Midland Coal	2,447
36		Algoma Steel	Cannelton Coal	2,349
37	59	Armco Steel		2,314
38	91	National Steel	National Mines	2,311
39		Pennsylvania Power & Light	Tunnelton Coal	2,296
			Rushton Mining	
40		Panhandle Eastern Pipeline	Youghiogheny & Ohio Coal	2,172

Source: Compiled from McGraw-Hill Co., *1976 Keystone Coal Industry Manual.*

TABLE D. 2
Forty Largest Coal Reserve Holders, 1976

Rank	Parent Company	Coal Subsidiary	Reserves (millions of tons)
1	Burlington Northern		11,400
2	Continental Oil	Consolidation Coal	10,800
3	Union Pacific	Rocky Mountain Energy	10,000
4	Newmont Mining Group	Peabody Coal	8,900
5	Exxon	Monterey Coal	7,000
6	North American Coal		5,000
7	Occidental Petroleum	Island Creek Coal	4,430
8	AMAX (St. Oil Calif.)		3,134
9	U.S. Steel		2,700
10	Gulf Oil	Pittsburgh & Midway Coal	2,600
11	Pacific Power & Light		2,500
12	Atlantic Richfield		2,200
13	Sun Oil		2,200
14	Penn-Virginia Corp.	Westmoreland Resources	1,949
15	Bethlehem Steel	Bethlehem Mines	1,800
16	Texaco		1,650
17	American Electric Power	Central Appalachian Coal	1,500
18	Kerr-McGee	Kerr-McGee Coal	1,500
19	Pittston Group		1,500
20	Norfolk & Western Railroad	Pocahontas Land	1,400
21	Eastern Gas & Fuel	Eastern Associated Coal	1,192
22	General Electric	Utah International	1,100
23	Hillman Coal & Coke		1,000
24	Houston Natural Gas	Zeigler Coal	1,000
25	Montana Power	Western Energy	1,000
26	Standard Oil of Ohio	Old Ben Coal	825
27	Greenwood Stripping		735
28	General Dynamics	Freeman-United Coal	600
29	Montana-Dakota Utilities	Knife River Coal Mining	600
30	D. D. Stewart	Kentucky Home Coal	600
31	Panhandle Eastern Pipeline	Youghiogheny & Ohio Coal	500
32	Columbia Gas System		484
33	Quaker State Oil	Valley Camp Coal	475
34	MAPCO, Inc.	Webster County Coal	473
35	Consolidated Natural Gas		450
36	Tennessee Valley Authority		412
37	Duke Power	Eastover Mining	401
38	Armco Steel		400
39	Coastal States Energy	Southern Utah Fuel	400
40	Penn Pocahontas Coal		400

SOURCE: Compiled from McGraw-Hill Co., *1976 Keystone Coal Industry Manual*. For relative consistency, these reserve figures were drawn from a single source. It should be noted, however, that in a study by the American Petroleum Institute (*The Performance of Oil Firm Affiliates in the Coal Industry*, March, 1977), coal reserve holdings by oil companies were considerably larger. Most especially, Mobil Oil was listed as controlling 2.5 billion tons, although it does not appear at all in the *Keystone* statistics. The holdings of Continental, Exxon, AMAX, Occidental, and Kerr-McGee were also larger by several billion tons.

TABLE D. 3
Petroleum/Gas Interests in the Coal Industry

Company	Coal Affiliate	Production	Reserves
Continental Oil	Consolidation Coal	x	x
Occidental Petroleum	Island Creek Coal	x	x
Standard Oil of Ohio	Old Ben Coal	x	x
Gulf Oil	Pittsburgh & Midway Coal	x	x
Ashland Oil–Hunt Oil	Arch Mineral Group	x	x
Exxon	Monterey Coal		
	Carter Oil	x	x
Kerr-McGee	Kerr-McGee Coal	x	x
Houston Natural Gas	Zeigler Coal	x	x
Eastern Gas & Fuel	Eastern Associated Coal	x	x
Shell Oil Company			x
Sun Oil	Cordero Mining	x	x
Texaco			x
Ethyl Corp.	Elkhorn Coal	x	x
Mobil Oil	Pan American Energy		x
Atlantic Richfield			x
Belco Petroleum	Hawley Fuels	x	x
Phillips Petroleum			x
Pennzoil	Zapata Corp.	x	x
Diamond Shamrock	Pickands Mather	x	x
McCulloch Oil	Braztah Corp.	x	x
Standard Oil (Calif.)	AMAX (20%)	x	x
Quaker State Oil	Valley Camp Coal	x	x
MAPCO, Inc.	Webster County Coal	x	x
Panhandle Eastern Pipeline	Youghiogheny & Ohio Coal	x	x
Coastal States Energy	Southern Utah Fuel	x	x
International Mining & Petroleum	Belva Coal	x	
Cities Service			x
Columbia Gas System			x
Consolidated Natural Gas			x
Tesoro Petroleum	Tesoro Coal	x	x
Tenneco Corp.			x
Seneca Oil			x
Great Basins Petroleum			x
Petroleum International			x
El Paso Natural Gas			x
General Energy Corp.	McCoy Elkhorn	x	
	Buckhorn Hazard Coal	x	x
Lone Star Gas			x
Natural Gas Pipeline of America			x
United Nuclear	Plateau Mining	x	
U.S. Natural Resources	Twilight Industries	x	
Western Transmission	Canterbury Coal	x	
Husky Petroleum			x
Transcontinental Oil	Greer Ellison Coal	x	
Northwest Pipeline			x
Clinton Oil		x	x
Tipperary Oil & Gas		x	x
Crystal			x
California Time Petroleum			x

TABLE D. 3 (continued)

Company	Coal Affiliate	Production	Reserves
Crestmont Gas & Oil	Black Lode Coal	x	x
Hiko Bell Mining & Oil			x
Quenta Petroleum			x
Woods Petroleum			x
Texas Alberta Oil			x

SOURCE: Compiled from McGraw-Hill Co., *1976 Keystone Coal Industry Manual*; U.S. Department of the Interior, "List of Outstanding Coal Leases on Federal Lands" (1974); American Public Power Association, National Rural Electric Cooperative Association, *Artificial Restraint on Basic Energy Sources (1971)*; Federal Trade Commission, *Concentration Levels and Trends in the Energy Sector of the U.S. Economy* (NTIS, 1974); American Petroleum Institute, *The Performance of Oil Firm Affiliates in the Coal Industry*; General Accounting Office, *The State of Competition in the Coal Industry*, EMD-78-22, 1977.

Table D. 4

Memberships and Activities of Coal Interests Most Involved
in Federal Environmental Policy Making

Company	NCA	AMC	NCPC	NIPCC	NPC	USCC	FEA	1958–59	1970–74
Gulf Oil (Pittsburgh & Midway	x	x	x	x	x	x	x	x	x
Continental Oil (Consol. Coal)	x	x	x	x	x		x	x	x
Kennecott Copper (Peabody)	x	x	x	x			x	x	x
Valley Camp Coal (Quaker St. Oil)	x	x		x	(x)	x		x	x
AMAX (St. Oil Calif. 20%)	x	x		x	(x)	(x)	x		x
Exxon (Monterey Coal)	x	x		x	x			x	x
U.S. Steel		x		x		x		x	x
ASARCO (Midland Coal)	x	x		x		x		x	x
Lykes-Youngstown (Buckeye)	x	x				x		x	x
Bethlehem Steel	x	x		x				x	x
Mobil Oil	x	x			x	x			x
Atlantic Richfield		x		x	x	x			x
Pittston Group	x	x	x	x			x		
North American Coal	x	x		x			x		x
American Electric Power	x	x	x					x	x

Source: Compiled from membership lists (cited in bibliography) for the National Coal Association (1972), American Mining Congress (1973), National Coal Policy Conference (1965), National Industrial Pollution Control Council (1972), National Petroleum Council (1972), U.S. Chamber of Commerce Natural Resources Committee (U.S. Congress, Senate, Committee on Public Works, *Hearings on Air Quality*, 90th Cong., 1st sess., 1967, III, 2162–63), and Federal Energy Administration Coal Advisory Committee (1975).

Bibliography

MANUSCRIPT COLLECTIONS

American Mining Congress. Coal Convention Registration Lists. American Mining Congress Records Office, Ring Building, Washington, D.C.

National Archives. Record Group 48. Department of the Interior, Office of the Secretary, Central Classified Files, 1937–1953, section 11–34.

National Coal Association. Convention Registration Lists. National Coal Association Offices, Washington, D.C.

National Coal Policy Conference. Directors and membership lists. National Coal Policy Conference Papers. Office of W. W. McClanahan, Co., Washington, D.C.

National Industrial Pollution Control Council. Administrative Records (ten cartons). Department of Commerce, Washington, D.C.

National Industrial Pollution Control Council. NIPCC Sub-council meetings, minutes summaries, 1970–1972. Freedom of Information Files. Department of Commerce Library, Washington, D.C.

National Petroleum Council. Administrative Records. Department of the Interior, Washington, D.C.

Pennsylvania Department of Environmental Resources. Bureau of Surface Mine Reclamation. Mining Permit Files, 1965–1973; Violations Records, 1965–1973; Violation Hearings Transcripts, 1965–1973. Harrisburg, Pennsylvania.

Pennsylvania Environmental Quality Board. Public Hearings on Air Pollution Regulations, 3 vols., 1971. Hearing Transcript, Meeting of Environmental Quality Board, January 27, 1972. Harrisburg, Pennsylvania.

U.S. Environmental Protection Agency. Air and Water Programs Office. Administrative Records. NAPCA Contract Records. Accession No. 412-73-5. Federal Records Center, Suitland, Maryland.

U.S. Environmental Protection Agency. 1971 Air Pollution Files. Freedom of Information Records Office. Environmental Protection Agency, Washington, D.C.

U.S. Environmental Protection Agency. Office of Air Quality Planning and Standards. Administrative Records. Research Triangle Park, Maryland.

West Virginia Surface Mining and Reclamation Association, Administrative Records. Charleston, West Virginia.

PUBLIC DOCUMENTS

Congressional Record, 1970–1977.

Council on Environmental Quality. *The President's 1971 Environmental Program*, March, 1971. Washington, D.C.: Government Printing Office, 1971.

Federal Energy Administration. Project Independence Blueprint Final Task Force Report. *Project Independence.* Washington, D.C.: Government Printing Office, 1974.

————. *Draft Environmental Impact Statement: Energy Independence Act of 1975 and Related Tax Proposals* (DES 75-2). Washington, D.C.: Government Printing Office, 1975.

Federal Register, 1969–1977.

Federal Trade Commission. *Concentration Levels and Trends in the Energy Sector of the U.S. Economy* (PB-231033/AS). Springfield, Va.: National Technical Information Service, 1974.

General Accounting Office, Office of Federal Elections. *Federal Election Campaign Act of 1971 (Pub. Law 92-235); Alphabetical Listing of 1972 Presidential Campaign Receipts.* 2 vols. Washington, D.C.: Government Printing Office, 1972.

————. *The State of Competition in the Coal Industry* (EMD-78-22). Washington, D.C.: General Accounting Office, 1977.

National Industrial Pollution Control Council. *Council Report, 1971.* Washington, D.C.: Dept. of Commerce, 1971.

————. *The Steel Industry and Environmental Quality.* Washington, D.C.: Dept. of Commerce, 1972.

Office of Science and Technology. *Patterns of Energy Consumption in the United States* (prepared by Stanford Research Institute). Washington, D.C.: Government Printing Office, 1972.

Papers of the Presidents, Richard Nixon, 1970. Washington, D.C.: Government Printing Office, 1971.

Pennsylvania Bulletin, volumes 1–2, 1971–1972.

Pennsylvania, Commonwealth of. *Legislative Journal*, 1961–1963.

Pennsylvania, Commonwealth of, Department of Environmental Resources. *Annual Report, 1970.* Harrisburg, Pa., 1971.

President's Materials Policy Commission. *Resources for Freedom.* Washington, D.C.: Government Printing Office, 1952.

Sulfur Oxide Control Technology Assessment Panel (SOCTAP). *Final Report on Projected Utilization of Stack Gas Cleaning Systems,* April, 1973. Washington, D.C.: Environmental Protection Agency, 1973.

Tennessee Valley Authority. *Environmental Statement: Policies Relating to Sources of Coal Used by the TVA for Electric Power Generation* (TVA-OHES-E15-71-4). Washington, D.C., 1973.

U.S. Bureau of Mines. *Annual Report to the Seccretary of the Interior, 1949.* Washington, D.C.: Government Printing Office, 1949.

U.S. Congress, House, Special Committee on Coal Research. *Coal.* 84th Cong., 2nd sess., June, 1956.

U.S. Congress, House, Special Committee on Coal Research. *Coal.* 85th Cong., 1st sess., February, 1957.

U.S. Congress, House, Committee on Interstate and Foreign Commerce. *Air Quality Act of 1967.* 90th Cong., 1st sess., October, 1967. House Report No. 728.

U.S. Congress, House, Committee on Interstate and Foreign Commerce, *Hearings on Air Pollution Control and Solid Waste Recycling.* 91st Cong., 2nd sess., March–April, 1970.

U.S. Congress, House, Committee on Small Business. *Hearings on Concentration by Competing Raw Fuel Industries in the Energy Market.* 92nd Cong., 2nd sess., October, 1971.

U.S. Congress, House, Committee on Interior and Insular Affairs. *Hearings: Regulation of Surface Mining—H.R. 60.* 92nd Cong., 1st sess., October, 1971.

U.S. Congress, House, Subcommittee on Public Health and Environment. *Clean Air Act Oversight.* 92nd Cong., 2nd sess., January, 1972.

U.S. Congress, House, Congressional Research Service (prepared for the Committee on Science and Technology). *Energy Facts II.* Washington, D.C.: Government Printing Office, 1972.

U.S. Congress, House, Committee on Interior and Insular Affairs. *Hearings on the Regulation of Surface Mining.* 93rd Cong., 1st sess., April, 1973.

U.S. Congress, House, Committee on Interior and Insular Affairs. *H.R. 11500, A Bill.* 93rd Cong., 1st sess. (committee print), November, 1973.

U.S. Congress, House, Committee on Interstate and Foreign Commerce, Subcommittee on Health and the Environment. *Clean Air Act Amendments of 1977.* 95th Cong., 1st sess., April, 1975.

U.S. Congress, House, Committee on Interstate and Foreign Commerce. *Clean Air Act Amendments of 1976.* 94th Cong., 2nd sess., May 14, 1976. House Report No. 94-1175.

U.S. Congress, House, Interior Committee, Subcommittee on Energy and the Environment. *Hearings—Reclamation Practices and Environmen-*

tal Problems of Surface Mining. 95th Cong., 1st sess., January–February, 1977. 4 vols.

U.S. Congress, House, Committee on Interstate and Foreign Commerce. *Clean Air Act Amendments of 1977*. 95th Cong., 1st sess., May, 1977. House Report No. 95-294.

U.S. Congress, House. Conference Report. *Surface Mining Control and Reclamation Act of 1977*. 95th Cong., 1st sess., July, 1977. House Report No. 95-493.

U.S. Congress, House. *Conference Report to Accompany H.R. 6161*. 95th Cong., 1st sess., August, 1977. House Report No. 95-564.

U.S. Congress, Senate, Select Subcommittee of the Committee on Public Lands and Surveys. *Synthetic Liquid Fuels*. 78th Cong., 1st sess., August, 1943.

U.S. Congress, Senate, Committee on Public Works. *Hearings on Air Pollution Control*. 88th Cong., 1st sess., September, 1963.

U.S. Congress, Senate, Committee on Public Works, Subcommittee on Air and Water Pollution. *Air Quality Act of 1967—Hearings on S. 780*. 90th Cong., 1st sess., 1967.

U.S. Congress, Senate, Committee on Public Works. *Senate Report No. 403*. 90th Cong., 1st sess., 1967.

U.S. Congress, Senate, Committee on Public Works, Subcommittee on Air and Water Pollution. *Hearings on Air Pollution*. 91st Cong., 2nd sess., 1970.

U.S. Congress, Senate, Committee on Public Works. *National Air Quality Act of 1970*. 91st Cong., 2nd sess., 1970. Senate Report No. 1196.

U.S. Congress, Senate, Subcommittee on Intergovernmental Relations. *Hearings on Advisory Committees*. 91st Cong., 2nd sess., December, 1970.

U.S. Congress, Senate, Committee on Government Operations. *Hearings on Advisory Committees*. 92nd Cong., 1st sess., July, 1971.

U.S. Congress, Senate, Committee on Interior and Insular Affairs. *Hearings on Surface Mining*. 92nd Cong., 1st sess., November, 1971.

U.S. Congress, Senate, Subcommittee on Air and Water Pollution. *Oversight Hearings—Implementation of the Clean Air Act*. 92nd Cong., 2nd sess., February, 1972.

U.S. Congress, Senate, Committee on Interior and Insular Affairs. *Hearings: Regulation of Surface Mining Operations*. 93rd Cong., 1st sess., March, 1973.

U.S. Congress, Senate, Committee on Public Works. *Hearings on Nondegradation Policy of the Clean Air Act*. 93rd Cong., 1st sess., July 24, 1973.

U.S. Congress, Senate, Committee on Government Operations. *Disclosure of Corporate Ownership*. 93rd Cong., 2nd sess., 1974. Senate Document No. 93-62.

U.S. Congress, Senate, Select Committee on Presidential Campaign Activities. *The Final Report—Senate Report No. 93-981.* 93rd Cong., 2nd sess., June, 1974.

U.S. Congress, Senate, Committee on Interior and Insular Affairs. *Surface Mining Briefing.* 94th Cong., 1st sess., February, 1975.

U.S. Congress, Senate, Committee on Public Works, Subcommittee on Environmental Pollution. *Implementation of the Clean Air Act—1975.* 94th Cong., 1st sess., April, 1975.

U.S. Congress, Senate, Committee on Government Operations, Subcommittee on Reports, Accounting, and Management. *Energy Advisory Committees.* 94th Cong., 1st sess., August, 1975.

U.S. Congress, Senate, Committee on Public Works, Subcommittee on Environmental Pollution. *Clean Air Act Amendments of 1977.* 95th Cong., 1st sess., February, 1977.

U.S. Congress, Senate, Committee on Environment and Public Works. *Clean Air Act Amendments of 1977.* 95th Cong., 1st sess., May, 1977. Senate Report No. 95-127.

U.S. Department of Health, Education, and Welfare. *Air Quality Criteria for Particulate Matter.* Washington, D.C.: Government Printing Office, 1969.

———. *Air Quality Criteria for Sulfur Oxides.* Washington, D.C.: Government Printing Office, 1969.

———. *Proceedings: National Conference on Air Pollution,* November 18–20, 1958. Washington, D.C.: Government Printing Office, 1958.

———. *Proceedings: National Conference on Air Pollution,* December 10–12, 1962. Washington, D.C.: Government Printing Office, 1962.

———. *Proceedings: Third National Conference on Air Pollution.* Washington, D.C.: Government Printing Office, 1966.

———. National Air Pollution Control Administration. *Guidelines for the Development of Air Quality Standards and Implementation Plans.* Washington, D.C.: Government Printing Office, 1969.

U.S. Department of Interior. *Demonstrated Coal Reserve Base of the United States on January 1, 1974.* Bureau of Mines Information Bulletin. Washington, D.C.: Bureau of Mines, 1974.

———. *Geological Survey Bulletin 1136,* January 1, 1960. Washington, D.C.: Government Printing Office, 1960.

———. *Land Utilization and Reclamation in the Mining Industry, 1930–71.* Bureau of Mines Information Circular IC8642. Washington, D.C., 1974.

U.S. Department of the Interior. *Strippable Reserves of Bituminous Coal and Lignite in the United States.* Bureau of Mines Information Circular IC8531. Washington, D.C., 1971.

———. *Surface Mining and Our Environment.* Washington, D.C.: Government Printing Office, 1967.

————. Bureau of Mines. *Minerals Yearbook, 1971.* Washington, D.C., 1971.

U.S. Environmental Protection Agency. *Air Quality Criteria for Nitrogen Oxides.* Washington, D.C.: Government Printing Office, 1971.

————. *The Clean Air Act,* December, 1971, P.L. 91-604 (agency print).

————. *Processes, Procedures, and Methods to Control Pollution from Mining Activities* (EPA-430/9-73-001). Washington, D.C.: Government Printing Office, 1973.

————. *Report of the Hearing Panel: National Public Hearings on Power Plant Compliance with Sulfur Oxide Air Pollution Regulations.* Washington, D.C.: Environmental Protection Agency, 1974.

————. *Technical Support Document—EPA Regulations for Preventing the Significant Deterioration of Air Quality* (EPA-450/2-75-001). Washington, D.C.: Environmental Protection Agency, 1975.

West Virginia Department of Mines. *Directory of Mines, 1972.* Charleston, West Virginia, 1973.

BOOKS AND ARTICLES

Adams, Henry. *The Education of Henry Adams.* Boston: Houghton Mifflin, 1918.

Allvine, Fred, and James Patterson. *Highway Robbery: An Analysis of the Gasoline Crisis.* Bloomington: Indiana University Press, 1974.

Ayers, Richard. "Enforcement of Air Pollution Controls on Stationary Sources under the Clean Air Act Amendments." *Ecology Law Quarterly* 4 (1975): 441–478.

Berle, Adolph. *The American Economic Republic.* New York: Harcourt, Brace, World, Inc., 1963.

Bernstein, Marver. *Regulating Business by Independent Commission.* Princeton: Princeton University Press, 1955.

Blair, John M. *The Control of Oil.* New York: Pantheon Books, 1976.

Bonine, John E. "The Evolution of 'Technology-Forcing' in the Clean Air Act." *Environmental Reporter* 6 (July, 1975): 1–29.

Bosselman, Fred P. "The Control of Surface Mining: An Exercise in Creative Federalism." *Natural Resources Journal* 9 (April, 1969): 137–165.

Bossi, Stephen. "Washington Farm Front." *Catholic Rural Life* 23 (March, 1974).

Braeman, John. "The Square Deal in Action: A Case Study in the Growth of 'National Police Power.'" In John Braeman, et al., *Changes and Continuity in Twentieth Century America,* Part I. Columbus: Ohio State University Press, 1964.

Chandler, Alfred. *The Visible Hand: Managerial Revolution in American Business.* Cambridge: Harvard University Press, 1977.

Citizens' Research Foundation. *Political Contributors and Lenders of*

268　　　　　　　　Bibliography

10,000 Dollars or More in 1972. Princeton, N.J.: Citizens' Research Foundation, 1974.

Cooley, Richard, ed. *Congress and the Environment.* Seattle: University of Washington Press, 1970.

Crenson, Mathew. *The Un-Politics of Air Pollution.* Baltimore: Johns Hopkins University Press, 1971.

Cuff, Robert. "Herbert Hoover, the Ideology of Voluntarism and War Organization during the Great War." *Journal of American History* 64 (September, 1977): 358–372.

Davies, J. Clarence. *The Politics of Pollution.* New York: Pegasus, 1975.

Davis, G. C. *The Federal Trade Commission: Promise and Practice.* Champaign-Urbana: University of Illinois Press, 1969.

Dun & Bradstreet, *1973 Million Dollar Directory.* New York: Dun & Bradstreet, 1974.

Edelman, Murray. *The Symbolic Uses of Politics.* Champaign-Urbana: University of Illinois Press, 1964.

Engler, Robert. *The Brotherhood of Oil: Energy Policy and the Public Interest.* Chicago: University of Chicago Press, 1977.

―――. *The Politics of Oil.* Chicago: University of Chicago Press, 1961.

Esposito, John C. *Vanishing Air.* New York: Grossman Publishers, 1970.

Foss, Phillip. *Politics and Grass.* Seattle: University of Washington Press, 1960.

Friedlaender, Ann F., ed. *Approaches to Controlling Air Pollution.* Cambridge: MIT Press, 1978.

Green, Mark J., ed. *The Monopoly Makers.* New York: Grossman Publishers, 1973.

Hawley, Ellis. "Herbert Hoover, the Commerce Secretariat, and the Vision of the Associative State, 1921–28." *Journal of American History* 61 (June, 1974): 116–140.

Hays, Samuel P. *Conservation and the Gospel of Efficiency.* New York: Atheneum, 1959.

―――. "Conservation and the Structure of American Politics: the Progressive Era." In A. G. Bogue and T. D. Phillips, eds., *The West of the American People.* Itasca, Ill.: Peacock Publishers, Inc., 1970.

―――. "The Limits to Growth Issue: An Historical Perspective." In Chester L. Cooper, ed., *Growth in America.* Westport: Greenwood Press, 1976.

―――. *The Response to Industrialism.* Chicago: University of Chicago Press, 1961.

Hofstadter, Richard. *The Age of Reform.* New York: Alfred Knopf, 1955.

Holden, Mathew. *Pollution Control as a Bargaining Process.* Detroit: Wayne State University Press, n.d.

Hurst, J. Willard. *Law and the Conditions of Freedom in the Nineteenth*

Century United States. Madison: University of Wisconsin Press, 1956.

Jacoby, Henry D., ed. *Clearing the Air*. Cambridge: Ballinger Publishing, 1973.

Jones, Charles O. *Clean Air: The Policies and Politics of Pollution Control*. Pittsburgh: University of Pittsburgh Press, 1975.

Kerr, K. A. *American Railroad Politics, 1914–1920*. Pittsburgh: University of Pittsburgh Press, 1968.

Kolko, Gabriel. *Railroads and Regulation, 1877–1916*. Princeton: Princeton University Press, 1965.

————. *The Triumph of Conservatism*. Chicago: Quadrangle Books, 1967.

McAteer, Davitt. *Coal Mining Health and Safety in West Virginia*. Washington, D.C.: United Mine Workers, 1970.

McConnell, Grant. *The Decline of Agrarian Democracy*. New York: Atheneum, 1969.

————. *Private Power and American Democracy*. New York: Alfred Knopf, 1966.

McGraw-Hill Co. *Keystone Coal Industry Manual*. New York: McGraw-Hill Co., 1970–1976.

McLellen, Jack. "Kaiparowits, Southern Utah at the Crossroads." *Sierra Club Bulletin*, August, 1975, pp. 6–7, 25–27.

Magida, Arthur. "Clean Air Act Deliberations—The Changing of the Guard." *National Journal* 8 (March, 1976): 341.

Meadows, Dennis, et al. *The Limits to Growth*. New York: Signet Books, 1972.

Miller, James. "Air Pollution." In James Rathlesburger, ed., *Nixon and the Environment*. New York: Village Voice Books, 1972.

Muir, John. *The Yosemite*. New York: Century, 1912.

National Academy of Sciences. *Rehabilitation Potential of Western Coal Lands: A Report to the Energy Policy Project of the Ford Foundation*. Cambridge: Ballinger Publishing Co., 1974.

Noone, James. "Coal Lobby Seeks House Action to Offset Senate's Tough Strip Mine Bill." *National Journal*, October 20, 1973.

————. "Energy Report/Strip Mining Lobby Groups Focus on House Interior Committee." *National Journal*, January 26, 1974.

Radosh, Ronald, and Murray Rothbard, eds. *A New History of Leviathan*. New York: E. P. Dutton, 1972.

Ralph Nader Congress Project. *Citizens Look at Congress*. New York: Grossman's Publisher, 1973.

Rodgers, William. *Corporate Country*. Emmaus, Pennsylvania: Rodale Press, 1973.

Rosenbaum, Walter A. *The Politics of Environmental Concern*. New York: Praeger Books, 1973.

Smith, Adam. *The Wealth of Nations*. New York: Penguin Books, 1977.

Stanley H. Ruttenburg and Associates. *The American Oil Industry: A Failure of Anti-Trust Policy*. New York: Marine Engineers' Beneficial Association, 1973.

Urofsky, Melvin I. *Big Steel and the Wilson Administration*. Columbus: Ohio State University Press, 1969.

Vietor, Richard H. K. "Businessmen and the Political Economy: The Railroad Controversy of 1905." *Journal of American History* 64 (June, 1977).

————. "The Evolution of Public Environmental Policy: The Case of 'No Significant Deterioration.'" *Environmental Review* 3 (Winter, 1979).

Vitullo-Martin, Thomas. "Pollution Control Laws: The Politics of Radical Change." In Leslie Roos, ed., *The Politics of Eco-Suicide*. New York: Holt, Rinehart, 1971.

Wiebe, Robert. *Businessmen and Reform*. Cambridge: Harvard University Press, 1962.

REPORTS, PAMPHLETS, SPEECHES, AND MISCELLANEOUS MATERIALS

American Mining Congress. "American Mining Congress Membership, 1974."

American Petroleum Institute. "Brief for Petitioners." United States Court of Appeals for the District of Columbia Circuit, No. 75-1665.

————. *The Performance of Oil Firm Affiliates in the Coal Industry*. Washington, D.C.: American Petroleum Institute, 1977.

American Public Power Association. *Artificial Restraints on Basic Energy Sources*. Washington, D.C.: Rawley & Scott, 1971.

Anderson, John T., et al. "Reserve and Resource Data on Coal, Uranium, and Oil Shale in the States of North Dakota, South Dakota, Montana, Wyoming, Colorado, Utah, Michigan, Ohio, Kentucky, Tennessee, and West Virginia." April 19, 1975. A report prepared for the American Petroleum Institute.

Battelle Memorial Institute. *A Systems Analysis Study of the Integrated Iron and Steel Industry*. Springfield, Va.: National Technical Information Service PB184577, 1969.

Benson and Benson, Inc., "A Profile of the *Audubon* Reader," October, 1970. A report prepared for *Audubon* magazine.

Christian Church, Division of Homeland Ministries, Office of G. A. Day, Director, Church and Community. Memoranda, resolutions, circulars.

Ellis, Howard. "The Economic Impact on Pennsylvania Residents Due to the Proposed Sulfur Dioxide Emission Standards for Combustion Units." N.p.: Gordon Associates, Inc., 1971.

Environmental Policy Center, Coalition Against Strip Mining. "Tabulation of Coal Reserves." Pamphlet. 1974.

Greenfield, Attaway & Tyler, Inc., *An Examination of the Accuracy and Adequacy of Air Quality Models and Monitoring Data for Use in Assessing the Impact of EPA Significant Deterioration Regulations on Energy Development* (EF75-58R). August 8, 1975. A report prepared for the American Petroleum Institute.

Illinois Mining Institute. *Proceedings: Diamond Anniversary Convention.* October 12–13, 1967.

Middleton, John T., Commissioner, National Air Pollution Control Administration. "Air Conservation in 1969: Who Will Make the Decisions?" A paper presented at the air pollution briefing in Phoenix, Arizona, February 4, 1969.

———. "Public Policy and Air Pollution Control." A paper presented at the Penjerdel Regional Conference, Swarthmore, Pennsylvania, June 11, 1969. Washington, D.C.: National Air Pollution Control Administration, 1969.

National Audubon Society. Audubon News Releases, 1972–1974. Public Information Office, National Audubon Society.

———. "National Audubon Membership Report, March, 1974." Public Information Office, National Audubon Society.

National Coal Association. "Coal and the Environment," 1973. Pamphlet.

———. *Coal Facts, 1972.* Washington, D.C., 1973.

———. *Coal Facts, 1974–1975.* Washington, D.C., 1976.

———. "Coal—Indispensable Support of Economic Growth: A Survey of the Impact of Coal on the Economy of Greater Wheeling." Washington, D.C.: National Coal Association, 1973.

———. *Directory of Organization and Services,* 1974.

———. "Proceedings: 48th Annual Convention, June, 1965." National Coal Association, Washington, D.C. Typescript.

———. "Proceedings: 55th Annual Convention, June, 1972." National Coal Association, Washington, D.C. Typescript.

———. "Proceedings: 56th Annual Convention, June, 1973." National Coal Association, Washington, D.C. Typescript.

National Coal Policy Conference. *A Guide to the Air Quality Act of 1967.* Washington, D.C., 1968.

———. *NCPC, Purpose, Platforms, and Objectives.* Washington, D.C., 1965.

National Petroleum Council. *Environmental Conservation,* vol. 2: *The Oil and Gas Industries.* Washington, D.C., 1972.

———. *U.S. Energy Outlook: Coal Availability.* Washington, D.C., 1973.

———. *U.S. Energy Outlook: A Summary Report.* Washington, D.C., 1972.

Pennsylvania Power and Light Company. "1973 Operating Report."

Perl, Lewis, National Economic Research Associates. "An Analysis of the Costs to the Electric Utility Industry of House and Senate Significant

Deterioration Proposals." December 12, 1975.
————. "Estimated Costs for the Electric Utility Industry of Nonsignificant Deterioration Amendments Currently Considered by the United States Senate." April 16, 1976.
Rowe, George R., assistant vice-president, commodity marketing, Burlington Northern, Inc. "Economics of Using Western Coal in Appalachian Markets." A paper delivered at 1974 Coal Convention of the American Mining Congress, Pittsburgh, Pennsylvania, May, 1974.
Sporn, Phillip. "Pionering with High Stacks on the OVEC and AEP Systems," The Tall Stack for Air Pollution Control. Pamphlet, n.p.,n.d.
Stanford Research Institute. "A Study of Surface Coal Mining in West Virginia." California: Stanford Research Institute, 1972.

INTERVIEWS

Beck, William. Drainage Permits Section, Bureau of Surface Mines Reclamation, Pennsylvania Department of Environmental Resources. Fulton Building, Harrisburg, Pa., July, 1973.
Chaney, Rex. Vice-president for information services, National Coal Association. Coal Building, Washington, D.C., February, 1974.
Cook, Charles. Government affairs representative, American Mining Congress. Ring Building, Washington, D.C., February 6, 1974.
Dunlap, Louise. Coordinator, COALition Against Strip Mining. Environmental Policy Center, Washington, D.C., February 6, 1974.
Greene, Ben. Director of Reclamation Bureau, West Virginia Department of Natural Resources. State Building, Charleston, West Virginia, November 13, 1973.
Guckert, William. Director of Bureau of Surface Mine Reclamation, Pennsylvania Department of Environmental Resources. Fulton Building, Harrisburg, Pa., July, 1973, August, 1973.
Handly, Robert. President of Citizens to Abolish Surface Mining. Charleston, West Virginia, November 13, 1974.
Herwig, Charles. Violations Section, Bureau of Surface Mine Reclamation, Pennsylvania Department of Environmental Resources, Fulton Building, Harrisburg, Pa., July, 1973.
Lusk, Ben. Executive director, West Virginia Surface Mining and Reclamation Association. WVSMRA Headquarters, Charleston, West Virginia, November 14, 1973.
McClanahan, William. Past director, National Coal Policy Conference. National Press Club, Washington, D.C., February 7, 1974.
Mohney, Frank. Executive director, Pennsylvania Coal Mining Association. Pennsylvania Coal Mining Association Headquarters, Harrisburg, Pa., August 14, 1973.
Snieder, James. Mining Permits Section, Bureau of Surface Mine Reclamation, Pennsylvania Department of Environmental Resources. Fulton Building, Harrisburg, Pa., July, 1973.

Sullivan, John. Office of Environmental Affairs, Department of Commerce. Main Commerce Building, Washington, D.C., May 16, 1974.

Tuerk, Edward. Office of Program Management Operations, Environmental Protection Agency, Washington, D.C., May 13, 1974.

Walker, Ray. President, Bradford Coal Company, Beigler, Pennsylvania. Interviewed in Clearfield, Pa., August 21, 1973.

Walters, Donald. Office of Air Quality Planning and Standards, U.S. Environmental Protection Agency, Research Triangle Park, North Carolina, June 10, 1975.

Woolridge, H. Rembrandt. President, Moshannon Falls Mining Company, Clearfield, Pa., August 21, 1973.

UNPUBLISHED PAPERS AND DISSERTATIONS

Huntington, Samuel. "Clientalism: A Study in Administrative Politics." Ph.D. dissertation, Harvard University, 1951.

Jones, Charles O. "Satisfying the Public: Speculative Augmentation in Federal Air Pollution Policy." Unpublished paper, University of Pittsburgh, 1973.

Scarpino, Philip. "A Quest for Order—Energy as a Factor in Change Over Time." Unpublished paper, University of Missouri-Columbia, 1977.

NEWSPAPERS AND MAGAZINES

Audubon
Audubon Leader
Bismarck Tribune (South Dakota)
Bluefield Daily Telegraph (West Virginia)
Business Week
Cleveland Plain Dealer
Charleston Gazette (West Virginia)
Coal Age, 1965–1977
Coal Mining and Processing, 1972–1977
Commentary and Research Service (Southern Coals Conference, 1973–1977
Conservation Report (National Wildlife Federation), 1975–1977
Denver Post
The Dominion-Post (Morgantown, West Virginia)
Enterprise (Wytheville, Virginia)
Forbes Magazine
Glance (Disciples of Christ)
Grand Forks Herald (North Dakota)
Green Lands Quarterly (WVSMRA), 1972–1974
The Intelligencer (Wheeling, West Virginia)
Louisville Courier-Journal

Martinsburg Journal, 1976
Mined Lands Conservation Conference (NCA), 1964–1970
Mining Congress Journal, 1970–1974
Morgantown Post (West Virginia)
New York Times, 1970–1977
Not Man Apart (Friends of the Earth), 1975–1977
Oil Daily
Philadelphia Enquirer
Pittsburgh Post-Gazette
Pittsburgh Press, 1959–1974
Raleigh Register (Beckley, West Virginia)
Time Magazine
United Mine Workers Journal
Wall Street Journal, 1973–1979

Index

Ad Hoc Emergency Committee for Clean Air (Pa.), 190
Advisory Council Act, 10
advisory councils, industry: role of, in coal's political structure, 36–37, 51–57
AFL-CIO, 221
Agriculture, Department of, 91
air pollution. *See* pollution, air
Air Quality Act (1967), 90, 128, 149, 197, 234; and concept of no significant deterioration, 199–200, 201, 202; implementing, 150–154; NCPC's *Guide to*, 44–45, 198–199; purpose of, 198; Senate hearings on, 144–147; shortcomings of, 155–156, 157; signing of, into law, 148
Alan Woods, 186
Alexander, Leslie, 104–105
Allegheny County Labor Alliance (Pa.), 59
Allegheny County Sportmen's League (Pa.), 59, 65, 66, 67–68, 79
Allegheny Power Systems (Pa.), 183
ambient air standards: issued by EPA, 161–168
American Association of University Women, Pennsylvania Division of, 188
American Bankers' Association, 7–8
American Cancer Society, 131

American Electric Power, 43, 132, 146, 178
American Energy Producers Association, 116
American Farm Bureau Federation, 7, 120
American Forestry Association, 95
American Iron and Steel Institute (AISI), 36, 37, 93, 136, 170
American Medical Association, 136
American Mining Congress (AMC), 27, 34, 46, 88, 158; and Air Quality Act, 144, 153, 154; on alluvial valleys, 119–120; and ambient air standards, 166, 167; and Clean Air Act, 136, 170; and concept of no significant deterioration, 223; conventions of, 50–51, 92; environmental cost-impact studies of, 53; on federal surface-mining legislation, 99, 106; on HEW air quality standards guidelines, 202; national effectiveness of, 182; and new source performance standards, 178; role of, in coal's political structure, 36, 49–51, 93; West Virginia coal producers' membership in, 38, 42
American Municipal Association, 137
American Petroleum Institute (API), 37, 167, 215–216, 223; and Air Quality Act, 145; and Clean Air

Act, 136, 170; concern of, for air pollution controls, 36
American Public Health Association, 135
American Public Power Association, 29, 104
American Smelting and Refining Company (ASARCO), 94, 166–167
Amoco, 223
Ancker-Johnson, Betsy, 207
Andrews, Hiram, 66
Andrus, Cecil, 123
Anthracite Institute, 190
Appalachian Peoples Service Organization, 95
Arizona Nurses' Association, 164
Ashland Oil, 54
Aspinall, Wayne, 16
Atchison, Topeka, and Santa Fe Railroad, 47
Atkins, Orin, 54–55
Atlantic Richfield, 119
Atomic Energy Commission (AEC), 16, 179
Audubon, 98
Audubon Leader, 97–98
Ayers, Richard, 164, 173–174, 177

Bagge, Carl, 3, 88, 105–106, 233; and Clean Air Act Amendments, 217; and concept of no significant deterioration, 196, 197; as leader of National Coal Association, 46, 47; letter of, to Jackson and Haley, 114; and provisions for selectively prohibiting strip mining, 103; on *Sierra Club* vs. *Ruckelshaus*, 204; on strip-mining bills, 110, 112, 117
Baker, Howard, 214
Bankers Trust, 33
banks, commercial: involvement of, in coal, 21, 30–35
Barber, Charles, 166
Barr, Joseph, 137
Bechtel, 104
Belco Petroleum, 25
Bentsen, Lloyd, 214

Berle, Adolph, 8
Bernstein, Marver, 82
best available control technology (BACT), 221
Bethlehem Steel, 23, 24, 133, 180, 186
Bituminous Coal Research, 140
Black Mesa Defense Fund, 95
Boston Company, 33
Boyle, W. A. ("Tony"), 43, 145
Breaux, John: amendment of, 225, 226
Brennan, Joseph, 186–187
Breth, Harris, 61, 66
Browder, Joe, 113
Broyhill, James, 214–215, 218, 219
Buchanan, William, 68
Buckley, James, 214
Bucyrus Erie, 26
Bumpers, Dale, 224–225
Bureau of Abatement and Control, 201
Bureau of Corporations, 8–9
Bureau of Indian Affairs, 19
Bureau of Land Management, 19, 91
Bureau of Mines, 14, 49, 50, 91
Bureau of Surface Mine Reclamation (BSMR). *See* Pennsylvania Bureau of Surface Mine Reclamation
Burlington Northern (BN) Railroad, 20, 21–23, 32, 121
Burns, Arthur, 117
Business Advisory Council, 156
Business Roundtable, 221–222, 232–233
Byrd, Harry, 116
Byrd, Robert, 16, 140

Calvert, Seymour, 141
Carolina Light & Power, 25
Carter, Jimmy, 118, 195, 220, 236; and Clean Air Act Amendments, 194, 225, 226; and Surface Mining Control and Reclamation Act, 123, 124
Caterpillar Tractor, 26, 27
cement industry: coal consumption of, 128

C. E. Powell, 63
Chamber of Commerce, Missouri, 216
Chamber of Commerce, Pennsylvania, 60, 184, 186
Chamber of Commerce, United States (USCC), 36, 207; and air pollution conference, 132, 133; and Air Quality Act, 145; and Clean Air Act, 136; Natural Resources Committee of, 32, 158
Chamber of Commerce, West Virginia, 42
Chappell, William, 219
Chase Manhattan Bank, 33–34, 105
Chesapeake & Ohio/Baltimore & Ohio Railroad, 39
Christian Church (Disciples of Christ), 96–97
churches: political involvement of, in strip-mining issue, 95–97
Citizens Committee on Natural Resources, 133, 135, 147, 197
Clayton, W. Graham, 39
Clean Air Act (1955), 134, 135
Clean Air Act (1963), 90, 135–137
Clean Air Act (1970), 3, 4, 56, 85, 93, 194; and concept of no significant deterioration, 200, 202–204; and EPA ambient air standards, 161–168; EPA enforcement of, 100, 234; implementation of, in Pennsylvania, 180–192; "Implementation Plan Guideline" (EPA) for, 10, 168–178, 235; mandate of, 11; Muskie, Nixon, and, 156–160; new source performance standards of, 91, 178–180; provisions of, 160–161
Clean Air Act Amendments (1977), 45, 194, 197, 233; events leading to, 208–226; provisions of, 236; signing of, into law, 226
Clean Streams Act (1965), 70
Club of Rome, 196
Coal Age, 137–140, 141, 149
coalition, coal: coal producers, 18–21; commercial banks, 21, 30–35; electric utilities industry, 21, 24–26;

metals industry, 21, 23–24; mining equipment manufacturers, 21, 26–27; oil and gas industries, 21, 27–30; railroads, 21–23
Coalition against Strip Mining (CASM), 94–95, 97, 108, 110, 125; commitment of, to abolish strip mining, 103, 113, 124; and east-west shift in coal production, 101; and National Farmers Union, 120; organization of, 90
Coal Mine Health and Safety Act (1969), 101
Coal Research Act (1959), 16–17
Coke and Coal Chemicals Association, 144
Commerce, Department of, 36, 91, 149, 179; and NIPCC, 52, 158; and revision of Clean Air Act implementation guidelines, 174–175, 176, 177
Commission on Religion in Appalachia, 95, 97
Congress: strip-mining bills introduced to, 88–92, 98–99, 113–117, 118
Conservation Foundation, 90, 164, 180
Consolidated Edison Company (Con Ed), 140
Consolidation Coal Company, 16, 18, 29, 56, 146; and air pollution conference, 132, 133; and banking's involvement in coal, 33; on bureaucratic burdens of federal strip-mining legislation, 122; and Clean Air Act, 187
Continental Illinois National Bank, 33, 34
Continental Oil, 18, 29, 30, 33, 56
Cooper, John Sherman, 171–172, 202
Council of Economic Advisers, 171
Council on Environmental Quality, 159, 171
Cross, Bert, 52–53

Daley, Richard, 137
Daly, Herman, 196

Dart Truck, 26
Delaware Valley Citizens' Council, 189
Denver National Bank, 105
Department of Environmental Resources (DER). *See* Pennsylvania Department of Environmental Resources
Dingell, John, 214–215
Dingell-Broyhill amendment, 218, 219
Dirksen, Everett M., 85, 87
Doig, Keith, 206–207
Domenici, Pete, 214
DuBridges, Lee, 153
Duke Power, 25
Dunlap, Louise, 90, 91, 103, 110, 115
Duquesne Light, 183

Eagleton, Thomas, 174, 184, 185
Earth Day (April, 1970), 6, 51, 85, 86, 157
east-west conflict, in strip-mining issue, 100–102, 119–122
Edelman, Sidney, 199–200
Edison Electric Institute (EEI), 37, 93, 167, 223, 232; and Air Quality Act, 145; and Clean Air Act, 170, 204; concern of, for air pollution controls, 36; environmental cost-impact studies of, 53; opposition of, to air standards, 158
Ehrlichman, John, 174
Eisenhower, Dwight D., 4, 14, 16, 17, 236
electric utilities industry: coal consumption of, 128; involvement of, in coal, 21, 24–26
Electric Utility Clean Air Coordinating Committee, 216
Elliott, John, 185
Ellis, Howard, 184
El Paso Natural Gas, 56
Energy, Department of, 28
energy crisis, 94, 95, 103; historical roots of, 194–197; strip-mining policy for, 112–126
Energy Independence Act (1975), 208

Environmental Defense Fund, 164, 165
Environmental Policy Center, 90, 95, 113; "Facts" booklet of, 115
Environmental Protection Agency (EPA), 10, 100, 108, 117, 154; Air Programs Office of, 165; ambient air standards issued by, 161–168, 203; and Clean Air Act, 160–161, 192–193, 234; and Clean Air Act Amendments, 220–221; and concept of no significant deterioration, 203, 204–205, 207, 212, 215; versus Department of Interior for federal control of strip mining, 90–91; health criteria promulgated by, 11; and implementation of Clean Air Act in Pennsylvania, 181; "Implementation Plan Guidelines" of, for Clean Air Act, 168–178, 197, 230, 235; and new source performance standards, 178–179; and NIPCC, 52, 53, 159, 233
Environmental Quality Board (EQB). *See* Pennsylvania Environmental Quality Board
Erlich, Paul, 196
Esposito, John, 157
Executive Order 11523, 52
Exxon, 18, 56, 145

Falkie, Thomas, 50
Federal Advisory Committee Act (1973), 54
Federal Campaign Financing Act (1971), 54
Federal Energy Administration (FEA), 111, 114, 207, 208; and Clean Air Act Amendments, 210; Coal Advisory Committee to, 37
Federal Energy Agency, 28, 50, 206
Federal Power Commission (FPC), 15, 46, 91, 149, 151; Bagge's appointment to, 47; and Clean Air Act, 175
Federal Register, 168, 173
Federal Reserve Board, 117
Federal Surface Mining Control and

Reclamation Act. *See* Surface Mining Control and Reclamation Act
Federal Trade Commission, 30
federal versus state preeminence, 99–100
Federal Water Pollution Control Administration (FWPCA), 199–200
Federation of American Scientists, Pittsburgh chapter of, 189
Federation of Western Outdoors Clubs, 95
Fidelity Bank of Philadelphia, 34, 39
Finance Committee to Re-elect the President (1972), 54
Finch, Robert H., 154, 202
First National City Bank (N.Y.), 32
Fitzpatrick, James, 134, 138
Flanigan, Peter, 174
Ford, Gerald, 116, 118, 195, 207, 208; and Clean Air Act Amendments, 209–220 passim; surface-mining control bill of, 114–115, 116–117; vetoes of strip-mining bills by, 86, 110, 111–112, 113, 117
Ford, Wendell, 123
Four Corners Power Project, 214
Freedom of Information Act, 10
Freeman Coal Company, 17–18
Friends of the Earth, 6, 95

Garn, Jake, 218, 219, 220, 224, 225
gas industry: involvement of, in coal, 21, 27–30
Geist, Paul, 214
General Dynamics Corporation, 17–18
General Electric, 18
Geological Survey, 17, 91
Given, Ivan, 138
Gordian Associates: study prepared by, 183–185, 192
grassroots political organization, coal's, 35, 38–43
Green Lands Quarterly, 42
Group against Smog and Pollution (GASP, Pa.), 182, 189
growth, industrial: coal as essence of,

227; historical roots of limiting, 194–197
Gruber, Charles, 134
Guckert, William, 234; and BSMR, 75–82 passim
Gulf Oil, 18, 56, 133, 180, 223

Haley, James, 93, 114
Haluska, John, 63, 65, 66
Hamilton, Walter, 166, 169–170, 176, 233
Hart, Gary, 214
Hart, Phillip, 29
Hawkins, David, 211–212
Hawley Fuels, 25
Hays, Jo, 66
Health, Education, and Welfare (HEW), Department of, 134, 149–150, 179, 228–229, 230; and Air Quality Act, 150–154; and Clean Air Act, 137; emission standards of, 140–149 passim; epidemiological studies of, 167; *Guidelines* of, 152–154, 201–202; sponsoring of air pollution conferences by, 131, 132. *See also* National Air Pollution Control Administration (NAPCA)
Hechler, Kenneth, 48–49, 88, 96–97, 98–99
Hetch Hetchy Valley (Yosemite), 198
Hinnaland, Dan, 120–121
Holden, Mathew, 83
Hoover, Herbert, 7
Hosmer, Craig, 99
Hot Springs National Park, 224–225
House Commerce Committee, 147, 149, 157; and Clean Air Act Amendments, 208–226 passim
House Committee on Small Business, 29
House Interior Committee, 48, 87, 88, 93, 99; and provisions for selectively prohibiting strip mining, 103–104; and surface-mining bill, 109; Udall's chairmanship of, 118
House Subcommittee on Environment, 99

House Subcommittee on Mines and
    Mining, 99, 109
Humble Oil (Exxon), 145
Huntington, Samuel, 82
Hurst, J. W., 235

Ickes, Harold, 14
interindustry associations: role of, in
    coal's political structure, 36
Interior, Department of, 19, 49, 93,
    106, 114, 179; and coal liquefac-
    tion, 14; versus EPA for federal
    control of strip mining, 90–92; and
    federal rules for strip mining, 118;
    implementation of federal strip-
    mining control act by, 11, 123;
    and National Petroleum Council,
    55; office of coal research in, 16, 17
Intermountain Power Project, 225
International Brotherhood of Electri-
    cal Workers, 59
Interstate Mining Compact Commis-
    sion, 104
Ireland, R. J., 136
Island Creek Coal, 16
Izaak Walton League, 95, 164

Jackson, Henry, 114; strip-mining bill
    introduced by, 87–88, 92, 98–99,
    102, 104–105, 107–108
Jackson, Thomas, 170
Johnson, Lyndon B., 47, 143, 148
Johnston, J. Bennett, 111
Jones, Fred, 81
Joy Manufacturing, 26–27, 43, 104
Justice, Department of, 29

Kaiser Aluminum, 94
Kanawa Valley Bank, 39
Kennecott Copper, 18, 94, 104, 159,
    222
Kennedy, Edward, 29
Kent State University, 215
Kerr-McGee, 56
Keystone Bituminous Coal Associa-
    tion (Pa.), 38, 182
Kleppe, Thomas, 118
Knight, Gary, 207

Kruger, George, 33–34

Labor, Department of, 179
Lahn, Richard, 212–213
Laudadio, John, 65, 66, 81
LaViers, Harry, 13
Lawrence, David, 61, 63, 64, 66
League of Conservation Voters, 48
Lewis, John L., 13
L. F. McCollum, 29
Limits to Growth (Dennis Meadows
    et al.), 196
Lindsay, John, 139–140
Lloyd, Walter, 187
Louisville and Nashville Railroad, 39
Love, John V., 207
Lukens Steel, 133, 186
Lusk, Ben, 42, 112
Lynn, James, 117, 175–176

McConnell, Grant, 82
McCracken, Paul, 171
McGovern, George, 230
MacKenzie, Vernon, 138, 143
McLean, John, 30, 33
Manasco, Carter, 15–16, 47
Mansfield, Mike, 92; amendment of,
    102–103, 110, 111, 120, 123, 124,
    126, 232
Marine Engineers' Beneficial Associa-
    tion, 29
Marion Power Shovel, 26–27
Meadows, Dennis, 196
Mellon Bank, 33, 34
mergers, 16, 17, 18
metals industry: involvement of, in
    coal, 21, 23–24
Metcalf, Lee, 52, 123
Metro Washington Coalition for
    Clean Air, 165
Middleton, John, 166, 167–168, 201,
    203; and revision of Clear Air Act
    implementation guidelines, 169,
    172–173, 174–175
Midland Coal Company, 166
Miller, James, 174
Milliken, Frank, 159, 222

Mined Lands Conservation Conference, 35, 48
mining equipment manufacturers: involvement of, in coal, 21, 26–27
Mink, Patsy, 99, 109
Mohney, Frank, 41, 77, 82
Moody, Joseph, 43, 142–143, 146
Morgan Guaranty Trust Company, 32, 33, 39
Morrison-Knudson, 104
Morton, Rogers, 50, 55, 91, 93, 210
Moss, Frank, 218–219, 220
Moss, Lawrence, 3
Muir, John, 197–198, 208
Mullan, Joseph, 158, 159
Murphy, Austin, 64
Muskie, Edmund, 44, 143–144, 202, 234; and Clean Air Act, 156–160; and Clean Air Act Amendments, 208–221 passim; hearings of, on Air Quality Act, 144–147; prefers ambient air quality standards, 143–144, 148

Nader, Ralph, 144, 147, 150, 157, 184; his Public Interest Research Group, 185
National Academy of Sciences, 103
National Air Pollution Control Administration (NAPCA), 10, 168, 197, 234; implementation of Air Quality Act by, 151–154, 155, 199–201
National Association of Counties, 137
National Association of Manufacturers (NAM), 36, 141; and air pollution conference, 132, 133, 135; and Air Quality Act, 145; and Clean Air Act, 136, 170
National Audubon Society (NAS), 91, 95, 97–98; *Audubon* magazine of, 98
National Catholic Rural Life Conference, 95–96
National Coal Association (NCA), 3, 15, 44, 158, 232; and air pollution conference, 132, 133; and Air Quality Act, 144, 148; *Bituminous*

Coal Facts of, 47; and Clean Air Act, 136; and Clean Air Act Amendments, 217; *Coal News* of, 47; *Congressional Highlights* of, 48; connections between banks and, 32, 34; conventions of, 27, 30, 138; on federal surface-mining legislation, 99–100, 106, 110; growing awareness of air pollution problem of, 138, 140; improved political profile of, 46–47, 49; and Jackson's strip-mining bill, 88; *Letter of the Law* of, 47–48; and Mined Lands Conservation Conference, 35, 48; *Mined Lands Quarterly* of, 48; and new source performance standards, 178; and revision of Clean Air Act implementation guidelines, 170; role of, in coal's political structure, 36, 46–49, 93; West Virginia coal producers' membership in, 38, 42
National Coal Policy Conference (NCPC), 17, 140, 142, 158; and Air Quality Act, 144–150 passim; demise of, 45–46; *Guide to the 1967 Air Quality Act* of, 44–45, 198–199; role of, in coal's political structure, 36, 43–45
National Conference(s) on Air Pollution: first (1958), 131–132, 180; second (1962), 132–135; third (1966), 141, 143
National Economic Research Associates (NERA), 216–217, 223
National Electric Reliability Council, 93, 104
National Environmental Policy Act (1970), 85, 156
National Farmers Union, 120
National Industrial Pollution Control Council (NIPCC), 10, 32, 156, 165, 222; *Council Report* of, 54; and EPA, 52, 53, 159, 233; Mining and Nonferrous Metals Subcouncil of, 158–159; and new source performance standards, 178; and revision of Clean Air Act im-

plementation guidelines, 169–170, 175; role of, in coal's political structure, 36, 51–55; and sulfur standards, 166
National League of Cities, 212
National Petroleum Council (NPC), 14, 30, 91, 206; Committee on Energy Outlook of, 33; role of, in coal's political structure, 36, 55–57; U.S. Energy Outlook of, 33, 56–57
National Recovery Administration, 8
National Rural Electric Cooperative Association, 29, 104, 204
National Tuberculosis Association, 131, 135
National Wildlife Federation, 95, 108, 135, 197
Natural Resources Defense Council (NRDC), 6, 174, 177, 179; and ambient air standards, 163, 164, 165; and Clean Air Act Amendments, 211; and concept of no significant deterioration, 204; national effectiveness of, 181–182
Nelson, Gaylord, 87, 88, 230
New Mexico Public Service, 214
new source performance standards (NSPS), 91, 178–180
New York Central Railroad, 60
nitrogen oxides, 151, 169
Nixon, Richard M., 10, 32, 54, 88, 93, 153; on Air Quality Act, 155; and Clean Air Act, 156–160; creation of NIPCC by, 36, 52, 156; and sulfur emissions tax, 171
nondegradation. See no significant deterioration
Norfolk & Western Railroad, 39
Norris, George, 25
Northern Plains Resources Council, 95, 120
no significant deterioration (NSD): concept of, 154, 164, 167, 176, 194, 196–197; controversy over, 209–226; discussion of, 197–208

Oak Creek (Ohio) Garden Club, 163

Occidental Petroleum, 18
Office of Coal Research (OCR), 91
Office of Management and Budget (OMB), 173, 174, 179
Office of Surface Mining, 236
Oglebay-Norton Coal Company, 32
oil industry: involvement of, in coal, 21, 27–30
OPEC (Organization of Petroleum Exporting Countries), 110, 206, 207
Opinion Research Corporation, 217
Overton, J. Allen, 92, 93, 114, 153, 233; on industry spending on air pollution, 136

particulates, 151–152, 169, 177
Peabody Coal Company, 16, 18, 99, 104, 145; and air pollution conference, 132, 133
Peele, Robert, 87
Penn Central Railroad, 23, 39, 187
Penn State, Center for Air Environmental Studies at, 141
Pennsylvania: formulating policies to implement Clean Air Act in, 180–192; political organization of coal interests in, 38–41. See also Surface Mining and Reclamation Act (1961, Pa.)
Pennsylvania Bureau of Surface Mine Reclamation (BSMR), 41, 82, 83–84; autonomy of, 80–81; implementation of Surface Mining and Reclamation Act by, 70–80
Pennsylvania Coal Mining Association (PCMA), 40–41, 42, 69, 79, 82; violations of Surface Mining and Reclamation Act by, 72–75, 77
Pennsylvania Conservation Association, 67
Pennsylvania Department of Environmental Resources (DER), 70, 77, 80–81; Citizens Advisory Council to, 188; and implementation of Clean Air Act, 181, 185, 190, 192
Pennsylvania Electric Association (PEA), 182–183, 185

Pennsylvania Electric Company, 183
Pennsylvania Environmental Council, 188
Pennsylvania Environmental Hearing Board, 72, 80, 81
Pennsylvania Environmental Quality Board (EQB), 181, 182–183, 234; and Gordian Associates study, 184, 185; and implementation of Clean Air Act, 186–192
Pennsylvania Federation of Sportsmen's Clubs, 59, 60, 70
Pennsylvania League of Women Voters, 188
Pennsylvania Power and Light, 34, 183
Pennsylvania Railroad, 43, 60, 145, 146, 180
Penn-Virginia Corporation, 39
Perl, Lewis, 216, 223
Phelps, Edwin R., 99–100, 105, 145–146, 204
Philadelphia Enquirer, 184
Philadelphia National Bank, 39
Pickands-Mather Company, 25, 88
Pittsburg and Midway Coal, 18, 56
Pittsburgh Press, 59, 81
Pittston Company, 16
pluralism: defined, 8
political organization, coal's: advisory councils and, 51–57; four-tiered structure of, 35–38; grassroots, 38–43; national, 43–51
pollution, air: coal's effects on, 4–5; coal's political efforts concerning, 36, 38–39; concern about dangers of, 127–131; conferences and hearings on (1958–1963), 131–137; health hazards resulting from, 127–128; and implementation of Air Quality Act, 150–154, 155–156; laws to control, 9; pressures for federal controls on (1963–1967), 137–150. *See also* Air Quality Act (1967); Clean Air Act(s)
Powder River Resources Council, 95
Pratt, Julius, 194, 196, 204
prevention of significant deterioration.

See no significant deterioration, concept of
Price-Anderson Act (1958), 15
producers, coal, 18–21
Project Independence, 207, 208, 209
Public Health Service, 143; Division of Air Pollution of, 138
Public Interest Research Group, 185

Quaker State Oil, 32

railroads: involvement of, in coal, 21–23; opposition of, to surface-mining regulatory legislation (Pa.), 60
Randolph, Jennings, 144, 149, 208–209, 218; amendments proposed by, 145, 146–147, 148
Rauch, Robert, 184, 185
regulation. *See* specific acts of legislation
regulatory criteria and technical standards: conflict over, 105
Richey, Herbert, 32, 158
Robertson, Norman, 34
Rochester and Pittsburgh Coal Company, 39
Rogers, Paul, 174, 214, 218, 220, 222, 223
Roosevelt, Franklin, 7
Roosevelt, Theodore, 8–9
Ruckelshaus, William, 166, 171, 172, 174, 193, 194. *See also Sierra Club vs. Ruckelshaus*
Ruttenberg, Stanley, 29

Saen, Frank, 60
St. Joseph Minerals' Massey Coal Company, 39
Saint Joseph (Minnesota) Rod and Gun Club, 163
Sall, George, 148, 150–151
Salt River Project (Ariz.), 104
Saunders, Stuart, 146
Sawhill, John, 50
Saylor, John, 16, 93
Schafer, Raymond P., 67
Schumacher, E. F., 196

Scott, Glen, 216
Scott, Hugh, 218
Scranton, William, 66, 67–68
secrecy: problem of, in government, 9–10
Seiberling, John: amendment of, 101–102, 109, 115, 124, 232
Senate Committee on Government Operations, 34–35
Senate Energy Committee, 123
Senate Interior Committee, 48, 88, 92, 98; and strip-mining bill, 106–109
Senate Public Works Committee, 3, 48, 135, 136, 164; and Clean Air Act Amendments, 208–226 passim; Subcommittee on Air and Water Pollution of, 143, 144, 177
Senate Select Committee to Investigate Presidential Campaign Activities, 54
Senate Subcommittee on Intergovernmental Relations, 52
Shapiro, Irving, 232
Shell Oil, 206–207
Short, Peter, 133
Sierra Club, 3, 6, 95, 108, 229; and ambient air standards, 163; and concept of no significant deterioration, 200, 204, 212–213; and federal guidance, 90; and new source performance standards, 91, 179
Sierra Club vs. Ruckelshaus, 196, 198, 203, 235; Supreme Court decision in, 203–204
Simon, William, 117
Smith, Adam, 5
Smith, Howard K., 134–135
South-East Coal, 13
Southern California Edison, 219
Southern Railway, 39
Sporn, Phillip, 146
Staggers, Harley O., 147, 214, 218
Stamp Out Smog in Los Angeles, 165
Standard Oil of Ohio, 18
standards: difference between emission and ambient, 143–144, 147; EPA's ambient, 161–168

Stans, Maurice, 53, 54, 156, 175, 203
State, Department of, 15
state versus federal preeminence, 99–100
steel industry: coal consumption of, 128; involvement of, in coal, 23–24
Stevens, Ted, 225
strip mining. See surface (or strip) mining
sulfur (di)oxides, 151–152, 169, 177; EPA's ambient air standards for, 163, 165–167; HEW's emission standards for, 140, 142, 145, 146, 147, 149
Sullivan, John, 54
Supreme Court, 196, 203, 212
surface (or strip) mining: coal's political efforts concerning, 36, 38–40; churches and issue of, 95–97; conservation groups and issue of, 97–98; controls of, 9, 21; debates on, 112–124; differences between environmental and coal coalitions on, 99–105; evolution of national policy for, 85–92; Ford's vetoes of bills on, 86, 110, 111–112, 113, 117; House and Senate passage of bills on, 105–111; ill effects of, 4–5; and Mansfield amendment, 102–103, 110, 111, 120, 123, 124, 126, 232; provisions for selectively prohibiting, 102–105; regulations and bills on, 88–92, 98–99, 113–117, 118; and Seiberling amendment, 101–102, 109, 115, 124, 232; technical standards for, 105. See also Surface Mining Control and Reclamation Act (1977, Federal); Surface Mining and Reclamation Act (1961, Pa.)
Surface Mining and Reclamation Act (1961, Pa.), 82; implementation of, by BSMR, 70–80; legislative battle over, 59–65; 1963 amendments to, 66–69
Surface Mining Control and Reclamation Act (1977, Federal), 56, 85, 126, 194, 233; administrative rules

resulting from, 234–235; provisions of, 123–124, 236; revisions of, 57

Sussman, Victor, 185, 190

Synthetic Liquid Fuels Act (1944), 14

Taft-Hartley Act (1947), 209

Tarkington, Andrew, 33, 56

Tate, Joseph, 122

Tennessee Citizens for Wilderness Planning, 87, 108

Tennessee Valley Authority (TVA), 88, 104, 151; and air pollution conference, 132; involvement of, in coal, 25–26; Massengale Mountain demonstration project of, 121; and new source performance standards, 178

Tennessee Valley Public Power Association, 29

Texaco, 223

Thayer, Harold, 141–142

3M Company, 52

trade associations: growth of, 7–8; role of, in coal's political structure, 35–36, 37, 57; state and regional, 35, 40

Train, Russell, 117, 171, 209, 210

Tuberculosis and Respiratory Disease Association of Philadelphia, 189

Tuerk, Edward, 165, 166, 174

Udall, Morris, 99, 102, 109, 121; as chairman of House Interior Committee, 118; on Ford's surface-mining control bill, 115; opposition to, 116; surface-mining bill of, reintroduced, 117–118, 120–123

Udall, Stewart, 88

Udall-Mink bill, 99, 101

Union Electric, 183

Union Financial Corporation, 32

Union Oil, 215

Union Pacific Railroad, 20

United Mine Workers (UMW) of America, 13, 17, 46, 59, 121–122; and Air Quality Act, 144, 145; and implementation of Clean Air Act in Pennsylvania, 182, 186–187; *Journal* of, 28–29; on oil's role in coal, 28–29; role of, in coal's political structure, 43, 44; and Seiberling amendment, 101; on sulfur content of coal, 140; support of, for surface-mining regulation, 59, 60, 63

United Papermakers and Paperworkers, 182

United Steel Workers, 59, 182

U.S. Conference of Mayors, 212

U.S. Steel Corporation, 23, 94, 181, 186; and air pollution conference, 133

Valley Camp Coal Company, 32, 158

Varner, Paige, 64, 66

Veneman, John G., 202

Wagner, Aubrey, 26, 88–90, 104, 121

Water Pollution Control Act (1972), 56

Water Quality Act (1965), 199

Western Systems Coordinating Council (WSCC), 93–94

Westinghouse, 27

Westmoreland Coal, 39

West Virginia: political organization of coal interests in, 38–40, 41–43

West Virginia Coal Association, 38

West Virginia Surface Mining and Reclamation Association (WVSMRA), 41–43, 112

Whip Inflation Now (WIN), 110

Whitaker, John, 93

Yablonski, Joseph, 64

Yom Kippur War, 110, 195

Zarb, Frank, 110–111, 117, 210–211